DATE		
SEP 22 2005		
11-8-06		

Anne Brontë

HER LIFE AND WORK

ADA HARRISON

AND

DEREK STANFORD

ARCHON BOOKS
1970

ISBN: 0-208-00987-6
Library of Congress Catalog Card Number: 73-121756
Printed in the United States of America

CONTENTS

Part One

ANNE BRONTË:
HER LIFE

by Ada Harrison

I

Is ANNE BRONTË WORTHY of a study in her own right? The question is inevitable, in view of the great volume of work on the Brontës already in existence, but it becomes superfluous if put another way. Is the author of *Agnes Grey* and *The Tenant of Wildfell Hall* worthy of a study in her own right?

Anne Brontë's work has stood the test of time; therefore its author has a natural title to our interest. At setting out, however, our interest is less lively than it should be, because, in a dim way, we feel that already we know Anne so well. It has been Anne's fate to be seen in an everlasting comparison, herself with her sisters and her work with their work. In this comparison she never claims attention; the result is that we know her without knowing her; she is a character who is present but does not speak.

It is piquant therefore to discover how good Anne's work is when we re-read it with an open mind, and to discover not only the author but the person herself in her own right.

Every Brontë is seen in two lights, as a writer and as a Brontë. Anne, as a heroine, needs no defence, so we may declare at once that she was less powerful both as a writer and as a Brontë than her sisters. She was very different from them. In the vivid Brontë canvas Anne is a pale figure, but that is not to say that she is a negligible figure; the light tones have their value, if only as relief. Anne, throughout, as well as her intrinsic value has great value as relief.

History causes us to see Anne in a constant state of juxtaposition to her sisters, and her own biographer, however fond, cannot alter her situation. Particularly he cannot remove Anne from juxtaposition with Charlotte. The Brontës all lived at home together for most of their lives. Whatever happened at Haworth was experienced by them all. Almost all we hear of their objective experience comes from letters written to or from Charlotte, and almost all we hear objectively about Anne, which is very little, comes from Charlotte's hand. Anne in this sense depends almost entirely on her elder sister. She peeps out from behind Charlotte; we never see her except through Charlotte's eyes. Charlotte's eyes were splendid and luminous, like all the Brontës' eyes, but they were lodged in her particular head. The biographer's task is therefore to interpret Anne as seen through them and to allow correctly for their distortion. It follows that his task, almost equally, is to understand Charlotte.

Charlotte loved her younger sister fondly, but she did not understand her and she underrated her. The biographer is out to get justice for his subject; there are moments when Charlotte is the enemy, but he should be safe from succumbing to them; for Charlotte also is his subsidiary subject; he is out to get justice for her as well.

The Brontës are a tragic study, for three of them died very young and all within the short space of nine months; they were deeply devoted to each other, and we participate in this long and explicit chapter of agony through Charlotte. While we are with them their power over us is tremendous. 'She hated her work but felt that she must pursue it', is Charlotte's description of Anne writing *The Tenant of Wildfell Hall*. These words strike a curious chord in anybody attempting to write about the Brontës. We do not hate our work, but there are times when we cannot escape a sense of oppression; harrowed by our long attendance at deathbeds and deranged by the powerful humourlessness that is one of the Brontës' chief characteristics, we fear that we may relay nothing but gloom. We continue, however. Hating our work, or rather suffering in it, is not an unusual condition for the writer, and the Brontës, as a subject, are the last to allow themselves to be let go.

*　　　*　　　*

On 17 January 1820 Miss Elizabeth Firth, of Kipping House, Thornton, near Bradford, wrote in her diary, 'Anne Brontë born; the other children spent the day here.' On 25 March she recorded, 'Anne Brontë christened by Mr Morgan. F. Outhwaite and I were godmothers.' And in her accounts is the entry, 'Gave at Anne Brontë's christening £1.'

Miss Firth was twenty-three, the daughter of a kind and substantial gentleman whose family had been long established at Thornton; she and Miss Outhwaite of Bradford had been schoolfellows; the little creature at the font, to whom Miss Outhwaite subsequently left a legacy of £200, was the sixth child of the Rev. Patrick Brontë, perpetual curate of Thornton, and the Rev. William Morgan was his old friend.

It was no doubt a pleasant celebration, though the Brontës lived very modestly. The curate was a tall, good-looking, and convivial Irishman; his wife, though now delicate and never handsome, was a tiny woman of a certain sweetness and distinction and there was no chance of shyness between the five elder children and the Firths. Miss Firth had given much time and affection to the Brontës during their five years at Thornton. 'Frock for one of the Brontës, 16/-' tells us that not only special occasions called forth presents, and the constant mention of tea-drinkings, visits, dinners, and shared excursions suggests an atmosphere of domestic intimacy and warmth.

By heredity the baby who was christened in 1820 had a good chance of being well endowed. Patrick Brontë, born Prunty or Brunty, one of the ten children of a farmer in County Down, had had the strength to rise in the world. He contrived to get some education, became a teacher and made his way to St John's College, Cambridge at the age of twenty-five. Here he was brought to the notice of William Wilberforce, and Wilberforce and Henry Thornton each allowed the deserving Irishman ten pounds annually until he was ordained. By now the Nelson surname was definitively assumed. As curate at Wellington in Shropshire, Brontë met William Morgan, who subsequently became engaged to Jane Fennell, daughter of Mr John Fennell, a Methodist local preacher of Woodhouse Green near Bradford; and on following him to Yorkshire, his friend in turn became engaged to Miss Maria Branwell, a Cornish cousin who was staying in the Fennells' house. The two couples were married in a double ceremony at Guisely, near Bradford, on 29 December 1812, each curate officiating for his friend.

The Rev. Patrick Brontë lived till he was eighty-four, and the extant records of him, stretching over nearly fifty years, show him, not unnaturally, in various lights. However, certain things about him were constant; he was a man of high principles, he was an Irishman and a puritan, he was sociable and susceptible, and he had a dramatic feeling for storm and stress. To this was added the parson and the Victorian father, sublimely exempt from both criticism and self-criticism.

For 25 February 1820 Miss Firth's diary records, 'Mr Brontë was licenced to Haworth', and continues, 'March 3rd, Mr and Mrs

Brontë to dinner, 8th, Mr Brontë in the evening, 13th, Mr Brontë in the evening, 17th, Mr Brontë called, 21st, Mr and Mrs Brontë to tea, 25th Anne Brontë was christened, etc. 31st Good Friday, No Service. We sat up expecting the Radicals.' Mr Brontë was passionately Conservative and had terrified Mr Firth with his prognostications of what might be expected from the Radicals. The journal continues: 'April 3rd, I called at Mr Brontës, 5th, Took leave of Mr Brontë before leaving home. June 6th, Mr Brontë came. Mr Brontë went home.'

Maria Branwell, whom Anne, her last child, most resembled, was twenty-nine when she married. We do not follow her, as we do her husband, through the vicissitudes and changes of a long life, for she died eighteen months after Anne was born. She appears only in the first act or, more accurately, in the prologue to the first act, for what we know of her comes from the letters she wrote to her husband while they were engaged. Long after her death these letters came into her daughter Charlotte's hand. 'Papa put into my hands a little packet of letters and papers, telling me that they were Mama's, and that I might read them. . . . It was strange now to peruse for the first time the records of a mind whence my own sprang; and most strange and at once sad and sweet to find that mind of a truly fine, pure, and elevated order. There is a rectitude, a refinement, a constancy, a modesty, a sense of gentleness about them indescribable. I wish she had lived and that I had known her.'

Reading her mother by the surest of testimonies, her own, Charlotte was right. The letters do show the qualities claimed for them. And they foreshadow how the youngest mind to spring from Maria Branwell's was to be endowed with the same rectitude, refinement, gentleness, and sense. The letters also show a certain strength, the freedom and lack of inhibition of a young woman loved and courted, and a conscious desire to handle the pen. Maria Branwell wrote a charming hand.

Though we can never guess how artists will derive, we can say, looking back, that this seems fairly likely soil for them to have sprung in. There was intelligence and vigour on the father's side and intelligence and sanity on the mother's. The Brontë children were Irish and Cornish and were brought up in Yorkshire, in a unique place. Three poetic strains of earth combined in them. Added to this, both parents, the father particularly, had a feeling for letters, an artisan or preparatory leaning towards the art in which the children were to excel. The Brontës drew in much from various sources, and fate added the inexplicable quickening touch.

Mrs Brontë was a native of Penzance. Her family was rather better off than her husband's and she brought an income of fifty pounds. The Branwells were staunch Methodists, and through them Methodism was destined to trouble the Brontës. In person Maria was elegant and nice, and this niceness was wholly transmitted to her daughters. Every visitor to the household in later years remarked it. Mr Brontë, bedridden in extreme old age, was still exquisitely kept; everything 'delicately clean and white' a caller said. The Brontë relics have the same quality.

Though their life together was lived before her day, Anne's parents loved each other. The hard-worked husband undertook the whole of the night-nursing during his wife's long last illness. Mrs Brontë's niece, Charlotte Branwell of Penzance, wrote in after years, 'Mr Brontë was perhaps peculiar, but I have always heard my dear mother say that he was devotedly fond of his wife and she of him.'

Mr Brontë's peculiarities, which seem to have been born of his Irish temper, were spectacular and much quoted. It seems that when he was upset or displeased he kept absolute silence, but relieved himself by punishing inanimate objects and notably by discharging a brace of pistols at his back door. Apropos of this habit we have one of the few recorded utterances of Mrs Brontë, 'Ought I not to be thankful that he never gave me an angry word?' In fact it seems that Mr Brontë, like most hot-tempered people, knew and feared his weakness and arranged a safety-valve for himself. Two pieces of bad behaviour which he did not succeed in checking were bound in the nature of things to be long and enthusiastically remembered against him. Mr Brontë had the puritan's detestation of any display of frivolity or frippery. On one occasion he is said in an access of rage to have cut a silk dress of his wife's to ribbons; on another, a servant, with her mind on the Parsonage children out on the moors above Haworth in the rain, had put some little coloured boots, which had been given them, to warm at the kitchen hearth. Their father's eye fell on the ungodly little boots and he thrust the whole row into the fire. These illustrations seem to suggest that Mr Brontë could control the Irishman but that the Irishman and the puritan together were too much for him.

The five children who spent the day of their sister Anne's birth at Kipping House were Maria, Elizabeth, Charlotte, Patrick Branwell, and Emily Jane. Maria, the eldest, was seven, and the whole six of them were born in less than eight years.

When Charlotte Brontë, no longer young, told her father that she wished to marry, he opposed the idea for several reasons, one of them being that she was too delicate for marriage. He was proved right, for her first pregnancy killed her. Mrs Brontë had also proved too delicate for marriage. For the sake of her health, her husband decided to move to Haworth, six miles off, where he would enjoy a stipend of £170 a year, plus £27 13s. maintenance, and a better house. The move was accomplished in the spring, and Anne, at about ten weeks old, was brought to Haworth Parsonage, which was the only home she ever knew and to which she was passionately attached. It had been hoped that the new situation would be good for Mrs Brontë – Haworth stood high; the Parsonage was the last house in the village and behind it were the open moors; but it was terribly exposed. By the decree of her husband, who had a mortal fear of fire, the windows were curtainless and the floors carpetless, and the only prospect was the churchyard 'crammed with upright tombstones that pressed upon the garden on two sides'. There was no help here for a woman born and bred in the softness of Cornwall. Mrs Brontë's last illness attacked her at the end of that year, and after a long struggle she died in September 1821. She had had her children kept away from her during the last months of her life and Anne was entirely without recollection of her mother.

The sociable cosiness of the Brontës' life ended abruptly when they left Thornton. Before they had time to settle in and establish themselves in their new home the family was first afflicted and then bereaved. Perhaps also the people of Haworth failed to rise to the Brontës' situation. It was a village of grim and honest traditions now adapting itself determinedly to the new industrial outlook; it had been famous for its evangelical fervour in the last century, and much of this remained and kept the church-and-chapel controversy in full vigour. The atmosphere was uncompromising and ungentle and those who kept themselves to themselves earned the highest praise. 'In Haworth,' Mr Brontë wrote, 'my family afflictions began. After a happy union of 9 years, and only one year's residence, my dear wife died – and left me with the care of six small children. Soon after my wife's sister came, and afforded me her assistance for twenty years.'

But Miss Elizabeth Branwell, one of Maria's elder sisters, was no substitute. She was too old for the change, and the task which she had undertaken as a duty never melted into a pleasure or a natural call.

As might have been expected, Anne, the youngest, and Branwell, the boy, were her favourites. A servant at the Parsonage at the time tells how the children were hushed – Mama ill next door and Papa writing sermons below in the parlour – and how they turned for comfort to each other, and how at the tenderest age used to walk out on the moors hand in hand. In the summer of 1821 Anne was barely eighteen months old. Her two main comforts and joys, love of her family and love of nature and the moors were discovered early and remained constant throughout her life.

It was natural that Mr Brontë, in his plight, should wish to remarry, and he made two attempts to do so. It is no surprise to discover that he addressed himself to Miss Elizabeth Firth, but she refused him, though she remained a good friend to his children. Two months after his wife's death Mr Brontë had written a long reply to the condolences of the Rev. John Buckworth, his first vicar in Yorkshire, and in it he gives us glimpses of himself. 'Do you ask how I felt under all these circumstances?' he inquires as he pours out an account of the harrowing illness. An ordinary enough question perhaps, except that later on in the letter he puts it again. 'Should you still inquire how I now feel, I would answer . . .' Clearly he is very ready to suppose that people would be interested in how he felt and very ready to enlighten them. Then there is his choice of metaphor. 'When I first came to this place, though the angry winds which had been previously excited were hushed, the troubled sea was still agitated, and the vessel required a cautious and steady hand at the helm.'[1] And later. 'No sooner was I there when another storm arose, more terrible than the former . . . one that shook every part of the mortal frame, and threatened it with dissolution. My dear wife was taken ill . . .'

This letter prepares us for the manner in which Mr Brontë continued his courting.

In his first post in Essex 'the good-looking young Irish curate made successful love to a young parishioner, Miss Mary Burder. . . . She was spirited away from the neighbourhood, and the lovers never met again.'[2] In 1823, after fourteen years, Mr Brontë remembered Mary Burder, and summoned courage to write to her mother, inquiring closely after her family, 'whether they be married or single'. Having received a reply after a delay of several months, he wrote to Miss

---

[1] There had been a great controversy and violent demonstrations by the parishioners at Haworth over the awarding of the living to Mr Brontë.

[2] Augustine Birrell, *Life of Charlotte Brontë*, 1887.

Burder herself, confidently reminding her that she once gave him her hand, and offering her his rekindled love, what he describes as his '*small* but *sweet* little family' and his two hundred a year. Miss Burder's reply would have demolished most men. Girding herself up after fourteen years, and cherishing, in conclusion, no feelings of resentment or animosity, she sweeps along, observing that a review of circumstances recalled to her recollection 'excites in my bosom increased gratitude and thankfulness to that wise, that indulgent Providence which then watched over me for good and prevented me from forming in very early life an indissoluble engagement with one whom I cannot think of as altogether clear of duplicity. . . . Whether those ardent professions of devoted lasting attachment were sincere is now to me a matter of little consequence.'

Mr Brontë could scarcely believe his eyes. 'Such a spirit of disdain, hatred, and revenge!' He persisted, still seeking a meeting and having faith perhaps in his personal charm. We hear no more. His letters are unpleasing and unctuous in tone. He exposed a bad side. But not only was Mr Brontë's Irish vanity egregious: his need was great; and as a harassed parish priest of forty-six he probably had little time to go wooing in fresh places.

The children were not to have a stepmother, and their father, after this shock to his hopes and his self-satisfaction, became withdrawn, and in his private life began to play the eccentric and the recluse. His public life continued to reflect the high principles he had always shown. Charlotte's biographer Mrs Gaskell, who held no brief for him, tells us 'he fearlessly took whatever side in local or national politics appeared to him right', and that 'not one opinion that he held could be stirred or modified by any worldly motive'. In later years during a strike of mill-hands, he supported the men in the teeth of the masters.

But underneath, the original man lived on. Patrick Brontë remained a nature needing society and affection, and, whatever his weaknesses, this need seems to have called forth a warm response from his family.

Some understanding of the self-absorbed, humourless, passionate, and high-principled father is necessary for the understanding of his children, for not only did he beget them but he was the constant figure in all their lives. Of the four who grew to maturity, Anne seems to have resembled him least. Though she was high-principled, she lacked rigidity, and though her sense of humour was not great, it was greater than that of her sisters.

18

Having been bereaved so early, the little Brontës were not in the ordinary sense childlike. They were the kind of children who excite the wonder and compassion of servants. Maria, the eldest, at seven, read and expounded the newspaper to the rest. Anne had first in her and then in Charlotte a little mother, and in every sense but the ordinary one was mothered a great deal. Charlotte's first extant work, a minute home-made book, with pictures, is a touching token of elder-sisterly love. 'There was a little girl and her name was Ann', wrote the author at the age of six. 'She was born at a little village named Thornton. . . .' 'Once Ann and her papa and mama went to sea in a ship', the tale concludes, 'and they had very fine weather all the way, but Ann's mama was very sick and Ann attended her with so much care she gave her her medicine.'

The choice of privilege has an ominous sound.

Certainly affection, and of the intenser sort, was never lacking, and Anne's writings suggest that it was of a more naturally demonstrative kind than came the way of her sisters.

Anne's build and appearance as a child can be guessed from a portrait of her at the age of thirteen, drawn by Charlotte, and a description of her a year earlier from the pen of Ellen Nussey, Charlotte's friend. The sisters were all spirit, with luminous eyes and mobile, irregular features; but Anne had higher claims to beauty than Charlotte and Emily, who at this moment had tight-frizzed hair and sallow skins. 'Anne, dear gentle Anne,' wrote Ellen after her first visit to the Parsonage, 'was quite different in appearance from the others, and was her aunt's favourite. Her hair was a very pretty light brown and fell on her neck in graceful curls. She had lovely violet-blue eyes, fine pencilled eyebrows and clear, almost transparent complexion.' Charlotte painted her in water-colours, in a blue stuff dress, cut low on the shoulders and with a black ribbon round her long neck. The hair in the picture is much darker than the truth, as can be seen from the soft silvery brown of a bracelet made from Anne's hair.

We may be certain that at a tender age, in spite of being her aunt's favourite, Anne was required to master all household tasks within her infant compass and was taught to sew. Miss Branwell, like her sister, was extremely particular and nice, and believed that household management was the core of a girl's education. Sewing at this time was designated women's work. 'Maria Brontë, aged ten. . . . Reads tolerably. Writes pretty well. Ciphers a little. Works badly.' 'Elizabeth

Brontë, aged 9. . . . Reads little. Writes pretty well. Works very badly. . . .' 'Emily Brontë, aged 6¼. . . . Reads very prettily and works a little.' So ran the entries in the register of the school to which the older children were sent. But in spite of official opinion we are struck by the neatness and finish of surviving samplers worked by Emily's and Anne's childish hands. Mary Taylor, a strongly feminist friend, wrote of Miss Branwell in later years, 'She made her nieces sew, with purpose and without, and as far as possible discouraged any other culture. . . . She used to keep the girls sewing charity clothing, and maintained to me that it was not for the good of the recipients, but of the sewers.'

The home to which Anne was so devotedly attached was certainly an improvement on her birthplace, Thornton, which was a commonplace little double-fronted house on the village street. Haworth Parsonage can hardly be seen except in the light of history and it stands literally in a graveyard; but viewed simply as a house it has a certain quality and charm. It is a very modest piece of what might be called Northern Georgian, two storeys high, with four rooms and a small hall below and five rooms above. In front, looking east, was an infertile patch of garden cut out of the churchyard. On the right of the hall was Mr Brontë's study and on the left the family living-room. The back rooms had no pretensions; behind the study was the kitchen and behind the living-room a store-room in which was kept, mainly, the peat burned on the fires. The flagged hall boasted an arch; beyond it rose the first flight of stairs, stone, and only seven in number; on the turn of the staircase was a little landing, furnished with a window-seat, as were all the rooms, and a few more stairs led to the floor above. No house could be more compact. The household consisted of the Rev. Patrick and Miss Branwell, the six young children and two young servants, and they no doubt disposed themselves about the bedroom floor as best they might. The tiny room over the hall belonged to the children; it was called not a nursery but a study, though no doubt some of them slept in it. Looking out the children saw the moor above the churchyard, church and village. There was no fireplace in the room and they repaired to the kitchen for a different kind of life and for warmth.

In their early years the little Brontë children lived entirely to themselves. They had each other, and this in one way sufficed, for, being what they were, they lived intensely. But Anne's circumstances greatly increased her natural sensitiveness and shyness; the love of home was exaggerated, homesickness was a terrible malady and isolation made common experiences an ordeal.

The moor, and running out or walking out upon the moor was a part of Anne's life from earliest days. Here the children were children, even if they were not boisterous. Emily at fourteen could still hang over a pool playing with tadpoles in a special delicious place which she and Anne called the 'Meeting of the Waters'. They grew up free of a great sweep of country in all season and all weathers. Anne writes of nature – the dangling leveret, the gossamers of an autumn morning, the hinds lying late in bed in winter because they have neither work nor food nor fire to get up for – with the matter-of-factness that is more telling than poetic verbiage and denotes that what she describes is as familiar to her as the furniture of a room.

Mr Brontë, well meaning and full of theories, was on his own showing an arid parent for a little girl. He relates an experiment with a mask. Each of the children was invited to wear this mask and answer his questions from behind it, his idea being that the anonymity would encourage them to speak with fuller freedom. The questions, as might have been expected, invited pious and precocious replies. Anne, no more than four, was asked what a child like her most wanted and earned commendation with the reply, 'Age and experience.' The little Brontës were quite clever enough, perhaps quite kind enough to humour a grown-up person and play his game; but the story has an interesting side, for when it came to Anne's turn to play the pedagogue she was often recognizable as her father's daughter.

There were theories also on physical upbringing. Mrs Gaskell tells us that Mr Brontë wished to make his children hardy, in which it may be observed no parent has ever more signally failed. Her informant told her that the children were not allowed meat. A champion of Mr Brontë at once rushed into the breach with the discovery that the children were allowed all the meat they wanted and that butter was the only article to be rationed. Perhaps meat was provided and the little Brontës, like many children, did not eat it. We hear that Charlotte, at school, never ate meat. All references to food at the Parsonage are somewhat Spartan. We hear of rice and milk, and porridge and milk, of plain joints and boiled apple-pudding, of Mr Brontë's own tastes being of the plainest: beef, mutton, tea, and bread and butter. When a beautiful dinner was put before Charlotte and Anne at the house of their publisher, it almost went without saying that in the state of excitement they were in they could not touch it. Like most highly-strung people the Brontës had nervous stomachs. The evidence does not suggest that Miss Branwell would have coaxed childish appetites or that Mr Brontë could ever forget that ten little Bruntys had come up sufficiently well on potatoes and milk.

Anne, who was never referred to except as mild and gentle, was also almost invariably referred to by her sister Charlotte as delicate. Anne was perhaps less delicate as a child than Charlotte thought her, but she cannot have been strong, and she doubtless had her share of the childish ailments and the coughs and colds, and also of the harsh old-fashioned remedies then in vogue. In the spring of 1824, whooping-cough and measles went through the house at the same time, and these attacks were destined to play a decisive part in all the Brontës' lives.

The girls were to go to school. Perhaps Miss Branwell felt that she had her hands too full (it seems this must have been one reason, for Emily was sent away at six) or perhaps it was felt that, for a poor parson's daughters, serious education, which was to be their livelihood, could not begin too soon. The place chosen was the Clergy Daughters' School at Cowan Bridge, terribly described as 'Lowood' by Charlotte in *Jane Eyre*. Maria and Elizabeth, aged ten and nine, and scarcely convalescent, went in July 1824. Charlotte followed in August and Emily in November. These piecemeal departures suggest that whooping-cough in each case was taking its course. History does not show whether Anne was destined to follow Emily – or when, or if Miss Branwell intended to keep the favourite little girl by her. Just before Emily's departure Mr Brontë wrote to a friend that the children were going to school, and that now, instead of his two young servants, he intended to keep an elderly woman. Tabitha Aykroyd was engaged, a childless widow of fifty-three, and Anne, at four, passed into her care. Tabby, as she became, remained at the Parsonage, with a short interval, until 1855, outliving all but Charlotte and her master. With their father, she was the great central figure in the Brontës' lives, a pillar of the house, supporting them until in her turn she needed their support, and loving them and ruling them in the fashion common to her kind.

The school, together with the late illness, combined with homesickness and natural weakness, was literally the death of the two elder children. After seven months at Cowan Bridge, Maria, and shortly afterwards Elizabeth were brought home to die. This they did within a fortnight of each other (the immediate cause being consumption) and on the day after Elizabeth's death Mr Brontë came to his senses and fetched Charlotte and Emily home. His conduct here foreshadows his actions in the last illnesses of Emily and Anne.

Thus the school idea for the time being was given up. Anne was not to be the only girl at home, relying for companionship on Branwell, who went to the grammar school at Marsh and did lessons with his father : she was to be one of a close trio of sisters. At five years old she had become acquainted with death, and exchanged one little mother for another, who at nine years old had a more adult acquaintance with death, and with persecution, and was to watch over her with adult anxiety.

II

ELIVERED FROM SCHOOL, the little Brontës were left at home in peace to grow, with their brother, into the Brontës of history. Anne at five was now a conscious member of the family. Perhaps the deaths of her sisters, in the house, suggested to her infant mind that this was what resulted when one left home and taught her to cling to it.

'My home is humble and unattractive to strangers,' Charlotte worte, 'but to me it contains what I shall find nowhere else in the wrold, the profound, the intense affection which brother and sisters feel for each other when their minds are cast in the same mould, their ideas drawn from the same source . . . when they have clung to each other from childhood and when disputes have never sprung up to divide them.' This was perhaps to be the truest of all for Anne, at least for the greater part of her life, for she was less adventurous than Charlotte and less independent than Emily, and with the return of her elders she began to take part in such a sisterly relationship as Charlotte describes. Emily and Anne were like twins; they were entwined, Ellen Nussey said of them when they were older. But with all members of such a family there is a great area held in common; the same things strike them and the same things move them; when little they are natural appendages of each other; there is no such thing as being alone.

Anne and her immediate family, reduced to four, appeared externally as four old-fashioned little oddities, talking with a strong Irish accent, dressed according to the notions of Mr Brontë and Miss Branwell (for whom fashion had not advanced since she left Penzance), and deeply involved in their own concerns. To Anne they must have appeared as it were internally as Charlotte, responsible, authoritative, tender, a little overpowering; Branwell, different and important because a boy, bubbling and clever with his Greek and Latin; and Emily, only eighteen months older, the true sister and other self. Anne for her own part was gentler and less emphatic than any of them. She was the youngest, surrounded by powerful characters, but indulgently treated and enjoying the privilege of always sharing their play. On the fringe of this world were the semi-grown-ups, the servants, and the actual grown-ups, Aunt Branwell and Papa. Papa showed his affection by coming into the dining-room where the children lived and telling them about the interesting and important things that went on in the world and that used to go on when he was a boy. Charlotte was later to tell a school-friend, Mary Taylor, that she had been interested in politics ever since she was five years old. Aunt Branwell gave the girls lessons every day in her room. She had her rules and her fixed hours, but beyond these she interfered very little, and she preferred to stay upstairs, away from the cold stone passage, which she detested, and the draughts. A message to her or about her in a letter from Charlotte to Branwell 'I hope . . . that the present delightful weather may . . . give Aunt pleasant reminiscences of the salubrious climate of her native place', suggests that her habit was to compare Haworth with Penzance to its disadvantage.

Consciously now Anne became aware that she was a Parsonage child living at the top of a steep stone village, and she looked out consciously at the surrounding world. Haworth Church stands at the bottom of the rough rectangle that rises to the top of the hill. This rough rectangle is the churchyard and in its top right-hand corner the Parsonage stands. Charlotte said that there were graves under the house, and this no doubt was literally true. A well-flagged walk or path, wide enough for a carriage, but very steep, runs up beside the long north wall of the churchyard to the Parsonage gate. This path is flanked on the other side by a line of low old buildings that in the Brontës' time were the Sunday schools and day schools, at the lower end of which was the sexton's house (where the curates lodged) and a couple of stone-tiled cottages and a little flagged court. The whole, church, churchyard, Parsonage, flagged path, and flanking buildings form a kind of hill-top precinct, in which Branwell Brontë, in his later days, caused to be included the public-house which adjoins the Church, the Black Bull. This precinct has become the Brontë precinct; it is redolent of atmosphere, but atmosphere was already there when the Brontës came – they breathed it in and left the place with themselves indissolubly attached.

Haworth itself is in some degree responsible for the Brontës, and Haworth itself partly explains the more-than-ordinary hold that home had upon them, even though, or perhaps because, the atmosphere of the precinct is largely the atmosphere of tombs. To a child coming home or leaving home or looking out from the nursery window of home, tombs were always in view. On the side of the churchyard below the garden-wall, the dead, for the most part under table-tombs, seemed to lie down, but on the far side they seemed to stand in serried ranks, as if the whole valley had died and been buried under upright tomb-stones. 'A churchyard so filled with graves,' wrote Mrs Gaskell, 'that the rank weeds . . . and the funeral grass scarce had room to spurt up between the monuments.'

Emily, in an early poem gives us the classic picture of the precinct.

> *. . . There is a spot, mid barren hills*
> *Where winter howls and drives the rain. . . .*

> *. . . The house is old, the trees are bare,*
> *Moonless above bends twilight's dome . . .*

> *. . . The mute bird sitting on the stone,*
> *The dank moss dripping from the wall,*
> *The thorn-trees gaunt, the walks o'ergrown*
> *I love them, how I love them all.*

Anne's environment in fact was one that powerfully affected the imagination, and, though essentially sombre, it reflected not only winter but all the beauties of changing weather and seasons as well.

The moor was also in view, the moment the child turned her back on the house, its lower slopes brilliantly green and patterned with black stone walls, and the brown of dried bracken and the black of dead heather above. 'The scenery of these hills is not grand,' Charlotte wrote; 'it is not romantic; it is scarcely striking. Long, low moors, dark with heath, shut in valleys where a stream waters here and there a fringe of stunted copse. Mills and scattered cottages chase romance from these valleys; it is only higher up, deep in amongst the ridges of the moors, that Imagination can find rest for the sole of her foot; and even if she finds it there she must be a solitude-loving raven, no gentle dove. If she demand beauty to inspire her she must bring it inborn; these moors are too stern to yield any product so delicate . . . [But] where the love of wild nature is strong the locality will perhaps be clung to with more passionate constancy, because from the hill-lover's self comes half its charm.'

This was the landscape, their love of which Charlotte felt it neces-sary to explain. But she speaks also of 'the brief flower-flush of August on the heather and the starry flowers that spangle for a few weeks the pastures of the moor sheep . . .', those gifts of softness in hard country, to be marvelled at, worshipped almost.

The village provided the necessities of life, but anything over and above had to be got from Keighley, nearly four miles away, where the railway was. The walk there and back early became a feature of the Brontës' lives. The Rev. Patrick Brontë, Charlotte, and Emily were by nature great walkers. Anne as a child went where Emily went, and later, though we hear of her as delicate, we also hear of her walking to the town and back, quite in the natural order of things.

Books, which were a necessity, came from Keighley, and were fetched from the Mechanics' Institute, which had a lending library. When Anne was six, we hear of *The Imitation of Christ*, a *Home Doctor*, an *Elementary Encyclopedia*, an *English Grammar*, *A General Geography*, *Sermons and Homilies to be read in Churches in the Time of Queen Elizabeth*, and *The Lay of the Last Minstrel*, all being in the Parsonage. When she was eight, Miss Branwell gave them Scott's *Tales of a Grandfather*, inscribed 'To my dear little nephews and nieces'. Scott, particularly Scott the poet, easy and charming reading and listening for a little girl, made a deep impression on Anne, and his echo is heard for a long time in her verses. All the children, reading freely, not going to school, associating with educated adults and with uneducated people who spoke a real language, effortlessly acquired a vocabulary and the power to move about, as it were, in their own tongue. It was noted in after years of Branwell, who was a brilliant talker, that he had the gift of dropping from the sublime not to the ridiculous but to the earthy, telling and matter-of-fact, that was, into the Irish or Yorkshire talk.

The children not only read, they also began to write. Charlotte has left a *History of the Year 1829*, her thirteenth year, and Anne's ninth. It is an informative document. 'While I write this I am in the kitchen of the Parsonage, Haworth; Tabby the servant is washing up the breakfast things, and Anne, my youngest sister (Maria was my eldest) is kneeling on a chair looking at some cakes which Tabby has been baking for us. Emily is in the parlour brushing the carpet. Papa and Branwell are gone to Keighley. Aunt is upstairs in her room and I am sitting by the table writing this in the kitchen.'

This gives us a pleasant picture of Anne, the baby, without an allotted task, joining in the cake-making and shortly to be given, or not given a hot cake. We see Emily already accepting or at least not resisting housework, of which she undertook much later on. The sudden mention of Maria startles us; Charlotte has not forgotten her, nor will Anne have been allowed to forget her. We learn also that Mr Brontë was broad-minded enough to take in a Whig as well as a Tory newspaper.

Charlotte then gives us the genesis of the children's writing. It began with their acting or assuming characters, as all children do more or less crudely, in order to have power and glory, that is to realize their natural human desires. The Brontë children began, as other children have done before and since, to write their plays down. But from this point they transcended nature, or acted with a naturalness that was transcendent. They carried the thing to tremendous conclusions. Charlotte initiates us. '. . . Our plays were established, "Young Men", June 1826; "Our Fellows", July 1827; "Islanders", December 1827. These are our three great plays that are not kept secret. Emily's and my best plays were established the 1st of December 1827; the others March 1828. Best plays mean secret plays; they are very nice ones. All our plays are very strange ones. Their nature I need not write on paper, for I think I shall always remember them. The "Young Men's" play took its rise from some wooden soldiers Branwell had; "Our Fellows" from Aesop's Fables: and the "Islanders" from several events which happened. I will sketch out the origin of our plays more explicitly if I can. First. "Young Men." Papa bought Branwell some wooden soldiers at Leeds; when Papa came home it was night and we were in bed, so next morning Branwell came to our door with a box of soldiers. Emily and I jumped out of bed and I snatched up one and exclaimed, "This is the Duke of Wellington! This shall be the Duke!" When I had said this, Emily likewise took up one and said it should be hers; when Anne came down she said one should be hers. Mine was the prettiest of the whole and the tallest and the most perfect in every part. Emily's was a grave-looking fellow and we called him "Gravey". Anne's was a queer little thing, much like herself, and we called him "Waiting-Boy". Branwell chose his and called him "Buonaparte".'

The scene is easy to visualize. Each child holds its chosen soldier in its hand, gazes at it, then laughingly begins to manipulate it and talk for it and make it live. It was this kind of thing that was carried as it were to infinity. Once the personages were endowed with life, the whole world was before them. And the dramas were not only spoken and acted; they were written down. In Charlotte and Branwell the passion to write was already alive. Children of eleven and twelve long to write but they have little to write about. The Brontë children, with their plays, linked their writing naturally to its object or to an enormous choice of objects. They gave themselves a territory which was a nursery in the double sense, a place where they could be children and also where they could nurse and develop their powers.

The play of the *Young Men* expanded splendidly. One day the children 'sent the Young Men, or the Twelves, as they often called the toys "all true heroes" on a voyage in "the good ship *Invincible* – seventy four guns" and allowed them to suffer shipwreck on the Guinea coast. The genii who haunted the "Gibble Kumri, or Mountains of the Moon" – the four young Brontës after reading *Arabian Nights* had assumed the roles of "Chief Genii", Talli, Branni, Emmi, and Anni, who ruled all subordinate spirits of land, water and air – saved the party from the murderous blacks and built for them a magic city, which they called Glass Town, or the Glass-town at the mouth of the Niger River.'[1]

Fire flashed round the heads of the Genii; they endowed themselves not only with the power to destroy the living, but also to resuscitate the dead. In the play the *Islanders,* beauty and splendour went to the limits of imagination. So did the darker side. There was a school for a thousand pupils, with underground punishment-cells, torture, guards to administer it, and little kings and queens hastening in balloons to the relief of their subjects. Every passion in fact was magnificently gratified, and it is reassuring to find the little Brontës who spoke from behind the mask giving themselves their fling like veritable children, even though children of genius. They could quarrel too. 'When mere children,' Mr Brontë recalled, 'Charlotte and her brother and sisters used to invent and act little plays of their own, in which the Duke of Wellington, my daughter Charlotte's hero, was bound to come off conqueror, when a dispute would not unfrequently arise among them. . . . When the argument got warm and rose to its height, as their mother was then dead, I had sometimes to come in as arbitrator. . . .'

The Duke of Wellington, or one or other of his sons, on whom the mantle descended, remained a constant figure. And other real life heroes came and went at ease among imaginary people. The invented people as time went on had highly romantic names, but in the beginning they were delightfully childish. Crashey, Ross (the actual

[1] *Gondal's Queen,* by Fannie E. Ratchford.

explorer), Crackey, Trackey, Gravey, Bravey, Sneaky (later Sneachi), were some of the names of the original wooden soldiers or Young Men. One can almost hear low Sneaky turning into high Italianate Sne-a-chi amid peals of laughter.

After a time the plays coalesced and the imaginary country of Angria emerged, with physical features, towns, population, heroes, history, and politics of its own, as well as the freedom to borrow whatever and whomsoever it needed from reality – an illimitable territory, only waiting to be written into life. Arthur Wellesley, Marquis of Douro, ruled over it, who signed himself at the height of his glory Arthur Augustus Adrian Wellesley, Duke of Zamorna and Emperor of Angria. 'Charlotte told me,' Mrs Gaskell reported, at that moment when Branwell in the last stages of drinking and drug-taking was wearing his family out, 'that the readings were of great and stirring interest to all, taking them out of the gnawing pressure of daily recurring cares and setting them in a free place.' The readings were the readings and discussion of the novels which the sisters had set themselves to write. The free place since childhood had been ready and waiting. In a wonderful sentence, 'Now I should be agonized if I had not the dream to repose on!' Charlotte invoked it again in a period of captivity in common life.

The children wrote their poems, stories, and the whole literature or libretti of their 'plays' in minute handwriting in minute home-made books – a few leaves stitched together into a cover of brown or blue sugar-paper, the archetypal tiny books. 'These little books hold in their tiny script the most accurate record of the evolution of genius extant in any language.'[1] There exist also several sixpenny notebooks purchased by Mr Brontë, one of which is inscribed, 'All that is written in this notebook must be written in a good, plain and legible hand.' This was a father of a better kind – sympathetic, generous, awarding a rich bribe on the very slenderest hope of satisfaction. A sixpenny notebook! How thick, how expensive, how inviting! It would be a miserable author indeed who could fail to write a masterpiece in that.

* * *

'A queer little thing, much like herself, and we called him *Waiting-Boy.*' Here, in one of those evocative phrases from her infant pen, is Charlotte's first description of Anne. We know Emily and Anne by their own works and by Charlotte's written descriptions of them, in

[1] *The Brontë Web of Childhood*, by Fannie E. Ratchford.

which we learn something about them and something about Charlotte. Unfortunately, from Emily and Anne we have no written responses. In their early days Charlotte stood to her younger sisters in a fixed attitude, that of masterful little mother. Emily moved out of range; not so Anne. Anne was the youngest, soft, gentle, quiet – Charlotte longed to protect her. Anne did no violence to her nature by staying where she was. Charlotte refers to Anne from first to last as little, sweet, resigned, gentle, pious, delicate, and passive. Half-mesmerized by this harping on one string, we hardly pause to wonder if there is anything amiss with it until we come upon Charlotte in juxtaposition with Anne for the last time and read her sweeping condemnation of Anne's major work. 'The choice of subject was an entire mistake,' she wrote of *Wildfell Hall* in her biographical notice of her sisters. Suddenly we remember Waiting-Boy. Without over-emphasizing the casual comparison, with someone young, passive, and under orders, we see that much here was shadowed forth. Charlotte, all her life, had a fixed idea about Anne; but although Anne stayed where she was, *vis-à-vis* her elder sister, she remained, as quiet people do, *what* she was.

Objectively we know from the history of the year 1829 that Anne chose Guernsey for her island, and for its chief men Michael Sadler, Lord Bentinck, and Sir Henry Halford. At seven she was quite up to the game and already educated into a consciousness of politics and current affairs. At nine she went on a visit with the rest of them to their great-uncle Fennell. The weather was bad and they could not go out much, and they indulged in the pastime of drawing, which they all adored. 'Branwell has taken two sketches from nature,' wrote Charlotte to their father, 'and Emily, Anne, and myself have likewise each of us drawn a piece from some views of the Lakes which Mr Fennell brought with him from Westmoreland. The whole of these he intends keeping.' . . . We have another pleasant glimpse of Anne with her sisters, happily making a 'copy' under the eye of a tactful old host who knows that appreciation is what artists need.

All the children adored drawing and a number of their childish essays in the art remain, including their faint childish drawings on the nursery wall. The girls were fond of making copies, in the manner of the period – an elaborate copy of an elm tree has survived, done when Anne was fifteen – and these exercises usually show more care than merit; it is clear that drawing, like the making of little books, was a regular activity and pleasure.

The drawings and the tiny books, a toy smoothing-iron, a charming white mug lettered in gold 'Emily Jane Brontë', Charlotte's paint-box and Anne's little collection of cornelians from the sea-shore (these two items of much later date), Mr Brontë's heel-spikes, the regular presence of animals, not only dogs and cats but also geese and a tame hawk, suggest the kind of people the Brontës were. Nobody who troubled to look round the Parsonage could think that the people who inhabited it failed to live, or, at least until fatal sickness took a hold on them or they were forced to leave their home, that they were unhappy.

At eleven a phase of Anne's childhood ended, as Charlotte again went to school, this time to Miss Wooler's at Roe Head, a very different place from Lowood. Emily and Anne no doubt saw her off, impressed, respectful, entwined, and deeply thankful to be left at home. Mary Taylor witnessed her arrival. She was seen 'coming out of a covered cart in very old clothes, looking very cold and miserable.' There were some gaps in her knowledge and she was to be placed in the second class with the younger girls. The ignominy was too much for Wellington and Douro, not to mention the little mother and the head of the Haworth study, and 'she received this announcement with so sad a fit of crying' that she had to be placed in the first class after all.

III

WITH CHARLOTTE'S DEPARTURE Branwell was left alone and the closeness between Emily and Anne increased. Charlotte and Branwell were partners; Emily and Anne were also partners and not through their position only; they had the intense affinity of complementary natures. It is easy to suppose that we know something of Charlotte, Branwell, and Anne. Emily is a difficult subject for research . . . we know that from her earliest youth her absolute needs were *nature* and *freedom*, and that human society in its non-necessary aspects was what, in Charlotte's words, she 'failed of enduring'. But what the girl who was to write *Wuthering Heights* and a handful of imperishable poems did need from human society, Anne supplied. Emily was strong, and strength and self-sufficiency more and more became her ideal. She liked the wildest aspects of nature and the most uncompromising aspects of life. Certainly Emily led and Anne followed, and *vis-à-vis* this sister Anne was passive. But the give-and-take of such a relationship is mutual.

> *I am the only being whose doom*
> *No tongue would ask . . .*

wrote Emily in 1839. But Anne's tongue, when they were girls, would have asked it, and Anne would have understood the answer given. As girls and children the sisters' bond was strengthened by a perfect association out-of-doors, and even when Emily was becoming conscious of her doom, or creating it, Ellen Nussey wrote of her, 'On the top of a moor or in a deep glen Emily was a child for glee and enjoyment.' Now, when Emily was thirteen and Anne eleven and a half, another association of unique intimacy was beginning. The passion to write was maturing in the younger girls in their turn, and in Emily at least, independence was maturing also. Charlotte being away and Branwell's leadership evidently not proving satisfactory, the two of them set up an island-country of their own . . . the stormy and Byronic

c

land of Gondal, which was to have a longer life than Angria, in fact was to live as writing-territory almost as long as its creators.

Though much remains of Angria, little is left of Gondal: with the exception of two lists by Anne's hand there is no Gondal prose; all has to be reconstructed from stray hints and references in Gondal poems; but a sentence exists that shows how vivid it was to the children and how the dream was established with the utmost naturalness as a parallel reality. It occurs in a fragment of a diary kept by Emily and Anne.

'November the 24, 1834, Monday.
Emily Jane Brontë   Anne Brontë[1]
I fed Rainbow, Diamond, Snowflake, Jasper pheasant (alias). This morning Branwell went down to Mr Driver's and brought news that Sir Robert Peel was going to be invited to stand for Leeds. Anne and I have been peeling apples for Charlotte to make an apple pudding and for Aunt's nuts and apples Charlotte said she made puddings perfectly and she . . . of a quick but lim[i]ted intellect. Taby said just now Come Anne pilloputate [i.e. pill a potato] Aunt has come into the kitchen just now and said Where are your feet Anne Anne answered On the floor Aunt. Papa opened the parlour door and gave Branwell a letter saying Here Branwell read this and show it to your Aunt and Charlotte. The Gondals are discovering the interior of Gaaldine. Sally Mosley is washing in the back kitchin.

It is past twelve o'clock Anne and I have not tid[i]ed ourselves, done our bed work, or done our lessons and we want to go out to play We are going to have for dinner Boiled Beef, Turnips, potatoes and apple pudding The kitchin is in a very untidy state Anne and I have not done our music exercise which consists of *b major* Taby said on my putting a pen in her face Ya pitter pottering there instead of pilling a potate. I answered O Dear, O Dear, O Dear I will derectly With that I get up, take a knife and begin pilling. Finished pilling the potatoes Papa going to walk Mr Sunderland expected.

Anne and I say I wonder what we shall be like and what we shall be and where we shall be, if all goes well, in the year 1874 – in which year I shall be in my 57th year. Anne will be in her 55th year Branwell will be going in his 58th year and Charlotte in her

---

[1] Emily Jane and Anne Brontë's signatures. The MS is in the handwriting of Emily Jane Brontë.

59th year Hoping we shall all be well at that time We close our
paper

Emily and Anne
November the 24, 1834'

A drawing of a lock of hair is crammed on to the side of the tiny
sheet on which the Paper is written, and underneath it is the legend
'A bit of Lady Jul[i]et's hair done by Anne'.

Though not written on a birthday, this is the first of Emily's and
Anne's so-called Birthday Papers, which they promised themselves
to write on Emily's birthday, 30 July, every four years. A similar
fragment has survived which celebrates Branwell's birthday, on 26
June 1837. These two fragments, a couple of letters and four actual
Birthday Papers, by Emily's and Anne's separate hands, are the only
personal writings of the younger sisters that we have. It is supposed
that Charlotte, going through their papers after they died, and preparing such works as she thought fit for publication, destroyed all
private letters and diaries. The four actual Birthday Papers were
found accidentally by Charlotte's husband, Arthur Bell Nicholls. 'The
four small scraps of Emily's and Anne's MSS,' he wrote to the Brontës'
first official biographer, Clement Shorter, 'I found in the small box
I send you. They are sad reading, poor girls!' The box was a little
black box, two or three inches long, containing four papers neatly
folded to the size of sixpence. But though to Arthur Nicholls all
reminiscences of the Brontës must have been sad reading, to us,
accustomed to Charlotte, serious even at the age of nine, the frivolity
and carelessness of this Paper are delightful. For two girls of fourteen
and sixteen, let alone two Brontës, it is an amazingly childish and
uninhibited production. The Gondals come in helter-skelter with the
rest, discovering the interior of Gaaldine with as much naturalness as
Sally Mosley does her washing in the back kitchen.

Of the two lists referred to, the first again show the dream and the
reality or the two realities running parallel. It is a short list of Gondal
place-names inserted alphabetically by Anne in the 'Vocabulary of
Proper Names' at the end of *Goldsmith's Geography*, which the girls
used. The list, squeezed in firmly in Anne's tiny squat 12-year-old
script, is as follows:

'Alexandia [sic] A kingdom in Gaaldine
Almedore, a kingdom in Gaaldine
Elseraden, a kingdom in Gaaldine

Gaaldine, a large island in the North Pacific
Gondal, a large island in the North Pacific
Regina, the capital of Gondal
Ula, a kingdom in Gaaldine, governed by four sovereigns
Zelona, a kingdom in Gaaldine
Zedora, a large Provence [sic] in Gaaldine governed by a viceroy'

We note Anne's preference for the romantic and mysterious letter Z.

Goldsmith's Geography is a dignified little book bound in calf, but it is closely scribbled over, none the less, with faces, calculations, and even a couple of remarks ('You ugly creature' and 'Nothing very particular'), evidently exchanged in writing during a tedious lesson. All the books the children used are scribbled on, which might be surprising if it did not point, like all the other evidence, to a tremendous prevailing scarcity of paper. Everything the girls wrote was crammed into the smallest possible compass, and much of it needs a magnifying glass to read. The Angrian and childish books were of their nature, little; smallness, 'niceness', preciousness, and secrecy were all bound up together; all writers have feelings about paper – some use it royally, others are diffident in deflowering a virgin page; but be that as it might, paper, for the Brontës, was manifestly very short. They crossed their letters, they tore the end-papers out of books, they never wasted a finger's breadth of the precious material. Paper was a basic commodity which they had always needed and were always going to need. Anne's last poem, 'I hoped that with the brave and strong', which contains twelve four-line stanzas, is written on a third of a half-sheet of note-paper. Though she had received her sentence from the doctor, and this was a poem almost of despair, she folded her sheet into a triptych and covered the first leaf, leaving the other two free for possible future compositions.

Anne's second list consists of twenty-six names of Gondal characters, pencilled in two columns on a scrap of paper.

'Arthur Exina	Alexandria Zenobia Hybernia
Gerald Exina	Isabella Senland
Edward Hybernia	Xirilla Senland
Gerald——	Lucia Angora
Alexander——	Catherine T. G. Augusteena
Halbert Clifford	Isabella Abrantez
Julia At [crossed out]	Eliza Hybernia
Archibald MacRay	Harriet Eagle

Gerald F [crossed out]	Isidora Montara
Henry Sophona	Helen Douglas
Eustace Sophona	Cornelia Alzerno
Adolphus St. Albert	Rosalind Fizhorch [Fitzgeorge?]
Albert Vernon	
Alexander D'	

Though the younger sisters' private writings have perished, Clement Shorter tells us that he received from Mr Nicholls 'countless manuscripts written in childhood' by Charlotte and Branwell. Branwell, even more precocious than his sisters, had been writing since he was ten. His partner now removed (though they kept Angria going by letter) and his juniors withdrawn out of his jurisdiction, Branwell must have found himself more than usually at a loose end. He was now fourteen, a brilliant boy, whose brilliance was destined to come to nothing, either because it was the kind of childish brilliance that burns itself out or because it could not survive the folly of his upbringing. In accordance with his father's theories, though the daughters might be sent to school, the son might not. He was kept at home, supposedly out of temptation, the admired only boy, coached by his father and thrown for companionship upon the village youth, whose society he was in fact forbidden. Branwell, who was the most Irish of the Brontës, as Anne was the least, was a tremendous enthusiast, for Angria and for everything. When he was sent as an escort with Charlotte on her first visit to Ellen Nussey at her home The Rydings, Ellen remarks, 'He was in wild ecstasy about everything.' The absence of Charlotte and the setting up of an independent Gondal must have sent him more often in the disapproved direction.

Charlotte returned home after eighteen months, during which, almost morbidly conscientious, she had scarcely allowed herself an hour's respite from study and self-improvement. Now she set about handing on to her sisters what she had acquired, though Anne still remained under the general tutelage of her aunt.

'An account of one day is an account of all. In the morning from nine o'clock till half-past twelve I instruct my sisters and draw, then we walk till dinner, after dinner I sew till tea-time, and after tea I either read, write, do a little fancy work or draw, as I please. Thus in one delightful, though somewhat monotonous course, my life is passed.'

The extract is from an early letter to Miss Ellen Nussey, for

Charlotte, in spite of shyness, oddity, self-consciousness, and old-fashioned clothes, had made two life-long friends at school, Ellen Nussey and Mary Taylor. She now begins the interchange of visits and the correspondence with Ellen which was to continue for the rest of their lives, and which contains most of what we know of external Brontë history. 'My Aunt and sisters desire their love to you,' she writes in conclusion to her letter. They had not yet met Ellen, but Charlotte had stayed with her and she had sent them a box of apples; and we can picture Anne, if not Emily, along with her instruction, learning from Charlotte the delights of that novel thing, an extra-mural friendship.

'On Tuesday next we shall have all the female teachers of the Sunday-school to tea.' The girls all taught in the Sunday-school, and visited and read to the sick, but though they did their duty by the village they did not linger; an old Bradford resident remembered that even when grown up, 'they were the most timid and sensitive creatures it was possible to gaze upon. They generally dressed in old-fashioned gowns of faded black silk, while their feet were encased in strong low-fitting shoes and various-hued stockings.'[1] Equipped for walking rather than for society, they preferred setting their faces upward toward the moor.

Such was Anne's life from twelve to sixteen, a remote and circumscribed existence, dominated at a distance by the rigid, opinionated, and affectionate old father, but happy enough for a shy girl whose resources were to be found in herself and her immediate circle, and strong in certain essentials – affection, security, natural beauty, and peace and freedom for the imagination. Though there was no outer social circle, the inner circle was close and stimulating; in each other the Brontës had what many infant authors lack, a ready and enthusiastic audience for their work.

Mr Brontë, a reader himself, encouraged reading, though we are not surprised to hear that Miss Branwell did not. In 1832 he engaged a drawing-master for his children and the organist at Keighley came to give them music-lessons. Anne may be said for these years to have lived a life in which the artificialities were reduced to nil and the realities always vividly present. The virtues of such a life are manifest; its weaknesses were that the total lack of artificiality and frivolity was itself slightly unnatural for an adolescent girl, and though Anne, unlike Charlotte, remained amazingly free from priggishness, this life

[1] W. Scruton, *Brontë Society Transactions*, Vol. 1, 1898.

did not allow her to grow out of her shyness, of which she was deeply conscious as a fault. From a remark of Charlotte we may gather that, unless her godmothers remembered her, Anne at this period can hardly have had the handling of a penny-piece of her own.

In the summer of 1833 Ellen Nussey paid a visit to the Parsonage. The friend took shape. Though she lived only twenty miles away, 'Papa,' wrote Charlotte in issuing the invitation, 'desires me to present his respects to Mrs Nussey and say that he should feel greatly obliged if she would allow us the pleasure of your company for a few weeks.' There was thus time for Ellen to become a friend of the family, which she did, and particularly of Anne; a friend once removed as it were, but from the beginning we are sensible that they entered and kept a definite relationship. Anne became 'Little Anne' also to Ellen, the youngest of the Brontës, the prettiest, the least forbidding. Ellen Nussey is our second source of Brontë history. It was to her that all early biographers, beginning with Mrs Gaskell, applied. She furnished them with information and also published some 'Reminiscences of Charlotte Brontë' in Scribner's *Monthly Magazine* for 1871, over the signature 'E'. These reminiscences contain the account of her first visit to Haworth.

Both Charlotte's friends came from more prosperous and more genial backgrounds than her own; through their eyes she could see her herself and her family as oddities. . . . 'You're like growing potatoes in a cellar,' Mary Taylor had exclaimed, and Charlotte had assented sadly, 'Yes, we are.' All the same she found no difficulty in asking both of them to stay, and the Parsonage found no difficulty in receiving them. For the first time the girls saw their tall, good-looking Irish father play the attentive host to one of their friends and their antiquated tiny aunt play the hostess, caring for the guest's comfort, while in the manner of elderly maiden ladies, she recalled her early triumphs in Penzance. For the rest they were free of the moors in June and July. . . . 'There was always a lingering delight in these spots,' wrote Ellen; 'every moss, every flower, every tint and form were noted and enjoyed. Emily especially had a gleesome delight in these nooks of beauty. . . . We laughed and made mirth of each other and settled we would call ourselves the quartette.'

A portrait exists of Ellen Nussey, which must have been painted at about the time of her first visit to the Parsonage. The face is gentle and attractive, with widely set eyes under a wide brow, 'a fair quiet face,' Charlotte writes, 'brown eyes and dark hair which she wore in curls.' There is a feeling of feminity and repose and grace. It is easy to guess what such a character had for the Brontës, and what the Brontës had for her.

The only likeness we have of Mary Taylor shows her in middle age. She was a strong, interesting character, the original of Rose Yorke, in *Shirley*. Her portrait shows a fine massive head, on which the lace cap sits strangely. As a girl she had evidently been attracted to Branwell Brontë. She was adventurous enough to emigrate to New Zealand, whence she sent memories of Charlotte back to Mrs Gaskell. She was feminist and critical, urging Charlotte to leave home and declaring after her friend's death that she had been sacrificed to her selfish old father. Charlotte loved and appreciated her, but she is not mentioned by Anne, who had so speedily developed an affection for Ellen Nussey. Though independent in mind, and by no means unfeminist, Anne was essentially unmilitant, and for this reason may not have felt particularly drawn to Mary Taylor.

Ellen's narrative is composed of memories of various visits, but the descriptions of the people refer to 1833. 'Tabby, the faithful trustworthy old servant . . . still kept to her duty of walking out on the moor with the "childer" if they went any distance from home, unless Branwell were sent by his father as a protector.' 'Emily Brontë had by this time acquired a lithesome graceful figure. . . . She had very beautiful eyes . . . kind, kindling liquid eyes; but she did not often look at you . . . she was too reserved. . . . She talked very little . . . Branwell studied regularly with his father and used to paint in oils, which was regarded as study for what might eventually be his profession. All the household entertained the idea of his being an artist. . . .' She describes the house. 'The interior of the now far-famed Parsonage lacked drapery of all kinds. . . . There was not much carpet anywhere except in the sitting-room and on the study floor. The hall-floor and stairs were done with sandstone, always beautifully clean, as everything was about the house. . . . Scant and bare indeed . . . yet mind and thought, I had almost said elegance, but certainly refinement, diffused themselves over all, and made nothing really wanting. . . .' The Brontës, in fact, nothwithstanding the prevailing austerity, had taste, as can still be made out by the visitor to Haworth Parsonage.

The poorness of the patch of garden struck the visitor from a fine house. 'The garden was nearly all grass, and possessed only a few stunted thorns and shrubs and a few currant bushes, which Emily and Anne treasured as their own bit of garden.' 'The living was of the simplest . . . a single joint followed invariably by one kind or another of milk pudding.'

'From childhood to womanhood,' Ellen Nussey told Clement Shorter, 'the three girls regularly breakfasted with their father in his study, the square room on the right of the entrance. In the dining-room on the left they spent the greater part of their lives. There they ate their midday dinner, tea, and supper. Mr Brontë joined them at tea, though he frequently dined alone in his study leaving Miss Branwell to preside.'

Some time after the first visit we hear that there was 'the addition of a piano. Emily, after some application, played with precision and brilliancy. Anne played also, but she preferred soft harmonies and vocal music. She sang a little; her voice was weak, but very sweet in tone.'

'During Miss Branwell's reign the love of animals had to be kept in due subjection. There was but one dog which was admitted to the parlour at stated times. Emily and Anne always gave him a portion of their breakfast. Later on there were three household pets . . . the tawny, strong-limbed "Keeper", Emily's favourite: he was so completely under her control, she could quite easily make him spring and roar like a lion . . . Flossy – long, silky-haired, black and white, Flossy – was Anne's favourite; and black "Tom", the tabby, was everybody's favourite.' In objective touches Ellen gives us a picture of Anne's other half, Emily, who could hold converse with nature, with animals, with the piano, but looked at or spoke to human beings very little. She tells us that at twilight she and Charlotte 'walked with arms encircling one another round and round the table' (this was a trick brought from Miss Wooler's), 'and Emily and Anne followed in similar fashion'. We may suppose that even if Emily was indifferent, Anne listened with interest to her seniors' talk of Roe Head and learned that Lowood was not the pattern of all schools.

Ellen herself rapidly became a favourite. 'Were I to tell you of the impression you have made on everyone here you would accuse me of flattery. Papa and Aunt are continually adducing you as an example for me to shape my actions and behaviour by, Emily and Anne say they never saw anyone they liked so well as Miss Nussey.' Even Tabby was 'absolutely fascinated'. All the Brontës for the rest of their days were to have the comfort of this friend.

In contrast with Ellen's picture of the Brontës on their best behaviour in the parlour in 1833, we have Emily and Anne's picture of the

Brontës in the kitchen in 1834, with Gondal, profoundly unsuspected by Ellen, very much in the picture also.

In that same year Ellen asks Charlotte to recommend her some books to read. Charlotte turns to the new pupil with enthusiasm. 'If you like poetry, let it be first-rate, Milton, Shakespeare, Thompson, Goldsmith, Pope (if you will though I don't admire him), Scott, Byron, Campbell, Wordsworth, and Southey.' Anybody's reading, as well as Anne's and Emily's, was safe in Charlotte's hands. 'Now Ellen don't be startled at the names of Byron and Shakespeare. Both these were great men. . . .' Unlike Byron, Shakespeare was out of fashion, but Charlotte at eighteen could recommend him. 'Omit the comedies of Shakespeare and the Don Juan. . . .' This advice was no doubt administered at home with a firm hand in the interests of Anne's purity. However we need not suppose that Anne, being a reader herself, was unduly subject to advice. The feast was spread and the company was free to choose its dishes. There were also the newspapers and *Fraser's Magazine*, which Aunt had 'consented' to take in 1831, and probably paid for. And it is interesting to remember that it was in *Fraser's Magazine* that Anne's longest poem 'The Three Guides' was published in 1848.

An opinion elicited by Ellen on dancing, 'It is allowed on all hands that the sin of dancing consists not in the mere action of shaking the shanks (as the Scotch say) but in the consequence that usually attends it – namely frivolity and waste of time,' suggests the state of mind, induced by Cornish Methodism, Irish Puritanism, and outlandish seclusion, that prevailed at Haworth Parsonage when Anne was verging on fifteen.

But opinions, not elicited, but poured forth incontinent on the subject of the coming election have a very different ring. 'The Election! The Election! That cry has rung even among our lonely hills like the blast of a trumpet. Under what banner have your brothers ranged themselves? . . . Use your influence with them, entreat them, if it be necessary on your knees to stand by their country and religion in this day of danger.'

Toryism, drunk in at the father's knee, was the last thing to be resisted and Anne was the last person to resist principles imbibed in this manner, but no doubt with her they were a little less vehement than with Charlotte. In an Angrian story of this period Charlotte makes Branwell describe his sisters. He is asked if they are as queer as he: 'Oh,' he replies, 'they are miserable silly creatures, not worth talking about. Charlotte's eighteen years old, a broad dumpy thing, whose head does not come higher than my elbow. Emily's sixteen, lean and scant, with a face about the size of a penny, and Anne is nothing, absolutely nothing.' 'What! Is she an idiot?' he is asked. 'Next door to it.' And later he says of himself that he is 'not satisfied with being a sign painter in the village as Charlotte and them things were with being sempstresses.'

We need read nothing more into this unpondered description of Anne than we already know, namely that she was entirely unobtrusive.

* * *

Eighteen-thirty-five saw the end of this quiet phase. The family was to break up. Branwell was not to be a sign-painter; he was to go to the Royal Academy schools as an art student, and in order to help maintain him in London Charlotte was to return to Roe Head in the capacity of governess, and Emily was to accompany her as a pupil.

Though the Brontës were profoundly independent in character they were also profoundly Victorian in outlook and the idea of wage-earning *per se* had absolutely no charm for them. It was simply a painful duty. 'Did I not once say Ellen you ought to be thankful for your independence? I felt what I said at the time and I repeat it now in double earnestness.' However Charlotte both loved and respected Miss Wooler; things might have been worse.

A portrait group exists[1] of the three sisters, painted by Branwell, and as it is generally attributed to the year 1835, it may have been executed at this moment when the family was about to disperse. Mrs Gaskell, whose biography was written immediately after Charlotte's death, and who knew Charlotte, said that the likenesses were good. Branwell was just eighteen in July 1835. He was not a good painter, even allowing for his youth, but something is to be learned from the battered canvas.

Anne and Emily gaze out of the picture with great eyes like hares. Their faces are of infinite sensibility. In Anne's the eyes are luminous, fearful, and yet steady. One feels that she will fear, but that she will go forward to meet what she fears, even though the features all seem ready in an instant to melt into tears. The mouth, almost unbearably sensitive, like Emily's, is round and prominent, with none of the particular firmness that we see in Charlotte's. A certain sensuousness resides there, and in the round chin.

[1] In the National Portrait Gallery.

On the girls' departure Mr Brontë recommended them again to his old friend Elizabeth Firth, now Mrs Franks, addressing whom seemed to bring out his bad strain. After touching on Miss Wooler's as 'this delusive and insnaring world' where his daughters could not 'lie beyond the reach of temptation', he mentions blandly that he designs to send Branwell alone as an art student to London, and 'my dear little Anne I intend to keep at home for another year under her aunt's tuition and my own. . . . My own health is generally but very delicate . . . indeed I have never been well since I left Thornton.' (This is now fifteen years ago.) 'My happiest days were spent there . . .' Then follows a long funereal passage on the good old times.

Anne was at home alone for only three months, for Emily, it was soon clear, could not exist at school. The regimented life, most of it passed indoors, among people, was literal captivity to her. '. . . Every morning, when she awoke,' wrote Charlotte, 'the vision of home and the moors rushed on her, and darkened and saddened the day that lay before her. Nobody knew what ailed her but me. I knew only too well . . . I felt in my heart she would die if she did not go home. . . .'

To have lived all their lives on a hill-top, in a churchyard, with their back to the open moor, unfitted the Brontës for living in other places. Emily it unfitted totally. We can imagine Anne's feelings on receiving her back. However the chance of education was not to be wasted and Anne returned to Roe Head in her sister's stead. She remained there till 1837, and left summarily after a scene between Charlotte and Miss Wooler, of which she herself was the subject. Anne was ill, very ill, Charlotte feared, and she did not think the headmistress took her sister's symptoms seriously enough. This is the sum of what we hear through Charlotte of Anne's two years at Roe Head, and we may suppose that no news from that anxious and defensive quarter is at least tolerably good news. In any event there was no fault to be found with the school.

Roe Head, about twenty miles from Haworth, was in the district of Hartshead, where Mr Brontë had been a curate before he went to Thornton, so it was not alien ground. If one did not insist on bleakness, it was a fine house on a splendid site, standing on the gentle slopes of Mirfield Moor overlooking the valley of the Calder. 'Young verdure, transparent emerald and amber gleams – Nunwood, the sole remnant of antique British forest, slept in the shade of a cloud – the distant hills were dappled. . . .'[1] This was the spring prospect, that gave place in

[1] *Shirley*, Chapter XII.

due course to rifts of mist, and splendid fumey sunsets, and snow. The twin fronts of the house were rounded, so that many of the rooms had bay windows, overlooking the view. The pupils, no more than eight in number, probably slept on the second storey, in front. There was a walled garden, a fine old coach-house and stable-buildings, and a grassy slope in front. Miss Wooler, the eldest of three maiden sisters, was described by Mr Brontë as a clever, decent and motherly woman; a great-nephew visiting the old ladies as an awed little boy found Aunt Wooler surprisingly understanding, and reported how when over ninety, she remarked tolerantly of Americans in search of Brontë gleanings, 'I cannot refuse to see them: it is very trying, but I must do my best.'[1] Ellen Nussey saw her through the pupils' eyes. 'She was short and stout, but graceful in her movements, very fluent in conversation and with a very sweet voice. . . . Personally Miss Wooler was like a lady abbess. She wore white, well-fitting dresses, embroidered. She was nobly scrupulous and conscientious. . . .'

This was the figure who had come out to welcome Charlotte as a new girl, and after having dispatched Emily no doubt came out, perhaps a little anxiously, to welcome Anne. We learn also from Ellen that the schoolroom, which was the big bow-windowed room on the right of the entrance, was very nice and comfortable for a schoolroom, and that (when she and Charlotte joined at least) 'a crimson cloth covered the long table down the centre of the room'. Charlotte too left an impression of this room. Chafing indoors there she wrote, 'A sweet August morning was smiling without. The dew was not yet dried off the field, the early shadows were stretching cool and dim from the haystacks and the roots of the grand old oaks and thorns scattered along the sunk fence. All was still except for the murmur of the scribes over their task. I flung up the sash. An uncertain sound of inexpressible sweetness came on a dying gale from the south. I looked in that direction . . . I listened . . . the sound sailed full and liquid down the descent; it was the bells of Huddersfield Parish Church.'

Roe Head was said to have a ghost, and Miss Wooler used to send the girls upstairs in turn on errands, so as to dispel their fear. She had two badges of conduct for her pupils, a black ribbon worn in the style of the Order of the Garter, and a silver medal.

Though as a school the establishment was serious, nothing less tyrannical or oppressive could be imagined. It was small, intimate and

---

[1] *Memories of Margaret Wooler*, by the Rev. Max Blakely of Scarborough. Brontë Society Transactions.

as it were personal to its director, who walked and talked with the girls out of doors, giving them a strong sense of the locality and its history, and joined them sometimes in their evening hour of relaxation. Miss Wooler paced the room and her pupils vied with each other to hang upon her arm . . . a rather girlish picture, but pleasant for its warmth. When the pupils had finished their tasks they were free to relax round the schoolroom fire or out of doors. They had plenty of air and exercise and outdoor games. As companions, they came from a good level of society, being not so rich that the desideratum was frivolous accomplishment, nor so poor that it was humble-pie. In the annals of school history, with its many black pages, it should not go unrecorded that Miss Wooler had a special dish prepared for Charlotte's dinner every day.

Anne remained shy; we do not hear of her bringing home any friends to stay; but remembering her attachment to Emily, and the closeness of the family, that is not surprising. Nor is it surprising to hear that in December 1836 she won a good conduct prize.[1] By nature, as well as by background, she was the kind of person who gazes at community life shrinkingly. And she was not naturally gay. But by every outside person's testimony she was appealing and likeable, and from every trace of her we see that she possessed genuine humility, which was lacking in both her sisters. We may fairly suppose that she had her own unobtrusive place in the schoolroom, and we may guess a little of what she experienced in those two years from sixteen to eighteen – softer country, some contact with society, the influence and friendship of Miss Wooler, and the companionship of young people who were young in different ways from what the Brontës were. We see her at Roe Head becoming mistress of some of the material she was to use in her books, and qualifying to become a governess as painlessly as she could have done anywhere.

Charlotte's presence must have helped her, most particularly in keeping homesickness at bay; but Charlotte's relations with Anne or with anybody at Roe Head during this period were bound to be influenced by her own state. Charlotte loathed her present duties as just now she would have loathed almost any duties. It was for her the moment of life when the dream was in the ascendant. Both the Angrian dream and the romantic dream possessed her, and the guilt

---

[1] It was a book called *On the Improvement of the Mind and Education of Youth*, and was inscribed, 'Prize for good conduct presented to Miss A. Brontë with Miss Wooler's kind love.'

of her indulgence possessed her equally. The desire to write and the confused desire to live, coupled with her sense of sin, her powerful sense of duty, and her struggles for divine assistance made of Charlotte a battlefield and she lacked the physical strength to sustain the battle. Perhaps the younger sister in some degree helped and pitied the elder.

For the understanding of Anne's future, it is necessary at this point to mention Branwell. In 1836 the brilliant boy had turned nineteen. Already for some time past, in default of a better audience, he had been regularly entertaining the company at the Black Bull at Haworth. Before trying for the Academy Schools he had been having lessons in portrait-painting with William Robinson of Leeds and he had delighted similar audiences there. Branwell had gifts: they were not very great or powerful gifts, though they might have sufficed to bring him some comfort and self-respect, but he had little notion of how to apply them. We see the ebullient, red-headed, tiny figure (like Charlotte he took after his mother), always wildly enthusiastic, gaily and brilliantly organizing the early literary life of the Brontës, protecting his sisters on the moors, driving them out in a gig, escorting Charlotte to The Rydings, visiting her at school, the adored brother and genius of the family. But from there, there was absolutely no advance, either in self-discipline or in realistic contact with the world. At nineteen Branwell thought, laudably enough, that it was time to see life, or to harness his talents and get some qualification. He practised both painting and writing. In 1835 he proposed to be an artist, but in 1835 and 1836 we also find him addressing two letters to the Editor of *Blackwood's*. Perhaps he tried literature when the outlook for art was unpropitious, or vice versa. His letters to *Blackwood's*, like the pompous little note he addressed to the Secretary of the Academy Schools, asking to bring his work, are unpleasing, but they are also touching. 'Sir – Read what I write. And would to Heaven you could believe it true, for then you would attend to and act upon it.' And 'Sir, Read now at least . . .' If the Editor read, he did not answer. Branwell went to London, probably in the spring of 1836, but he did not get into the Academy and most likely never went near it. In another burst of confidence and optimism, no doubt fostered by Charlotte, he wrote to *Blackwood's* again in January 1837 and also to Wordsworth, and Charlotte wrote to Southey at about the same time. Wordsworth, Southey tells us, was disgusted with Branwell's letter, and of Charlotte's he wrote, 'I sent a dose of cooling admonition to that poor girl whose letter reached me at Buckland.' However, he had been moved to send something, and Charlotte, notwithstanding the coldness, ('Literature can never be the business of a woman's life') wrote again. 'Sir, I cannot rest till I have answered your letter.' This time Southey sent a better reply. 'Dear Madam, Your letter has given me great pleasure, and I should not forgive myself if I did not tell you so.' He asks her to visit him if she is ever in the Lakes and signs himself her sincere friend.

Such a letter from the Poet Laureate could not do otherwise than set Charlotte up in her own esteem and that of her family. The dose had in fact been administered to Branwell. A dose of this kind, especially if repeated, is utterly mortifying, but it is not enough to quench a nineteen-year-old poet if he is serious. Branwell was not quenched, but the tone of the letters, together with his behaviour in London, suggest that already he was feeble and would easily drift on that course, which was to be the end of him and was to bring so much wretchedness to Anne.

In the summer of 1836 Charlotte and Anne spent a few days at the end of term with the still-affectionate Franks, who apropos this visit received a letter from Charlotte to say that her father could not spare them for more than a week-end, and at the same time a letter from the Rev. Brontë to say that they were to stay as long as possible. 'We propose coming by the four or five o'clock coach on Friday afternoon,' wrote Charlotte, 'and returning by an early morning coach on Monday, as Papa, I fear, will scarcely be willing to dispense with us longer at home.' And 'My dear Madame,' wrote Mr Brontë, 'My dear little Charlotte has informed me that you and Mr Franks have been so kind as to invite her and Anne to pay you a visit for a week, but that through impatience, as is very natural they have curtail'd that invitation to a few days. I have written to them to countermand this intention.' Home, after a term's absence, was the only place that had any charm for the sisters. Ellen, whose family had moved in the interval from The Rydings to Brookroyd, was to have joined them at Haworth in the Christmas holidays, but a serious accident to Tabby prevented the visit and Anne shared Charlotte's disappointment. 'It mortifies and disappoints me most keenly,' Charlotte wrote, 'and I am not the only one who is disappointed. All in the house were looking forward to your visit with eagerness.' Over Tabby's illness an issue arose with Miss Branwell in which Anne showed herself no more passive than her sisters. Miss Branwell wished Tabby, when she was out of danger, to be nursed at her home. The sisters, according to Mrs Gaskell, 'made one unanimous and stiff resistance. Tabby had tended them in their childhood. They, and none other, should tend her in her infirmity and age. At tea-time they were sad and silent and the meal went away untouched by any of the three. So it was at breakfast . . . they "struck" eating till the resolution was rescinded.' Mrs Gaskell had written of earlier relations with Miss Branwell. 'Next to her nephew, the docile, pensive Anne was her favourite. Of her she had taken charge from her infancy; she was always patient and tractable and would submit quietly to occasional repression, even when she felt it keenly. Not so her elder sisters. . . .' This description of Anne was furnished of course by Charlotte, and it may have been Anne's childish submission that impressed on Charlotte's mind the idea of her sister's passivity. Clearly for her or for Emily such a thing would have been impossible. But old Miss Branwell was fond of Anne; perhaps Anne was fond of, or at least lenient towards old Miss Branwell. In any case we learn that Anne could submit when her own comfort was the issue and resist for the sake of another person, a firmness corroborated by Ellen Nussey, who tells us that though they differed greatly in character and disposition 'they were each and all on common ground if a principle had to be maintained.'

Charlotte rallied at home but sank again when she returned with Anne to school and to the drudgery of her daily existence. Duty to the Brontës always had first call, but the fulfilling of it was terribly destructive to them. She owned, to Mary Taylor, 'that after clothing herself and Anne there was nothing left, though she had hoped to be able to save something. She confessed it was not brilliant, but what could she do?' Accepting her lot, she sought frantically for divine aid to help her bear it, but was confronted by her lack of faith and confessed herself 'smitten at times to the heart' with the conviction that '———'s ghastly Calvinistic doctrines are true.'

Charlotte's struggles at this moment would not be pertinent if it had not been suggested that '———'s ghastly Calvinistic doctrines' referred to Anne. The form of the phrase alone seems enough to refute the idea. It is impossible to imagine her imputing such authority to her youngest sister at the age of sixteen. However Calvin and his doctrines deeply concerned Anne; the phrase leads in a direction we must follow.

Studying Anne through Charlotte, we read in Charlotte's preface to her sister's poems, published with *Wuthering Heights* and *Agnes Grey* after her death,

> 'In looking over my sister Anne's poems I find mournful evidence that religious feeling had been to her but too much like what it was to Cowper; I mean of course in a far milder form. Without rendering her a prey to those terrors that defy concealment, it subdued her mood and bearing to a perpetual pensiveness; the pillar of a cloud glided constantly before her eyes; she ever waited at the foot of a secret Sinai, listening in her heart to the voice of a trumpet sounding long and waxing louder. Some perhaps would rejoice over these tokens of a sincere though sorrowing piety in a deceased relative; I own, to me they seem sad, as if her whole innocent life had been passed under martyrdom of an unconfessed physical pain. . . .'

Charlotte tells us with the authority which, backed up by her love and her moving prose we find at the outset hard to question, that Anne suffered from religious melancholy, in fact that the doctrine of predestination preyed on her mind as it had done on Cowper's, though to a less terrible degree. But moved as we are by Charlotte, in the interests of Anne we must not take her on trust. The Brontës were not Methodists, but Methodism was in their consciousness and in their blood. Their mother had been a Methodist; their Aunt Branwell was one still, and perhaps it was to her 'ghastly Calvinistic doctrines' that Charlotte referred. We have only to read the Rev. Patrick's poems to hear many an echo of Wesley's hymns: we can hear echoes of them even in Branwell. Haworth was strongly Methodist ground: the famous and unforgotten William Grimshaw of Haworth had been a pillar of Methodism and Wesley had taken tea at the then Parsonage, and preached in the splendid stone barn adjacent in Grimshaw's day. John Newton in his life of Grimshaw says, 'Haworth is one of those obscure places which like the fishing-towns of Galilee favoured with our Lord's presence would scarcely be known at a distance were it not connected with the name of Grimshaw.' The Brontës would have concurred in this. Charlotte evinces plenty of knowledge of Methodism in *Shirley* and some of its threads and the threads of the Grimshaw legend are undoubtedly woven into *Wuthering Heights*.

Cowper also was in the Brontës' consciousness and in their blood, not only because of his work but because it was John Newton who had preached Methodism to Cowper at Olney. Mary Taylor mentions the special attachment all the Parsonage family felt for the poet:

'*The Castaway* was known to them all, and they all at times appreciated or even appropriated it.' Methodism was divided into two camps, those who believed in predestination with Calvin and Whitefield, and those who, like Wesley, did not. Cowper's tragic poem is the witness to his hopeless acceptance of predestination and the seeming fact that he was damned.

> *No voice divine the storm allayed*
> *No light propitious shone :*
> *When snatched from all effectual aid,*
> *We perished, each alone :*
> *But I beneath a rougher sea*
> *And whelmed in deeper gulphs than he.*

To Anne, Calvin and Cowper and religion itself were important in a different way from what they were with Charlotte. Charlotte tried to grasp at the consolations of religion in desperate moments, as now, in the profound stultification of governess-ship at Roe Head, or when physical lowness made death seem nearer than usual. Charlotte in later life was observed to be obsessed, and little wonder, with the thought of death : graves, though she lived among them, made her turn cold ; she brooded as it were positively upon death, wondering what suffering there was at the moment of dissolution and how long it might last. She felt herself in terrible need of the faith that eluded her. Mary Taylor tersely sums up her state with the remark that 'Charlotte was free from religious depression when she was in tolerable health'. In 1836 she could not avoid falling a victim to it.

With Anne, religion was not an emergency measure. She was, all the time, a sincere Christian. Thus, being imbued like the others with Methodism and with Cowper, problems of faith and salvation were serious and continuous with her, not fitful and terrible as they were with Charlotte. For Cowper she felt a peculiar love and affinity, and at the age of twenty-two addressed a poem to him, full of compassionate fellow-feeling. A few months afterwards she wrote 'A Word to the "Elect" '. It is clear that the subject of salvation deeply occupied her thoughts and had done since she was a girl. In the illness that preceded her removal from Roe Head in 1837, a minister was sought to visit her, and Anne had asked urgently that it should be the Rev. James La Trobe who was a bishop of the Moravian Church. The Moravians had a congregation at Mirfield and were held in high respect by Miss Wooler. The Rev. La Trobe left the following letter.

'She [Anne Brontë] was suffering from a severe attack of gastric fever, which brought her very low, and her voice was only a whisper; her life hung on a slender thread. She soon got over the shyness natural on seeing a perfect stranger. The words of love, from Jesus, opened her ear to my words, and she was very grateful for my visits. I found her well acquainted with the main truths of the Bible respecting our salvation, but seeing them more through the law than the Gospel, more as requirement from God than His gift in His son, but her heart opened to the sweet views of Salvation, pardon, and peace in the blood of Christ, and she accepted His welcome to the weary and heavy-laden sinner, conscious more of her not loving the Lord her God than of acts of enmity to Him, and had she died then I should have counted her His redeemed and ransomed child. It was not till I read Charlotte Brontë's Life that I recognized my interesting patient at Roe Head, where a Christian influence pervaded the establishment and its decided discipline.'

With the passing of her first youth, Anne, never confident or gay, was saddened by her hard lot as a governess and by disappointment in love. Doubt and melancholy threatened her, and she was conscious of it; there was little consolation in her life; but she did not succumb. On the contrary she expressed her struggle and finally also expressed her triumph, that is her achievement of faith in the face of oncoming early death.

Charlotte is wrong in imputing religious melancholy to Anne. Nobody who suffered from religious melancholy could have written *Agnes Grey* and *The Tenant of Wildfell Hall*. Charlotte saw her sister religious, passive, as she called it, silent, sometimes sad, and she failed to appreciate Anne's novels. Silence, to a nature that looks for a warm response, is sometimes hard to bear and always hard to understand. Charlotte added the sum up wrong. Anne husbanded her spirits; for when we re-read her work, hammered by Charlotte's constant description of the author, we find it unexpectedly lively.

In the spring of 1837 Miss Wooler moved her school to Heald's House, Dewsbury Moor, a lower and less healthy site than Roe Head. 'Dewsbury is a poisonous place for me,' Charlotte said of it in recollection, not only because the town itself was horrible, low-lying, dank, industrial, and not sufficiently removed – but because the 'teach, teach, teach' continued, and because she returned against her better judgement after the scene with Miss Wooler over Anne. Heald's

House actually once again was charming – a long, two-storeyed Queen Anne front, backed on to a conglomerate ancient stone foundation.

It is pleasant to see Anne herself, in retreat from school and any incidental troubles, inditing, with Emily, in the June holidays, what amounted to a Birthday Paper for Branwell.

'Monday evening June 27 1837
at [a] bit past 4 o'clock Charlotte working in Aunt's room Branwell reading Eugene Aram to her Anne and I writing in the drawing-room Anne a poem beginning "fair was the evening and brightly the sun["] I Augustus – Almedas life 1st v. 1-4 the page from the last a fine rather coolish then grey cloudy but sunny day Aunt working in the little Room papa – gone out. Tabby in the kitchin – the Emperors and Empresses of Gondal and Gaaldine preparing to depart from Gaaldine to Gondal for the coronation which will be on the 12th of July Queen Vittoria [sic] ascended the throne this month Northangerland in Moncey's Isle Zamorna at Eversham. all tight and right in which condition it is to be hoped we shall all be on this day 4 years at which time Charlotte will be 25 and 2 months – Branwell just 24 it being his birthday – myself 22 and 10 months and a peice [sic] Anne 21 and nearly a half I wonder where we shall be and how we shall be and what kind of a day it will be then let us hope for the best

Emily Jane Brontë – Anne Brontë'

Just below these lines is a pen-and-ink drawing of two female figures seated at a table, one labelled 'Emily', the other 'Anne'. On the table is a box marked 'the Tin Box' and two sheets marked 'the papers' and 'The Papers'. Below and to the right of the drawing is the following continuation :

'Aunt. Come Emily its past 4 o'clock Emily, Yes Aunt Anne Well do you intend to write in the evening. Emily well what think you (we agreed to go out first to make sure if we get into a humour)[1] we may stay in

'I guess that this day four years we shall be in this drawing room comfortable I hope it may be so Anne guesses we shall all be gone somewhere together comfortable we hope it may be either.'[2]

[1] A humour to write, presumably.
[2] *Gondal's Queen* by Fannie E. Ratchford.

If the 1834 paper appears childish, the 1837 paper, with its mimic coronation and its general untidiness appears at first sight amazingly so. On a second glance, however (leaving aside the particularity about birthdays, which in two young women of seventeen and a half and nineteen must be admitted to be downright infantile), we receive an impression of genius unbuttoned and the childishness of the unchildish. Emily, who writes the paper, for all her slapdash spelling, cannot quite keep the poet down. 'A fine rather coolish then grey cloudy but sunny day.' She begins to say a word about Nature, and has to pause and think, to make it exact, and ends up by making it so much better than exact. Her few lines of pen-and-ink sketch, it may be noted, is the most spirited piece of art of all that came out of the Parsonage.

In the autumn of that year Emily made her one attempt at offering a financial contribution. 'My sister Emily is gone into a situation as teacher in a large school of near forty pupils, near Halifax,' Charlotte wrote. 'I have one letter from her since her departure; it gives an appalling account of her duties – hard labour from six in the morning until near eleven at night with only one half-hour of exercise between. This is slavery. I fear she will never stand it.'

Emily stood it for a few months. Anne was brought away from Dewsbury at the end of that year. 'You were right in your conjectures respecting the cause of my sudden departure' Ellen Nussey learned on 4 January 1838. 'Anne continued wretchedly ill – neither the pain nor the difficulty of breathing left her – and how could I feel otherwise than very miserable? I looked upon her case in a different light from what I could wish any uninterested person to view it – Miss Wooler thought me a fool – we came to a little *éclaircissement* one evening – I told her one or two rather plain truths . . . and the next day, unknown to me, she wrote to Papa . . . Papa sent for us the day after he had received her letter. . . . Meantime I had formed a firm resolution – to quit Miss Wooler and her concerns for ever. . . . Anne is now much better – though she still requires a great deal of care – however I am relieved of my worst fears respecting her.'

The letter reflects Charlotte's anxiety and excitement. Miss Wooler was distressed and anxious too, according to eye-witnesses, as well she might have been with the Brontës on her hands, and as her immediate writing to their father proves. The breach was fully healed, however, and affection returned and prevailed. Miss Wooler offered her house at the sea-side in Anne's last illness and it was Miss Wooler who gave Charlotte away to Arthur Nicholls as a bride.

In June all the family were at home again, Charlotte having left Dewsbury Moor on the doctor's orders. Mary Taylor and her younger sister Martha, the one authentically childish figure who moves across the horizon at Haworth, are paying them a visit. 'They are making such a noise about me that I cannot write any more. Mary is playing on the piano; Martha is chattering as fast as her little tongue can run, and Branwell is standing before her, laughing at her vivacity.'

In spite of the cheerful picture, Charlotte fancies that the flush on Mary Taylor's cheek is hectic and that her breath comes short. Her letter reminds us how great a threat and scourge consumption was a hundred years ago, and how most likely she could hardly remember a time when the word was not part of her consciousness. Anne had been very ill at school; her sister's anxiety is not to be wondered at. But Anne on her eighteenth birthday was better, she was at home, breathing the air of the moors and of Gondal, poetry swelled in her and she took up her pen. She wrote 'The Captive's Dream' on 24 January and 'The North Wind' two days after. Neither of these poems is joyful in subject, though they are not unjoyful either. They are pure Gondal poems, exercises on a chosen theme, poems, that is, not of experience but of inexperience. On 9 and 10 July and on 21 August Anne wrote three more poems, again pure Gondal, and strongly echoing Scott. The last, 'Verses to a Child', is the classic picture of the forsaken mother addressing her babe, and is still a poem of inexperience, like the other two. But as the productions of an eighteen-year-old girl who will one day be a novelist, the poems have an interest. There is a good sense of form in them and an agreeable looseness and freshness; their length and the fact that two of them were written on successive days show that the writer had creative energy and the power to sustain creative excitement.

In the spring of 1839, Anne went out to her first situation, technically equipped. She was on her own now, to make and record her life out of the given constituents, namely, what she herself had, what she had inherited, and what she met. This exactly she did. She had two posts, in both of which she suffered, and she wrote two books, the first almost entirely the record of these experiences and the second also partly inspired by them. And it is chiefly the quality of these two books that make her worthy of study.

Anne was nineteen when she entered her first situation and she died at twenty-nine. For nearly six of the intervening ten years she was a governess. Charlotte intermittently followed the same profession.

The biographer, when he comes to study these years, sits down before a feast of misery. Governess, in the eighteen-thirties, was almost the only career open to women. Were there any, we wonder, who could advance upon it cheerfully? Perhaps there were. The Brontës advanced upon it like martyrs, with all the purity of spirit, with much of the fortitude, with some of the endurance but with none of the elation. Of Charlotte it must be said that for the profession of private governess she was almost divinely ill-equipped. The main qualification, a superior intelligence, she had, but her intelligence was not merely superior, it was probably the first female intelligence in England, and a creative intelligence at that. A fully-introspective creative temperament went with it; she was also thin-skinned, awkward in society, delicate, critical, and possessed of the highest standards, both for other people and herself.

What of Anne? In some ways her plight was even worse. She was even more delicate and shrinking; she positively feared society; in one sister's experience at Law Hill and in the other's sufferings at Roe Head, governess-ship already had a bad history. All the same she must have had certain private consolations. She was not going into a school, like Emily, and as her temperament was milder in every way than Charlotte's, she might expect to fall less hard. Also there would be some actual solace, of a kind Charlotte never expected to enjoy – the children. If the ordeals of the drawing-room and the dining-room were to be terrible, there would still be the schoolroom, her own domain, and that her imagination peopled warmly.

' "I should like to be a governess," declared Agnes Grey to her mother.

'My mother uttered an exclamation of surprise, and laughed. My sister dropped her work in astonishment, exclaiming, "*You* a governess, Agnes! What can you be dreaming of?"

' "Well, I don't see anything so *very* extraordinary in it. I do not pretend to be able to instruct great girls; but surely, I could teach little ones; and I should like it *so* much. I am so fond of children. Do let me, Mama." '

And later she says,

'How charming to be entrusted with the care and education of children! Whatever others said, I felt I was fully competent to the task; the clear remembrance of my own thoughts in early childhood would be a surer guide than the instructions of the most mature adviser. I had but to turn from my little pupils to myself at their age and I should know at once how to win their confidence and affections.'

When it came to Anne's turn to set out, she grasped the nettle firmly. She went on 8 April to the family of Mrs Ingham, of Blake Hall, Mirfield, which was of course familiar ground. On 15 April Charlotte apologizes for her delay in writing to Ellen:

'We were very busy in preparing for Anne's departure – poor child! she left us last Monday no one went with her – it was her own wish that she might be allowed to go alone – as she thought she could manage better and summon more courage if thrown entirely upon her own resources. We have had one letter from her since she went – she expresses herself very well satisfied and says that Mrs Ingham is extremely kind; the two eldest children alone are under her care, the rest are confined to the nursery – with which and its occupants she has nothing to do. Both her pupils are desperate little dunces – neither of them can read and sometimes they even profess a profound ignorance of their alphabet, the worst of it is the little monkies are excessively indulged and she is not empowered to inflict any punishment – she is requested when they misbehave themselves to inform their Mama – which she says is utterly out of the question, as in that case she might be making complaints from morning till night – So she alternately scolds, coaxes, and threatens – sticks always to her first word and gets on as well she can – I hope she'll do, you would be astonished to see what a sensible clever letter she writes – it is only the talking part that I fear – but I do seriously apprehend that Mrs Ingham will sometimes consider that she had a natural impediment of speech.'

Anne's courage and her infinite willingness to forbear emerge from this letter. Charlotte's patronage jars a little. However, Anne was only nineteen, and the elder sister was not accustomed to the idea of the younger in a position of authority. Clearly Anne is putting a brave face on it, but it is noteworthy that disciplined, mild, and uncomplaining though she was, this is the only time that she succeeded in achieving a brave face. Her experiences as governess were by her own account unrelievedly wretched and *Agnes Grey* is her account of them, which if not literal is certainly profoundly true. 'My sister Anne,' wrote Charlotte in a horrible sentence, 'had to taste the cup of life as it is mixed for the class termed "Governesses".' The cup was mixed as expected, but worse. Intense shyness and homesicknesses were expected; we have no poems, nothing, from Anne's pen during the time she was at Mirfield; but the homesickness she describes in *Agnes Grey* and in the poems written at Thorp Green, her second situation, tell what she must have suffered in her first. Bed was the only refuge.[1] But what was worse than expected was the sense of isolation, and worst of all, and painfully unexpected, the failure with the children.

A governess, by virtue of her position, is lonely. She is not a servant, she is a lady; but there are no other ladies of her status in the house; she is somewhat in the position of the chaplain of olden days, who left the table before the pudding. But the chaplain was often partnered with the lady's maid. The governess has no such consolation; she depends on the mistress, and perhaps ladies of the 1830s were not unduly sensitive about dependence of this kind. Mrs Ingham at first sight was kind, and the last report on her was that she was 'a mild, placid woman'. But that Anne was utterly lonely in her situation is clear. 'She will wish herself a housemaid or a kitchen girl,' wrote Charlotte, 'rather than a battered, trampled, desolate, distracted governess.' And Miss Rigby, in a famous review of *Jane Eyre*, put it with more detachment. 'There is no other class which so cruelly requires its members to be, in both mind and manners, above their situation, in order to fit them for their situation. She, the governess, is a bore to almost every gentleman as a tabooed woman. . . . She is a bore to most ladies and a reproach too.'

In passing it must be said that the employers of the Brontës were hardly to be envied. These sensitive, drooping, well-bred girls might well bring out the worst in a coarse-grained employer. And if the employers were not coarse-grained, they might easily come to feel inferior.

Inferior without exception Charlotte found them. While she was being put down for posterity as 'a shy nervous girl, ill at ease, who desired to escape notice and to avoid taking part in the conversation', and 'sitting apart from the rest of the family poring in her short-sighted way over a book',[2] she herself was sending back scathing animadversions to Ellen on her first employer's (Mrs Sidgwick's)

---

[1] Anne's poem, 'Past Days'.
[2] A communication to the *Westminster Gazette*, May 1901. The recollection is by Mrs William Slade, mother of Mrs Strickland who met Charlotte Brontë at the Whites when she (Mrs Slade) was at boarding school.

coldness, 'hearts dug out of a lead mine or cut from a marble quarry', and on her second employer's (Mrs White's) heat. 'If any little thing goes wrong, she does not scruple to give way to anger in a very coarse unladylike manner. . . . I think passion the true test of vulgarity or refinement.' (We see that for the moment a certain little *éclaircisse-ment* with Miss Wooler is not in mind.) In her saga Anne clearly drew on Charlotte's experiences as well as on her own. 'To my astonishment I was taken to task by Mrs Sidgwick (for lack of cheerfulness) with a stress of manner and a harshness of language scarcely credible. . . . Like a fool I cried most bitterly . . . I could not help it. . . .' The terms in which Mrs Murray rebukes Agnes Grey are similar. Charlotte indignantly found herself overwhelmed with 'oceans of needlework . . . and above all, dolls to dress'. Agnes's experiences were much the same.

But none of this compares with the distress over the children them-selves. Anne was a child-lover, in the ordinary sense. She was a soft, feminine character for whom domesticity had charms. She dreamed of a child in her lap and at her breast like almost every girl, and confessed as much in her poem 'Dreams'. There is no evidence that Anne was a child-lover in the particular sense, but she had easily visualized a governess loving and managing little children, as she suggests in the beginning of her book. We see now that she allows Agnes Grey to indulge these hopes in irony. They are going to be dashed by actualities at once. Her life at the Inghams, Charlotte wrote, 'was one struggle of life-wearing exertion to keep the children in anything like decent order'. And Anne wrote that the task of governess was beyond the imagination of anybody 'who had not felt something like the misery of being charged with the care and direction of a set of mischievous turbulent rebels, whom his utmost exertions cannot bind to their duty; while at the same time, he is responsible for their conduct to a higher power, who exacts from him what cannot be achieved without the aid of the superior's more potent authority: which, either from indolence or the fear of becoming unpopular with the said rebellious gang, the latter refuses to give.'[1]

There, in a few lines, we have the picture, and we can look at it from both angles. The parents cut the ground from under the gover-ness's feet by spoiling the children and refusing to endorse her authority. The children were little savages. Duty was a tremendous matter to Victorians and particularly to Victorian Brontës. (We remember

[1] *Agnes Grey.*

George Eliot, exclaiming of God, Immortality, and Duty, how inconceivable was the first, how unbelievable the second, 'yet how peremptory and absolute the third'.) The rebel gang, Tom, Mary, and Fanny Bloomfield were aged seven, six, and four respectively, but Duty was what they had to be brought to envisage none the less. Little children are often little savages, but Anne Brontë had never been such a child, and the child she had been was mother to the young woman she was now.

However, with the courage and endurance which she never lacked in spite of her mildness ('Patience, Firmness, and Perseverance were my only weapons') and in full inexperience, Anne held on, though the methods she employed do cause us to smile ruefully now and again.

'I determined to refrain from striking him [Tom] even in self-defence: and, in his most violent moods my only resource was to throw him on his back, and hold his hands and feet till the frenzy was somewhat abated. To the difficulty of preventing him from doing what he ought not, was added that of forcing him to do what he ought. . . . Yet Tom was by no means the most unmanageable of my pupils; . . . Mary Ann apparently preferred rolling on the floor to any other amusement; down she would drop like a leaden weight; and when I, with great difficulty, had succeeded in rooting her thence, I had still to hold her up with one arm, while with the other I held the book with which she was to read or spell her lesson. As the dead weight of the big girl of six became too heavy for one arm to bear, I transferred it to the other; or if both were weary of the burden, I carried her into a corner, and told her she might come out when she should find the use of her feet, and stand up; but she generally preferred lying there like a log till dinner or tea-time, when as I could not deprive her of her meals, she must be liberated and would come crawling out with a grin of triumph on her round red face.'[1]

In the famous incident of the nestlings, however, the governess comes off with nothing but credit. (Tom Bloomfield has been given a nestful of young birds by his uncle, and gleefully declares his intention of torturing them to death.) 'So saying, urged by a sense of duty and at the risk of both making myself sick and incurring the wrath of my employers − I got a large flat stone, that had been reared up for a

[1] *Agnes Grey*, Chapter III.

mouse-trap by the gardener, then, having once more vainly endeavoured to persuade the little tyrant to let the birds be carried back, I
asked what he intended to do with them. With fiendish glee he com-
menced a list of torments; and while he was busied in the relation
I dropped the stone upon his intended victims and crushed them flat
beneath it.' There we have Anne exactly, frail, but gloriously un-
deterred; inspired by principle, she can act; she even makes Agnes
declare that if the boy's uncle presents him with another nest, she will
drop another stone on it. In the end a sad and not unusual thing
happened. The children became to Anne what they had always been
to Charlotte, the enemy. 'The children,' Charlotte wrote of the
Whites, with beautiful simplicity, 'are not such little devils incarnate
as the Sidgwicks.' Agnes's pupils *could* not be offended, or hurt, or
ashamed; they could not be unhappy in any way, except when they
were in a passion'. They were 'unimpressible, incomprehensible
creatures. You cannot love them, and if you could your love would be
utterly thrown away'.[1]

The best-known incident in the history of the Brontës as governesses is that of the penitent child crying to Charlotte, 'I love 'oo,
I love 'oo, Miss Brontë!' and the child's mother icily remarking,
'Love the governess, my dear?' The moment comes when, having
perused Charlotte and reread *Agnes Grey*, we exclaim to ourselves with
equal incredulity, 'Love the children?'

Anne was at Mirfield for eight months. The Inghams of history,
who were not the Bloomfields but those who begot the Bloomfields
in Anne's imagination, were an old Yorkshire family, civilized, lively,
numerous (the children finally totalled twelve), and much addicted to
blood sports. Blake Hall was a fine square stone house with panelled
rooms, and was beautifully situated in a well-wooded park. Charlotte
wrote, after her sister had been there for two months, 'Mr Carter
was at Mirfield, and saw Anne. He says she was looking uncommonly
well.' Mrs Ingham is remembered as 'not at all a cross person'. On one
occasion some of the children had scarlet *ponchos* sent them from South
America. They put them on, and telling Anne that they were going
to be devils, they mounted their ponies and galloped off, leaving her in
tears. On another occasion Mrs Ingham went into the schoolroom
and found two of the children tied to the table-legs, so that Anne
could write in peace.

Anne's leaving of Blake Hall was a matter of mutual arrangement.

[1] *Agnes Grey*, Chapter VI.

Her employers did not find her suitable for her post, and the evidence does not suggest that they wished her to continue in it. Charlotte described her leaving as 'Anne is not to return', and the fact that Emily troubled to remark, in 1845, that Anne left her second post 'of her own accord' suggests that this was not the way in which she left her first one. The Inghams remembered Anne all their lives, but the rather significant adjective 'ungrateful' was applied by them to her.

Anne's case at Blake Hall was evidently one of grave incompatibility, weighted with the native sorrows of a governess's lot in 1839. Rudimentary psychology suggests that the incident of the nestlings was founded on fact, or similar fact, for though people fond of blood sports often claim to be kindest of all to animals, they sometimes behave like little Master Bloomfield while they are learning to be kind; and while Brontës had the advantage of being able to gratify their lower appetites in Angria, Bloomfields and their like had not. The fortunate Inghams could exercise their imaginations by being red-cloaked devils on horseback; Anne would have adored this kind of thing in Angria or Gondal; as a pursuing nineteen-year-old governess, unmounted, in the actual world, it left her in tears.

Psychology also suggests that Anne worked off ill-feeling against her employers by making the Bloomfields jumped-up tradespeople. The Brontës put a heavy accent on good breeding, as people in the weaker position often do. Charlotte's censorious letters written while she was a governess show her behaving in this way.

It might have been expected that Anne would have delighted in Blake Hall with its soft prospects of grass and trees, but the Brontës showed only a grudging appreciation of mild country. Every place except Haworth suffered from the disability of not being home. (Charlotte has no sooner said that Anne is looking uncommonly well at Mirfield than she adds, 'Poor girl, *she* must wish to be at home'.) It may be remarked here that the Brontës' extreme homesickness and intolerance of what they were not used to seems to link up with the peculiar childishness betrayed by Emily and Anne in the Birthday Papers.

> 'The surrounding country itself was pleasant as far as fertile fields, flourishing trees, quiet green lanes and smiling hedges with wild flowers scattered along their banks could make it, but it was depressingly flat to one born and nurtured among the rugged hills of ——.'[1]

[1] *Agnes Grey*, Chapter VII.

That the Inghams found Anne ungrateful seems natural enough for 1839. Gratitude was a quality that employers, quite innocently, would expect dependents to show. The significant adjective which Anne herself uses, of Agnes, is 'neglected'. And here too, no doubt her employers were quite innocent. It needs no imagination to see that Anne's mistress had many calls upon her time. It is very likely that she never once imagined that the governess, as a person, had any call upon it.

Anne inevitably was found unsuitable for her post. She and her pupils can have had little common language. She describes her methods in her book, and they were entirely pious. Agnes never ceases to appeal to the pupils' better selves; the idea of a child going to bed unkissed is unthinkable. The Bloomfields tore these methods to shreds; they probably succeeded little better with the Inghams. Blood sports or no blood sports, they were lively and numerous and no doubt a close child-community. A goodnight kiss from a governess? What difference could it make?

Anne's biographer has heard repeatedly of her passivity. The moment when she sits writing in the schoolroom with two Inghams tied to two table-legs is his moment of pure joy. He cannot expect Mrs Ingham to have seen eye to eye with him. If, after that, Anne left by mutual agreement, no one could be surprised.

By the end of Agnes Grey's short sojourn with the Bloomfields we have learnt something about Anne. We see what a contrast she is to her sisters, and we find it a relief. Anne was not such a tremendous writer as Charlotte or Emily; but she was a different kind of artist and wrote a different kind of prose. Charlotte and Emily are romantic, poetic, and dramatic. Anne is simple, fresh, brief, and flat; but her style has its own intensities and, perfected, is just as telling as any other style. Anne in fact did not seek to pile it on; she sought to pile it off. And how well, now, we may feel that we begin to understand her. She was a Brontë, but she was a different Brontë from her brother and sisters, and her brother and sisters produced reactions in her. We are quite willing to believe that she was quiet and withdrawn by nature, but we see also how much room there was for a 'passive' person in the Brontë conclave. Charlotte, Emily, Branwell, and the Rev. Patrick were all intense. Anne too by nature was quite sufficiently intense; but she reacted against intensity of the family kind; we can see not that she lacked opinion and volition, but that she held her peace until it was necessary to break it, observed intently, and let be.

IV

BETWEEN HER FIRST situation and her second, Anne Brontë
fell in love. It was with one of her father's curates, the Rev.
William Weightman. Curates, up to date, especially Irish
curates of whom the girls had had experience, had not proved likely
men, but William Weightman was different. He comes upon the
scene in a letter of Charlotte's of 17 March 1840, and is already well
established in the circle. High spirits, evinced as a heavy-handed
gaiety, inform all Charlotte's utterances about him. Clearly there
has been a flutter in the dovecote. Ellen Nussey has participated, but
the Taylor girls have not, and feel ill-used. 'My dear Mrs Eleanor,'
Charlotte's letter runs,

'I wish to scold you with a forty horse power for having told
Martha Taylor that I had requested you "not to tell her everything", which piece of information of course has thrown Martha
into a tremendous ill-humour besides setting the teeth of her curiosity
on edge with the notion that there is something very important in
the wind which you and I are especially desirous to conceal from
her. Such being the state of matters I desire to take off any embargo
I may have laid on your tongue, which I plainly see will not be
restrained and to enjoin you to walk up to Gomersal and tell her
forthwith every individual occurrence you can recollect, including
Valentines, "Fair Ellen, Fair Ellen", "Away fond love", "Soul
divine" and all – likewise if you please the painting of Miss Celia
Amelia Weightman's portrait and that young lady's frequent and
agreeable visits – By the bye I enquired into the opinion of that
intelligent and interesting young person respecting you – it was a
favourable one. She thought you a fine looking girl and a very
good girl into the bargain – Have you received the newspaper which
has been despatched containing the notice of her lecture at Keighley? Mr Morgan came, stayed three days and went – by Miss
Weightman's aid we got on pretty well – it was was amazing to see

with what patience and good temper the innocent creature endured that fat Welshman's prosing – though she confessed afterwards that she was almost done up by his long stories.

'We feel very dull without you, I wish those three weeks were to come over again. . . .

'I am obliged to cut short my letter – every-body in the house unites in sending their love to you – Miss Celia Amelia Weightman also desires to be remembered to you – Write soon again, and believe me yours unutterably . . . Charivari.'

Ellen had settled to go to stay early in January. There had been a not unusual making and unmaking of plans between her and Charlotte, complicated by a sudden objection to visitors in winter on the part of Miss Branwell. However, Ellen evidently spent three weeks at the Parsonage, which must have included St Valentine's Day, and she has left us a vivid footnote to her visit.

'. . . Celia Amelia, Mr Brontë's curate, a lively handsome young man fresh from Durham University, an excellent classical scholar. He gave a very good lecture on the Classics at Keighley. The young ladies at the Parsonage must hear his lecture, so he went off to a married clergyman to get him to write to Mr Brontë and invite the young ladies to tea and offer his escort to the lecture and back again to the Parsonage. Great fears were entertained that permission would not be given . . . it was a walk of four miles each way. The Parsonage was not reached till 12 p.m. The two clergymen rushed in with their charges, deeply disturbing Miss Branwell, who had prepared hot coffee for the home party, which of course fell short when two more were to be supplied. Poor Miss Branwell lost her temper, Charlotte was troubled, and Mr Weightman, who enjoyed teasing the old lady, was very thirsty. The great spirits of the walking party had a trying suppression, but twinkling fun sustained some of them.

'There was also a little episode as to Valentines. Mr Weightman discovered that none of the party had ever received a Valentine – a great discovery! Whereupon he indited verses to each one, and walked ten miles to post them, lest Mr Brontë should discover his dedicatory nonsense, and the quiet liveliness going on under the sedate espionage of Miss Branwell. Then I recall the taking of Mr Weightman's portrait by Charlotte. The sittings became alarming for length of time required, and the guest had to adopt the gown, which the owner was very proud to exhibit, amusing the party with his critical remarks on the materials used, pointing out the adornments, silk, velvet, etc.'

Gaiety, and of a more vital kind, is abroad at the Parsonage for the first time since the Taylors' visit in 1837.

Anne left Mirfield in December 1839. On 1 January 1840, she wrote a poem, 'Self-Congratulation' signed Solala Vernon. It is a dialogue, in which the identity of the speakers is somewhat obscure. The first line is 'Ellen, you were thoughtless once,' (in the original MS 'Maiden, thou wert thoughtless once,') and the cause for self-congratulation is that the heroine of the poem has not betrayed her feelings.

> *Last night as we sat round the fire*
> *Conversing merrily,*
> *We heard without approaching steps*
> *Of one well known to me!*
>
> *There was no trembling in my voice*
> *No blush upon my cheek,*
> *No lustrous sparkle in my eyes*
> *Of hope or joy to speak:*
> *But oh, my spirit burned within,*
> *My heart beat full and fast!*
> *He came not nigh, he went away*
> *And then my joy was past.*
>
> *And yet my comrades marked it not;*
> *My voice was still the same;*
> *They saw me smile, and o'er my face*
> *No signs of sadness came.*
> *They little knew my hidden thoughts*
> *And they will never know*
> *The aching anguish of my heart,*
> *The bitter burning woe.*

Anne has received the shaft, which she transfers to Solala Vernon or perhaps even at some later date to Ellen Nussey, who had not met Mr Weightman by 1 January, but who was shortly to become one of those on whom he gazed with interest. Clearly he gazed at them all with delightful interest, which they returned in various ways. Anne, though the world does not suspect it, has succumbed to the charm of the lively, handsome young man, after knowing him at most a month. What a walk home that must have been after the lecture ! Ellen does not mention that it was raining, so we are free to hope that there was frost and stars. We may be sure that there was elation. This was just the way in which the Brontës could enjoy attractive male company. It was not as if they had been asked to a dance. Perhaps also it is not too much to guess that if poor old Miss Branwell lost her temper and Charlotte was conscience-stricken, it was Anne who, along with Ellen and the curate, remained quietly twinkling with fun.

One of the Valentines mentioned by Ellen was no doubt addressed to Anne and was certainly the first treasure of this kind that she ever possessed.

In her next letter, of 7 April, Charlotte addresses Ellen as 'My dear Mrs Menelaus', Menelaus being the successful suitor of the peerless Helen – Ellen, the inference is, being about to become the chosen of the peerless Weightman. The letter ends 'Good-bye to you, and let me have no more of your humbug about Cupid, etc. . . . You know as well as I do it is all groundless trash', which suggests that if Charlotte was rallying Ellen, Ellen was also rallying Charlotte. Nobody, it may be noted, was rallying Anne. It was assumed that she was not in on such acts. The substance of the letter describes another kind of excitement at Haworth.

'Little Haworth has been all in a bustle about Church Rates since you were here – we had a most stormy meeting in the schoolroom – Papa took the chair and Mr Collins and Mr Weightman acted as his supporters, one on each side – There was violent opposition, which set Mr Collins' Irish blood in a ferment. . . . He and Mr Weightman both bottled up their wrath for that time but it was only to explode with redoubled force at a future period – We had two sermons on Dissent and its consequences preached last Sunday one in the afternoon by Mr Weightman and one in the evening by Mr Collins – the dissenters were invited to come and hear and they actually shut up their Chapels and came in a body ; of course the churches were crowded. Miss Celia Amelia delivered a nobly eloquent high-Church, Apostolic succession discourse – in which he banged the dissenters most fearlessly and unflinchingly. . . .'

It is to be noted that the dissenters attended. This was in the Haworth tradition, however high feeling might run. Grimshaw had thrown open his pulpit to Wesley : Mr Brontë, after he became blind, went to a missionary meeting of Wesleyans, leaning on Charlotte's arm. The letter concludes, 'I have been painting a portrait of Agnes Walton for our friend Miss Celia Amelia – you would laugh to see how his eyes sparkle with delight when he looks at it like a pretty child pleased with a new plaything———' And the postscript adds, 'Mr Weightman has given another lecture at the Keighley Mechanics Institute.'

In a letter headed June 1840 we hear that

'Mary Taylor's visit has been a very pleasant one to us and I believe to herself. She and Mr Weightman have had several games at chess, which generally terminated in a species of mock hostility – Mr Weightman is in better health but don't set your heart on him, I'm afraid he is very fickle – not to you particularly, but to half a dozen other ladies, he has just cut his enamorata at Swansea, and sent her back all her letters – his present object of devotion is Caroline Dury, to whom he has just despatched a most passionate copy of verses, poor lad, his sanguine temperament bothers him grievously.

'The Swansea affair seems to me somewhat heartless as far as I can understand it though I have not heard a very clear explanation, he sighs as much as ever. I have not mentioned your name to him – nor do I mean to do so until I have a fair opportunity of gathering his real mind.'

By 14 July Charlotte's misgivings about the curate are increasing. . . .

'I am very glad you continue so heartwhole I rather feared our mutual nonsense might have made a deeper impression on you than was safe. Mr Weightman left Haworth this morning, we do not expect him back again for some weeks – I am fully convinced Ellen that he is a thorough male-flirt, his sighs are deeper than ever and his treading on toes more assiduous. – I find he has scattered his impressions far and wide – Keighley has yielded him a fruitful field of conquest, Sarah Sugden is quite smitten so is Caroline Dury – she however has left – and his Reverence has not ceased to idolize her memory – I find he is perfectly conscious of his irresistibleness and is as vain as a peacock on the subject – I am not at all surprised at all this – it is perfectly natural – a handsome – clean – prepossessing – good-humoured young man – will never want troops

68

of victims amongst young ladies. . . . I have no doubt he will get nobly through his examination, he is a *clever* lad.'

By 20 August Mr Weightman had not returned.

'By the bye, speaking of Mr Weightman I told you he was gone to pass his examination of Ripon six weeks ago. He is not come back yet and what has become of him we don't know. Branwell has received one letter since he went speaking rapturously of Agnes Walton describing certain balls at which he had figured and announcing that he had been twice over-head and ears desperately in love – It is my devout belief that his Reverence left Haworth with the intention of never returning – If he does return it will be because he has not been able to get a living – Haworth is not the place for him, he requires a change of faces – difficulties to be overcome. He pleases so easily that he soon gets weary of pleasing at all. He ought not to have been a parson. Certainly he ought not.'

Shrewd and penetrating, though at times also artless and even ridiculous, Charlotte exercises her gift and brings the young man before our eyes. She herself is not wholly indifferent to him, as she betrays in her letter to Ellen of 12 November, which is written on a piece of paper on which Weightman had been drawing, and it is irresistible to remark that it was Charlotte, of them all, who might have made him a good wife. Coupling him with herself, however, was far from her conscious thoughts, almost as far as coupling him with Anne. Weightman and Ellen, Weightman and Agnes Walton, Weightman and Caroline Dury, Weightman and Sarah Sugden, Weightman and the enamorata of Swansea, finally Weightman and the strongly-feminist Mary Taylor . . . Charlotte romps on, oblivious of what was going on under her nose – the more oblivious perhaps inasmuch as it concerned her younger sister. Anne a governess! Anne a married woman! And Anne, no doubt, was paradoxically grateful for the lack of attention.

Clearly the young man was very attractive, not only to the generality of women but to the Brontës as well. For he was extremely intelligent, as well as handsome, uninhibited, and amiable. He pleased without effort, but he was also capable of making the effort, as when he drew poor prosing Mr Morgan's fire upon himself. He had the Irish virtues in an English frame, which happened to be just the thing to please the Brontës best. Charlotte paid him the tribute of much analysis, ostensibly with a view to discovering if he was worthy of her darling Ellen; Emily paid him the tribute of civility, unknown from her to curates; and Anne, so much nearer than either to the generality of women, simply fell in love. There is no evidence that he particularly returned her interest, and the letter received by Branwell just before she went to her second situation was far from suggesting it, but the very fact that though he formed so many attachments he was not pledged to any of them must have allowed her to hope.

Anne went off for the second time in the August of that year. Her pupils in this situation were older, the two daughters of the Rev. Edmund Robinson of Thorp Green, near the village of Little Ouse-burn, between Boroughbridge and York. She was not destined to be happy here either, but the struggle was not one of life-wearing exertion in the sense that it had been at the Inghams. A German dictionary and a German Reader inscribed with Anne's name and 'Thorp Green' suggest that serious study was attempted. While she is learning the ropes in her new post Charlotte writes to Ellen about the curate in a fashion that foreshadows the way Anne was to write about him as a character of fiction.

'. . . I seldom see him, except on a Sunday, when he looks as handsome, cheery, and good-tempered as usual. I have indeed had the advantage of one long conversation since his return from West-moreland when he poured out his whole warm, fickle soul in fondness and admiration of Agnes Walton. Whether he is in love with her or not I can't say; I can only observe that it sounds very like it. He sent us a prodigious quantity of game while he was away. A brace of wild ducks, a brace of black grouse, a brace of partridges, ditto of snipes, ditto of curlews, and a large salmon. There is one little trait respecting him which lately came to my knowledge, which gives a glimpse of the better side of his character. Last Saturday night he had been sitting an hour in the parlour with Papa, and as he went away I heard Papa say to him – 'What is the matter with you? You seem in very low spirits tonight?" "Oh, I don't know I've been to see a poor young girl who, I'm afraid, is dying." "Indeed, what is her name?" "Susan Bland, the daughter of John Bland, the Superintendent." Now Susan Bland is my oldest and best scholar in the Sunday-school; and when I heard that, I thought I would go as soon as I could to see her. I did go on Monday afternoon, and found her very ill and weak, and seemingly far on her way to that bourne whence no traveller returns. After sitting with her some time, I happened to ask her mother if she thought a little port wine would do her good. She replied that the doctor had recommended it, and that when Mr Weightman was last there he had sent them a bottle of wine and a jar of preserves. She added that he was always good to poor folks, and seemed to have a deal of feeling and kind-heartedness about him. This proves that he is not all selfishness and vanity. No doubt there are defects in his character, but there are also good qualities. . . .'

Mr Weightman does not appear again in Charlotte's correspondence until 3 March 1841. Charlotte is now a governess at Mrs White's, of Upperwood House, Rawdon. St Valentine's day has brought a reminder of the curate. 'I daresay you have received a Valentine this year from our bonny-faced friend, the curate of Haworth. I got a precious specimen a few days before I left home, but I know better how to treat it than I did those we received a year ago.' Whether or not Anne received a Valentine we do not know. A Gondal poem dated 1 January suggests that she had gone home for Christmas, when she must have seen the curate. On 21 March, Charlotte sends to Ellen her own Valentine (from Weightman). 'I send you the precious valentine. Make much of it. Remember the writer's blue eyes, auburn hair, and rosy cheeks'; and on 1 April, still harping on the subject, she asks Ellen in a postscript, 'Have you lit your pipe with Mr Weightman's valentine?' Next day she writes to Emily. 'I had a letter from Anne yesterday. She says she is well. I hope she speaks absolute truth.' On 10 June she is anxious to be home for her holiday, '. . . or I shall miss the chance of seeing Anne this vacation – she came home I understand last Wednesday and is only to be allowed 3 weeks holidays – because the family she is with are going to Scarborough. *I should like* to see her to judge for myself the state of her health. I cannot trust any other person's report no one seems minute enough in their observations – I should also very much have liked you to see her.' On 1 July she writes, 'I am at home now, and it feels like Paradise. . . . P.S. I have lost the chance of seeing Anne. She is gone back to "the land of Egypt and the house of Bondage".'

And now Charlotte mentions to Ellen for the first time the possible deliverance of them all from Egypt and bondage by their setting up a school of their own.

'. . . To come to the point. Papa and Aunt talk, by fits and starts, of our – *id est* Emily Anne and myself – commencing a school. I have often, you know, said how much I wished such a thing;

but I never could conceive where the capital was to come from for making such a speculation. I was well aware indeed that aunt had money, but I always considered that she was the last person who would offer a loan for the purpose in question. A loan however she offered, or intimates that she perhaps *will* offer, in case pupils can be secured, an eligible situation can be obtained, etc. This sounds very fair but still there are matters to be considered which throw something of a damp upon the scheme. I do not expect that aunt will risk more than £150 on such a venture; and would it be possible to establish a respectable (not by any means a *showy*) school and to commence housekeeping with a capital of only that amount? Propound the question to your sister Ann, if you think she can answer it; if not, don't say a word on the subject. As to getting into debt, that is a thing we none of us could reconcile our minds to for a moment. We do not care how modest, how humble a commencement be, so it be made on sure ground, and have a safe foundation. In thinking of all possible and impossible places where we could establish a school, I have thought of Burlington.[1] Do you remember whether there is any other school there besides that of Miss J——? This is, of course, a perfectly crude and random idea. There are a hundred reasons why it should be an impracticable one. We have no connections, no acquaintances there; it is far from home, etc. Still, I fancy the ground in the East Riding is less fully occupied than in the West. Much inquiry and consideration will be necessary, of course, before any place is decided on; and I fear much time will elapse before any plan is executed.

'Our reverend friend William Weightman is quite as bonny, pleasant, light-hearted good-tempered, generous careless fickle and unclerical as ever. He keeps up his correspondence with Agnes Walton. During the last spring he went to Appleby and stayed upwards of a month.'

To marry glorious husbands, one of whom was in their midst, was for Charlotte and Anne at least, the romantic dream; to have a school of their own, by which they could be self-supporting but their own mistresses, was the practical dream, and had become doubly dear to them all through experience of Egypt and bondage; but as Charlotte guessed, it would be slow to assume reality.

Meanwhile Anne had been at home for three weeks in June,

[1] The old name for Bridlington.

without Charlotte but with William Weightman. Then she was obliged to join her employers at the seaside. On 30 July, Emily's birthday, she was still at Scarborough and from there she wrote the first authentic Birthday Paper which survives.

'July the 30th. A.D. 1841.

'This is Emily's birthday. She has now completed her 23rd year, and is, I believe, at home. Charlotte is governess in the family of Mr White. Branwell is a clerk in the railroad station at Luddenden Foot and I am a governess in the family of Mr Robinson. I dislike the situation and wish to change it for another. I am now at Scarborough. My pupils are gone to bed and I am hastening to finish this before I follow them.

'We are thinking of setting up a school of our own, but nothing definite is settled about it yet, and we do not know whether we shall be able to or not. I hope we shall. And I wonder what will be our condition and how or where we shall all be on this day four years hence; at which time, if all be well, I shall be 25 years and 6 months old, Emily will be 27 years old, Branwell 28 years and 1 month, and Charlotte 29 years and a quarter. We are now all separate and not likely to meet again for many a weary week, but we are none of us ill that I know of and are all doing something for our own livelihood except Emily, who however is as busy as any of us, and in reality earns her food and raiment as much as we do.

> How little know we what we are
> How less what we may be!

Four years ago I was at school. Since then I have been a governess at Blake Hall, left it, come to Thorp Green, and seen the sea and York Minister. Emily has been a teacher at Miss Patchett's school, and left it, Charlotte has left Miss Wooler's, been a governess at Mrs Sidgwick's, left her, and gone to Mrs White's. Branwell has given up painting, been a tutor in Cumberland, left it, and become a clerk on the railroad. Tabby has left us, Martha Brown has come in her place. We have got Keeper, got a sweet little cat and lost it and also got a hawk. Got a wild goose which has flown away and three tame ones, one of which has been killed. All these diversities and many others, are things which we did not expect or foresee in the July of 1837. What will the next four years bring forth? Providence only knows. But we ourselves have sustained very little alteration since that time. I have the same faults that I had then, only I have more wisdom and experience, and a little more self-possession than I then enjoyed. How will it be when we open this paper and the one Emily has written? I wonder whether the *Gondalians* will still be flourishing, and what will be their condition. I am now engaged in writing the fourth volume of *Solala Vernon's Life.*

'For some time now I have looked upon 25 as a sort of era in my existence. It may prove a true presentiment, or it may only be a superstitious fancy : the latter seems most likely, but time will show.'

Emily writes from home.

'A PAPER to be opened when Anne is 25 years old, or my next birthday after if all be well. Emily Jane Brontë. July 30th, 1841.

'It is Friday evening, near 9 o'clock – wild rainy weather. I am seated in the dining-room alone, having just concluded tidying our desk boxes, writing this document. Papa is in the parlour – aunt upstairs in her room. She has been reading Blackwood's Magazine to papa. Victoria and Adelaide[1] are ensconced in the peat-house. Keeper is in the kitchen. Hero[2] in his cage. We are all stout and hearty, as I hope is the case with Charlotte, Branwell, and Anne, of whom the first is at John White, Esq., Upperwood House, Rawdon; the second is at Luddenden Foot; and the third is, I believe, at Scarborough, inditing perhaps a paper corresponding to this.

'A scheme is at present in agitation for setting us up in a school of our own; as yet nothing is determined, but I hope and trust it may go on and prosper and answer our highest expectations. This day four years I wonder whether we shall still be dragging on in our present condition or established to our hearts' content. Time will show.

'I guess that at the time appointed for the opening of this paper we, i.e. Charlotte, Anne, and I, shall be all merrily seated in our own sitting-room in some pleasant and flourishing seminary, having just gathered in for the mid-summer holyday. Our debts will be paid off, and we shall have cash in hand to a considerable amount. Papa, aunt, and Branwell will either have been or be coming to

---

[1] Two geese.   [2] A hawk.

visit us. It will be a fine warm summer evening, very different from this bleak look-out, and Anne and I will perchance slip out into the garden for a few minutes to peruse our papers. I hope either this or something better will be the case.

'The Gondalians are at present in a threatening state, but there is no open rupture as yet. All the princes and princesses of the Royalty are at the Palace of Instruction. I have a good many books on hand, but I am sorry to say that as usual I make small progress with any. However, I have just made a new regularity paper! and I mean *verb sap* to do great things. And now I must close, sending from far an exhortation, "Courage, courage", to exiled and harassed Anne, wishing she was here.'

What shall one choose to bury with the foundations of the building, or write to be opened after four years? Clearly Anne feels a certain self-consciousness. These birthday papers are very different from the pages of a journal, which is what we long for so avidly from Anne's or Emily's hand. The journal is the pure kernel of writing; it is fragmentary and spontaneous, its form makes absolutely no demands, and it treats both objective and subjective or emotional matters with equal directness. These papers – although written only for the other self – are something different, as the name itself implies. At first glance they are disappointingly objective, and seem childish; then one remembers that they *are* childish, the writing of them is a habit carried on from childhood, and the form, so similar in both cases – the present, the future, looking back, looking forward, the animal kingdom, and Gondal – all suggests a pattern that has been followed before. And they are objective, because, though written for the other self, there are places where even the other self cannot go. Anne was in love; all that had to be omitted; she writes about what is left over. However, there is something to be learnt. We are immediately struck by the difference in tone of the two papers. Anne was in bondage, Emily was free. We are struck also, even knowing Anne's nature and training, by her emotional terseness and self-control. She was fated for the present to be a governess and accepted it without complaint; if she succeeded in changing her present situation she could ameliorate her lot but little . . . she dismisses it all in eleven words. In the same way she disciplines her hope for the future. 'I hope we shall.' She accepts and is resigned, but her spirits are not high; and who could wonder, for she is once more on the outward journey not only from

home but from a home whose claims on her heart the presence of
William Weightman has incalculably increased.

Read together, the papers declare the closeness of the bond between
the sisters: 'Having just concluded tidying our desk-boxes. . . .' One is
amazed that even Emily and Anne can do this for each other. Super-
sensitive, Anne hastens to dismiss even an imaginary suggestion that
Emily does not earn her keep. Almost exactly the same things occur to
them to write about. And this paper of Emily's, precisely since it
comes from her hand, is precious as revealing something that all the
sisters had in common, their normality. Normality may perhaps be
defined as acceptance of or resignation to a sufficient number of the
forms or norms of everyday existence. Emily was the most remarkable
member of a remarkable family. She is generally allowed to have been
a genius, and genius is not superlative talent; it is a difference in kind,
not in degree, and isolates its possessor. By her twenty-third birthday
she was already Emily Brontë; and had written some of her most
famous and characteristic poems; yet she runs on easily about Aunt
reading *Blackwood's* to papa, and herself and her sisters keeping a little
school. Emily's inner existence demanded freedom – her departure
from normality, if we like to call it so, was her faculty for pining and
dying at Miss Wooler's or Miss Patchett's – but everyday life as such
was perfectly easy of acceptance. It was the same for them all. The
Brontës, being rarefied, appreciated normality. They were such odd
animals, Charlotte said, that they preferred to black their own grates
to having a stranger in the house. But it was not in this that their
oddity consisted, but rather in their mixture of power and vulnerability,
which was a result of their extreme artistic sensitiveness. Charlotte was
sincere when she told Mrs Gaskell that she was thankful for Miss
Branwell's drilling, and Mrs Gaskell was right in observing that for
the sisters' impulsive natures to have learnt obedience to external laws
was positive repose. The Victorian woman's domestic routine was
normality and they did not question it. Nor can posterity complain.
The outer life did not repress the inner life but rather intensified it
and gave it greater relish. The daily routine was duty; writing was
pleasure; it was the prize, it was life itself, escape to the free place.

Returned from Thorp Green in perfect weather, Anne wrote
'Lines Written at Thorp Green', lamenting that the beauty about her
must turn to bleak winter before she could see home again, and ten
days later her heart forced her out into the open and to the confession
that homesickness was not what ailed her.

Oh did'st thou know my longings
For thee from day to day,
My hopes so often blighted,
Thou wouldst not thus delay![1]

Meanwhile Charlotte, back with the Whites, wrote to Ellen Nussey that the school scheme had not advanced, 'but Emily and Anne and I keep it in mind – it is our polar-star and we look to it under all circumstances of despondency', and reveals that from letters received from the Taylors, who were in Brussels, the first spark of an adventurous idea had been kindled in her mind. Her postscript refers to Anne and would wring our hearts even more than they are wrung already if it did not reveal Charlotte again in a naïvely human attitude . . . unconsciously keeping up her own spirits with the supposition that somebody else is worse off.

'I am well in health – I have one aching feeling in my heart (I must allude to it though I had resolved not to) – it is about Anne – she has so much to endure – far, far more than I have – when my thoughts turn to her – they always see her as a patient, persecuted stranger – amongst people more grossly insolent, proud, and tyrannical than your imagination unassisted can ready depict – I know what concealed susceptibility is in her nature – when her feelings are wounded I wish I could be with her to administer a little balm. She is more lonely – less gifted with the power of making friends even than I am – drop the subject.'

For once the picture seems a little over-painted.

And now the spark of Charlotte's idea is beginning to grow into a flame. She writes to Miss Branwell to ask if she will allow her proffered loan to be used to finance herself and possibly Emily for a six months' trip abroad to acquire a thorough familiarity with French and to get what they can of Italian and German. 'I say Emily instead of Anne; for Anne might take her turn at some future period, if our school answered.' Anne, though a likelier subject for higher education, was in good employment: there were doubts of all kinds to assail Charlotte, but it is interesting that Emily acquiesced, as later she was to acquiesce, after demur, in allowing the publication of her poems. Indeed it is Charlotte's turn to wring our hearts, begging for nourishment for them all, openly and simply. 'Of course I know no other friend in the world to whom I could apply on this subject except

[1] 'Appeal'.

yourself. I feel an absolute conviction that, if this advantage were allowed us, it would be the making of us for life. Papa will perhaps think it a wild and ambitious scheme; but who ever rose in the world without ambition? When he left Ireland to go to Cambridge University, he was as ambitious as I am now. I want us *all* to go on. I know we have talents, and I want them to be turned to account. I look to you, Aunt, to help us. I think you will not refuse.'

Miss Branwell did not refuse and Charlotte pressed on with energy. On 7 November she wrote to Emily, 'Grieve not over Dewsbury Moor.' (Miss Wooler had made Charlotte an offer.) 'You were cut out there to all intents and purposes, so in fact was Anne; Miss Wooler would hear of neither for the first half-year. Anne seems to be omitted in the present plan, but if all goes right I trust she will derive her full share of benefit from it in the end. . . . When does Anne talk of returning? How is she? What does William Weightman say to these matters? How are papa and aunt, do they flag? How will Anne get on with Martha?'

Anne was obviously to come home and keep house while her sisters were away. But on 10 January Charlotte, returned on Christmas eve after a surprisingly affecting farewell to her employers, writes to Ellen '. . . Anne has rendered herself so valuable in her difficult situation that they have entreated her to return to them, if it be but for a short time. I almost think she will go back. . . .'

Anne went back; and this is her tragic moment. It must have been apropos of her return to Thorp Green that she wrote 'Oh they have robbed me of the hope', the poem from *Agnes Grey*, which is undated.

> *Oh, they have robbed me of the hope*
> *My spirit held so dear :*
> *They will not let me hear the voice*
> *My soul delights to hear ;*
>
> *They will not let me see that face*
> *I so delight to see,*
> *And they have taken all thy smiles*
> *And all they love from me.*
>
> *Well, let them seize on all they can*
> *One treasure still is mine,*
> *A heart that loves to think on thee*
> *And feels the worth of thine.*

For once Anne finds it in her heart to upbraid. She had made up her mind to leave Thorp Green, but *they* . . . Aunt? Papa? her employers? had persuaded her to return. Charlotte, full of fire, was pressing forward to adventure: Emily was following her, and Anne must turn her back on Haworth and return to bondage. She had lost her chance, which perhaps with her sisters removed, not indeed as rivals, but as mere presences, might have been a better chance. 'Mr Weightman is still here,' Charlotte concludes, sweetly insensible, to Ellen. 'I have a curiosity to see a meeting between you and him. He will again be desperately in love, I am convinced. Come.' And her final long breathless letter to her friend, written in the rush of sewing and general preparations for departure to Brussels, rounds off with the curate for the last time: 'Your darling, "his young reverence" as you tenderly call him is looking delicate and pale poor thing don't you pity him? I do from my heart, when he is well and fat and jovial I never think of him – but when anything ails him I am always sorry – He sits opposite to Anne at Church sighing softly and looking out of the corners of his eyes to win her attention – and Anne is so quiet, her looks so downcast – they are a picture – He would be the better of a comfortable wife like you to settle him, you would settle him I believe – nobody else would.'

Monstrous! the reader is forced to exclaim at this point. In the very act of watching the curate exchanging the sighs and glances of love with Anne in church, Charlotte presents him once again to Ellen. Her behaviour is ironically natural – this precious thing, this treasure, in which she has narrowly escaped being interested herself – it is on the friend to whom one is bound with such sublime and jealous ties, rather than on the family that one bestows it. Anne simply could not enter her head.

Anne of course sensed this; ironically she was doubtless thankful; actually she must have felt what even the mildest nature feels at being blandly ruled out as a candidate for marriage.

V

⸻ ❧ ⸺

WILLIAM WEIGHTMAN DIED on 6 September 1842, after a short illness. In the picture Charlotte gives us of him and her sister in church, we actually see them together for the first and the last time. Anne's love-story, like the rest of her story, passed in silence. Unsuspected and keeping her own counsel, she had been faithful to the curate for nearly three years. He, for three years had been faithful to nobody, and was still unattached. We wonder whether the sighs and glances which he sent in Anne's direction were mere routine, or whether after much adventure he was coming into harbour. But he himself was never given a chance to discover. Anne's desire to stay was matched against the desire of the Robinsons to have her back, her distrust of self-indulgence, and all the arguments that the supposed voice of duty could muster on the other side, and it did not prevail.

William Weightman was buried in Haworth Church and Mr Brontë preached a sermon over him. It was printed: *A Funeral Sermon for the late Rev. William Weightman M.A. – preached in the Church of Haworth on Sunday the 8th of October* 1842 *by the Rev. Patrick Brontë A.B. Incumbent. The Profits, if any, to go in aid of the Sunday School. Price Sixpence.* It was the first sermon that he had ever read during the twenty years that he had ministered to the people of Haworth, for extempore preaching was colloquial and better understood, 'but some have requested I would publish what I may say'. Anne, at Thorp Green, we know fervently if wordlessly requested it. 'Therefore,' continued Mr Brontë, 'I deem it proper . . . to write down my thoughts, but in such plain terms that whatever they were, they might be understood without the aid of extraordinary learning.' This he does, with a surprising lack of pomposity, and yet with a certain Biblical strength and resonance that makes the prose of all the Brontës not ashamed to own its paternity. He took for his text 'The sting of death is sin', and having exhorted his hearers, he turned to

William Weightman. 'These were the scriptural doctrines preached, practised, and maintained by him whose loss we deplore. In his preaching and practising, he was, as every clergyman ought to be, neither distant nor austere, timid nor obtrusive, nor bigoted, exclusive nor dogmatical. He was affable but not familiar; open, but not too confiding. He thought it better and more scriptural to make the love of God, rather than the fear of hell, the ruling motive for obedience. He did not see why true believers, having the promise of the life that now is, as well as that which is to come, should create themselves artificial sorrows to disfigure the garb of gospel peace with the garb of sorrow and sighing.' After a few more hints reflecting William Weightman's history and sojourn, during which he 'more than answered my expectations and probably yours', Mr Brontë continues: 'There are many who for a short time can please, and even astonish, but who soon retrograde and fall into disrepute. His character wore well; the surest proof of real worth. He had, it is true, some peculiar advantages. Agreeable in person and manners, and constitutionally cheerful, his first introduction was prepossessing. But what he gained at first he did not lose afterwards. He had those qualities which enabled him later to gain ground. He had classical attainments of the first order. . . . When I stated to him that it would be desirable he should descend to the level of the lowest and most illiterate of his audience . . . he would good-naturedly promise to do so – and in this respect, there evidently was a gradual but sure improvement. As it ought to be with every Incumbent and his clerical coadjutor, we were always like father and son – according to our respective status – giving and taking mutual advice – under the superintendence of our common Lord and Master.

'In visiting, and cottage lectures, a most important part of a minister's duty' (we think of Mr Weston in *Agnes Grey*), 'he was as active and sedulous as health and circumstances would permit – He had the rare art of communicating information – without austerity, so as to render instruction, even to the youngest and most giddy, a pleasure, not a task. . . . Our late lamented friend ran a bright and short career. He died in the twenty-sixth year of his age – amidst the joyous and sanguine anticipations of friends, the good wishes of all around and as may naturally be supposed the glad hopes of himself, he was summoned for his removal from this world. . . .'

Poor William Weightman, cut off at twenty-six! Even in Mr Brontë he inspired a touchingly paternal fondness. Anne loved him faithfully for the rest of her life.

And while I cannot quite forget
Thou, darling, canst not quite depart.[1]

A touch of his own easy quality, which must have enthralled her, comes now and again into the poems she wrote in his memory.

Yes, thou art gone, and never more
Thy sunny smile shall gladden me
But I may pass the old church door
And pace the floor that covers thee. . . .

May stand upon the cold, damp stone
And think that, frozen, lies below
The lightest heart that I have known,
The kindest I shall ever know.[2]

The curate had been nursed by Branwell, who was at home, having occupied and left two situations as a clerk on the railway, and who was already an uncertain quantity. Charlotte's references to him have been doubting for a long time. On 2 April 1841 she had written to Emily, 'I have not heard from Branwell yet. It is to be hoped that this removal to another station will turn out for the best. As you say, it *looks* like getting on at any rate.' He is referred to several times as failing to turn up, and on the eve of her departure for Brussels Charlotte tells Ellen, 'I have some hopes of seeing Branwell and when I should be able to see him afterwards I can't tell he has never been at home for the last five months.'

Branwell was no uncertain quantity to himself, however. Having regained Haworth he wrote to his friend Francis Grundy, '. . . I would rather give my hand than undergo again the . . . malignant yet cold debauchery, the determination to find out how far mind could carry body without both being chucked into hell . . .', and Grundy was subsequently to comment, 'That Rector of Haworth little knew how to bring up and bring out his clever family, and the boy least of all. . . . So the girls worked their way to fame and death, the boy to death only !'

But Branwell, no more than the rest of them, was wanting in heart. Not only did he nurse the curate; his aunt too, this unhappy autumn, was taken ill. 'My dear Sir,' he wrote to Grundy on 25 October. 'There is no misunderstanding. I have had a long attendance at the death-bed of the Rev. William Weightman, one of my dearest friends,

[1] 'Severed and Gone,' 1847.   [2] 'A Reminiscence,' 1844.

and now I am attending at the death-bed of my aunt, who has been for twenty years as my mother. I expect her to die in a few hours. . . . As my sisters are far from home, I have had much on my mind.' And in a second letter, '. . . I have been waking two nights witnessing such agonizing suffering as I would not wish my worst enemy to endure, and I have now lost the guide and director of all the happy days connected with my childhood.' As if this were not enough, Martha Taylor died at almost the same moment in Brussels. She and William Weightman were the gayest, one might almost say the only gay figures in the Brontë circle, and the circle, being small, had been very close.

Anne was not at home when Weightman died nor did she reach home before the death of her aunt; but when Charlotte and Emily arrived from Brussels on 8 November they found her there: 'We sailed from Antwerp on Sunday; we travelled day and night and got home on Tuesday morning – and of course the funeral and all was over. We shall see her no more. Papa is pretty well. We found Anne at home; she is pretty well also.' '. . . Aunt, Martha Taylor, and Mr Weightman are now all gone; how dreary and void everything seems.' Ten days later Charlotte wrote again: 'Do not fear to find us melancholy or depressed. We are all much as usual.' The death of Miss Branwell was not a major grief, certainly not to Charlotte, who no doubt after all they had been through abroad was feeling the comfort of being at home. Anne perhaps for the moment felt likewise. On 10 November she wrote her poem to Cowper. We can imagine her in the drained and musing yet exalted mood that supervenes upon such a period taking down and re-reading Cowper, who was peculiarly a part of home, and being moved to think of him with new intimacy and tenderness. And on the same day (her creative energy could be remarkable) she took up and finished 'In memory of a happy day in February'. The poem had been begun in a moment of confident faith, and Anne found that this was the moment to resume it.

> *I knew that my Redeemer lived*
> *I did not fear to die.*
> *I felt that I should rise again*
> *To immortality.*

She believed; and after the threefold visitation of death she fortified herself by declaring her faith in the after-life. She returned to Thorp Green on the same day as Charlotte went on a visit to Ellen Nussey, and was back again at Haworth for Christmas. It must have been in the Christmas holidays that she wrote the unpublished poem 'To——', her first known love-poem to William Weightman after his death, simple, frank and, although her bereavement was so recent, less painful than some of the poems she was to write in his memory later.

To——

I will not mourn thee, lovely one,
Though thou art torn away.
'Tis said that if the morning sun
Arize with dazzling ray

And shed a bright and burning beam,
Athwart the glittering main,
Ere noon shall fade that laughing gleam,
Engulphed in clouds and rain;

And if thy life as transient proved
It hath been full as bright,
For thou wert hopeful and beloved;
Thy spirit knew no blight.

If few and short the joys of life
That thou on earth couldst know
Little thou know'st of sin and strife
Nor much of pain and wo

If vain thy earthly hopes did prove
Thou canst not mourn their flight
Thy brightest hopes were fixed above
And they shall know no blight.

And yet I cannot check my sighs
Thou wert so young and fair . . .
More bright than summer morning skies
But stern Death would not spare

He would not pass our darling bye
Nor grant one hour's delay
But rudely closed his shining eye
And frowned his smile away

That Angel smile that late so much,
Could my fond heart rejoice,
And he has silenced by his touch,
The music of thy voice,

I'll weep no more thine early doom
But O I still must mourn
The pleasures burried in thy tomb
For they will not return!

The poem, full of mis-spellings, is dated December 1842. The last two verses suggest that Anne and Weightman had, after all, seen much of each other at some period, doubtless the June holidays of that year, and that they had had at least some chance of being happy together.

'Lines Composed in a Wood on a Windy Day' tell us that Anne was in sufficient spirits on her return to work to be excited by an effect of nature. There is not much strength in the poem, but a few vivid words, 'the long withered grass in the sunshine is glancing', and even more the explanatory footnote. 'Composed in the Long Plantation on a Wild Bright Windy Day', show us how Anne, although less storm-ridden than the rest of the family, loved wild weather, as she loved the sea, and hard country and snow.[1]

But there were no high spirits and not much confident faith in the poems of the year 1843. Anne was now living it out. She was sunk back at Thorp Green, Weightman was dead, Charlotte had returned to Brussels (alone this time) for a second year, so the prospect of deliverance by their school-scheme was distant as ever. Branwell joined her as tutor at Thorp Green in January 1843. But we feel and she herself feels that there is danger of her sinking into the trough, and she tries desperately to support herself by faith.

On 28 May she wrote 'A Word to the Elect'. She did not believe in election, but now more than ever she knew the force of John Knox's words, 'The very elect are sometimes without all feeling of consolation.'

On 10 September she wrote 'A Doubter's Prayer'.

[1] 'The North Wind',

I've blown the pure untrodden snows
In whirling eddies from their brows,

and frequent other references to snow, particularly in the Gondal poem, 'The Student's Serenade'.

Oh, help me God! For thou alone
Canst my distracted soul relieve,
Forsake it not, it is Thine own
Though weak, yet willing to believe.

On 31 October she finishes 'The Captive Dove' begun in the spring of the previous year, and self-revelatory.

But thou, poor solitary dove
Must make unheard thy joyless moan
The heart that Nature formed to love
Must pine, neglected and alone.

'The Consolation', written on 7 November, is the confession that home is the only consolation that Anne, at twenty-three, can look for, and 'Past Days', written two weeks later, is on much the same theme.

Charlotte returned from Brussels in the New Year. Miss Branwell in her will had not only left Charlotte and Emily her workboxes and Anne her watch, she had left her small patrimony to be divided between these three nieces and a Cornish niece, so that the Brontës were now a little better off. 'Everyone asks me what I am going to do,' wrote Charlotte to Ellen at the end of January, '. . . and everyone seems to expect that I should immediately commence a school. In truth it is what I should wish to do. I desire it above all things. I have sufficient money for the undertaking . . . yet I cannot permit myself to enter upon life. . . . It is on Papa's account; he is now, as you know, getting old, and it grieves me to tell you that he is losing his sight. I have felt for some months that I ought not to be away from him : and I feel now that it would be too selfish to leave him (at least as long as Branwell and Anne are absent) in order to pursue selfish interests of my own.' As we are aware of the agonizingly selfish interest (her love for her Belgian professor, M. Héger), which had drawn Charlotte back to Brussels for a second year, we feel for her at this moment. The result was, however, that Anne stayed at Thorp Green. 'Anne and Branwell have just left us to return to York,' Charlotte concluded. This was in the beginning of 1844. 'They are both wondrously valued in their situations.' Anne was to be at Thorp Green for another eighteen months, making nearly five years in all. Time and custom have gradually blunted Charlotte's susceptibility on her account. Also Charlotte herself was suffering, as her poignant letters to M. Héger and her later confession to Ellen Nussey show. ('I returned to Brussels after Aunt's death against my conscience . . . prompted by what then seemed an irresistible impulse. I was punished for my selfish folly by a total withdrawal for more than two years of happiness and peace of mind.') 'I got home safely,' Charlotte writes to her friend after a visit in March, 'and . . . found Emily and Papa well, and a letter from Branwell intimating that he and Anne are pretty well too.' On 23 June we have, 'Anne and Branwell are now at home, and they and Emily add their request to mine that you will join us . . . do not let your visit be later than the beginning of next week or you will see little of A. and B. as their holidays are very short. They will soon have to join the family at Scarborough.' On 16 July, 'We were all very glad to get your letter this morning. *We*, I say, as both Papa and Emily were anxious to hear of the safe arrival of yourself and the little *Varmint*.' The little varmint was Flossy Jnr., daughter of the spaniel Flossy given to Anne by the Robinsons. Charlotte is resigned for Anne; things are not too bad for her. There is the regular round, Thorp Green, Haworth, Scarborough; the Robinsons have given her a dog. Charlotte herself, who has been limited by her master to a letter every six months, was writing in January 1845, 'Mr Taylor est revenu je lui ai demandé s'il n'avait pas une lettre pour moi – "Non, rien." "Patience" dis-je – "sa sœur viendra bientôt" – Mademoiselle Taylor est revenue "Je n'ai rien pour vous de la part de M. Héger" dit-elle "ni lettre ni message . . ."' The letter ends 'On souffre en silence tant qu'on en a la force et quand cette force manque on parle sans trop mesurer les paroles'. The pang was still as keen after a year. Charlotte has not too much thought to spare for the sufferings of other people.

The school scheme had progressed as far as the circulation of a printed prospectus; and on Mr Brontë's account it had been decided that the establishment, when it came into being, should be at the Parsonage, which was to be enlarged for the reception of pupils. However no pupils presented themselves. Ellen, as might have been expected, was sympathetic and helpful. 'I am driving on with my small matter as well as I can,' Charlotte wrote to her on 29th July 1844. 'I have written to all the friends on whom I have the slightest claim and to some on whom I have no claim – Mrs Busfeild for example. . . . She was exceedingly polite . . . but feared I should have some difficulty in making it succeed on account of the situation. Such is the answer I receive from almost every one. . . .' 'Dear Nell' [on 15 August], 'I sent you two more circulars. . . .' On 16 September, 'I send you two more circulars because you ask for them, not because I hope their distribution will produce any result. I hope that if a time should come when Emily, Anne, and I should be able to serve you, we shall not forget that you have done your best to serve us.' On 2 October, 'I, Emily, and Anne are truly obliged to you for the efforts you have made on our behalf, and if you have not been successful, you are only like ourselves. Everyone wishes us well but there are no pupils to be had. We have no present intention, however, of breaking our hearts on the subject, still less of feeling mortified at defeat.'

For those not in bondage the disappointment no doubt was less keen.

At Christmas Anne is invited with Charlotte to the Nusseys at Brookroyd. We do not know whether she ever received the invitation, but it was confidently refused on her behalf. 'I cannot, dear Nell, make any promises about Anne and myself going to Brookroyd at Christmas − her vacations are so short she would grudge spending any part of them from home.' In the same letter, much concerned at the tale of little Flossy's depredations, Charlotte adds, 'You and Anne are a pair for marvellous philosophical powers of endurance − no spoilt dinners − scorched linen, dirtied carpets − torn sofa-covers, squealing brats, cross husbands would ever discompose either of you.' Charlotte seems to be hardening in the habit of taking Anne and all that concerns her for granted. The last we hear of Anne that year during the Christmas holidays is that she is 'always good, mild and patient', as usual.

Anne gives her own account of herself in the four poems that follow 'The Student's Serenade' in 1844.

The first is the touching lament for her love, 'A Reminiscence'. The second, 'Memory', is a gentle and nostalgic nature-poem. Anne is resigned, she tells herself at twenty-four, to doing without all the ordinary joys that a girl hopes for; but in 'Fluctuations' and 'Prayer' we see how her resolution fails her and she cries out to God for help and faith. The fifth poem is again concerned with the joys of home.

This, actually is Anne's history during her long sojourn at Thorp Green − loss of love, separation from home, and the struggle, aided by her intimate life of writing and her sincerely striving faith, to bear these sorrows. She might have borne them for even longer than she did, but at some point into her life at Thorp Green Branwell's life intruded.

Branwell, at the beginning of 1844 was valued in his situation, as well he might have been, with his gifts. At the end of that year he is reported by Charlotte to be less irritable than he was in the summer; he writes home; he turns up for the holidays; he has been in regular employment for two years. So far, so good; better in fact than might have been expected. But there was something to be added, which was by no means good, and which was perhaps exactly what might have been expected – Branwell had fallen in love with his employer's wife.

The explosion occurred or was reported by Charlotte on 31 July 1845, a few days after her return home from a visit to Ellen.

'It was ten o'clock at night when I got home. I found Branwell ill; he is so very often owing to his own fault. I was not shocked at first, but when Anne informed me of the immediate cause of his present illness I was very greatly shocked. He had last Thursday received a note from Mr Robinson sternly dismissing him, intimating that he had discovered his proceedings, which he characterized as bad beyond expression, and charging him on pain of exposure to break off instantly and for ever all communication with every member of his family. We have had sad work with Branwell since. He thought of nothing but stunning or drowning his distress of mind.'

Branwell gives his own version of his affairs in October, in a letter to Francis Grundy.

'In a letter begun in the spring and never finished, owing to incessant attacks of illness, I tried to tell you that I was tutor to the son of (Mr Edmund Robinson, Thorp Green Hall) a wealthy gentleman whose wife is sister to the wife of ——, M.P., for the county of ——, and the cousin of Lord ——. This lady (though her husband detested me) showed me a degree of kindness which, when I was deeply grieved one day at her husband's conduct, ripened into declarations of more than ordinary feeling. My admiration of her mental and personal attractions, my knowledge of her unselfish sincerity, her sweet temper and unwearied care for others, with but unrequited return where most should have been given . . . although she is seventeen years my senior, all combined to an attachment on my part and led to reciprocations which I had little looked for. During nearly three years I had "troubled pleasure soon chastised by fear". Three months since, I received a furious letter from my employer, offering to shoot me if I returned from my vacation, which I was passing at home; and letters from her lady's-maid and physician informed me of the outbreak, only checked by her firm resolution that whatever harm came to her, none should come to me. . . . I have lain during nine long weeks utterly shattered in body and broken down in mind. . . .'

From this moment of history (the end of July) we may look backwards and discover what we can. Anne and Branwell had come home as usual for their summer holidays in June. But Anne was not going back to Thorp Green. 'Branwell and Anne are both come home,' Charlotte tells Ellen, 'and Anne I am rejoiced to say has decided not to return to Mr Robinson's – *her* presence at home certainly makes me feel more at liberty.'

Anne had given no reason or had not given the right reason for her resignation to Charlotte, and Charlotte felt free to plan a decent holiday, which took the form of three weeks with Ellen at her brother's Rectory at Hathersage, near Sheffield. Emily and Anne were also planning a little trip together. 'The opening of the railroad is now postponed till July the 7th,' wrote Charlotte on 24 June. 'I have told Emily and Anne that I should not like again to put you off – and for that and some other reasons they have decided to give up the idea of going to Scarborough, and instead, to make a little excursion next Monday or Tuesday to Ilkley or elsewhere. . . . If all be well they will be back on Wednesday – therefore if the day be fine on Thursday and all other things right, I hope no other obstacle will arise to prevent my going to Hathersage. . . .' Having dispatched Charlotte, Emily and Anne were anxious for her to get the full benefit from the change, and Emily wrote one of her few, cheerful notes to Ellen to that effect. 'Love to her and you from Anne and myself,' she concluded, 'and tell her all are well at home. Yours E. J. Brontë.' Charlotte arrived home on or about 22 July. She had travelled in the train with a Frenchman, and had heard and spoken the language in which she loved, for the first time since she left Brussels. The sight of Branwell brought her back summarily to earth.

Anne had held her peace about affairs at Thorp Green until obliged to speak. Close as the Brontës were, it is interesting to reflect at this moment how much they were in the dark about each others' real lives. . . . Charlotte eating her heart out for M. Héger, Branwell at the feet of Mrs Robinson, Anne still mourning William Weightman (her passion no doubt revived by witnessing Branwell's), and keeping her brother's secret. A more miserable and embarrassing position than hers at Thorp Green can hardly be imagined. It was no doubt thanks to her excellencies that Branwell had been included in the Robinson household. This was the outcome. She declared loyally that the fault lay with Mrs Robinson, whom she considered a mixture of perverseness, weakness, and deceit, but this scarcely made the situation more tolerable. Anne was a delicate, well-bred girl and a dependent, and though we know from her novels that she was a realist and by no means squeamish about the facts of life, to be thrust into association with some of the most unpleasant of them, and at her brother's hands, was a horrible ordeal. Mrs Robinson 'was so bold and hardened,' Mrs Gaskell wrote, 'that she did it (made love to Branwell) in the very presence of her children, just approaching to maturity; and they would threaten her that if she did not grant them such and such indulgences they would tell their bed-ridden father how she went on with Mr Brontë.'

Mrs Gaskell refers to Mrs Robinson openly as Branwell's paramour and says that she sent him money, £20 at a time. These are details that could hardly have been furnished by Charlotte or her father, who between them supplied much information to Charlotte's biographer, and on the instruction of Mrs Robinson's lawyer the passages in question were retracted. They indicate something of Anne's situation, however. It could not be endured indefinitely, and by June she had decided to end it. In addition to all else, her chagrin at having her long service at the Robinsons forcibly concluded in this manner must have been intense. The actual decision to leave was probably taken soon after 20 May, on which date she had written 'If this be All', a poem of complete discouragement. Its form suggests that she had made some positive movement to intervene and been repulsed on all sides.

> *Oh God, if this indeed be all*
> *That life can show to me . . .*
>
> *Working and toiling without gain*
> *The slave of other's will*
> *With constant care and frequent pain,*
> *Despised, forgotten still:*
>
> *Grieving to look on vice and sin*
> *Yet powerless to quell*
> *The silent current from within*
> *The outward torrent's swell*

While all the good I would impart
The feelings I would share
Are driven backward to my heart
And turned to wormwood there.

The stricken Branwell was sent to Liverpool and thence to Wales for a week with John Brown the sexton, and in the lull Emily's birthday came round and it was time to open the 1841 Birthday Papers and to indite those of 1845. It was probably on the last night of July that the ceremony took place and the two new papers were neatly folded to the size of sixpence and stuffed into their little black box.

Emily's paper runs:

'Haworth, Thursday, July 30th, 1845.
'My birthday – showery, breezy, cool. I am twenty-seven years old today. This morning Anne and I opened the papers we wrote four years since, on my twenty-third birthday. This paper we intend, if all be well, to open on my thirtieth – three years hence, in 1848. Since the 1841 paper the following events have taken place. Our school scheme has been abandoned, and instead Charlotte and I went to Brussels on the 8th of February 1842.

'Branwell left his place at Luddenden Foot. C. and I returned from Brussels, November 8th, 1842, in consequence of aunt's death.

'Branwell went to Thorp Green as a tutor, where Anne still continued, January 1843.

'Charlotte returned to Brussels the same month, and after staying a year, came back again on New Year's Day 1844.

'Anne left her situation at Thorp Green of her own accord, June 1845.

'Anne and I went our first long journey by ourselves together, leaving home on the 30th of June, Monday, sleeping at York, returning to Keighley Tuesday evening, sleeping there and walking home on Wednesday morning. Though the weather was broken we enjoyed ourselves very much, except during a few hours at Bradford. And during our excursion we were, Ronald Macalgin, Henry Angora, Juliet Angusteena, Rosabella Esmaldan, Ella and Julian Egremont, Catharine Navarre, and Cordelia Fitzaphnold, escaping from the palaces of instruction to join the Royalists who are hard driven at present by the victorious Republicans. The Gondals still flourish bright as ever. I am at present writing a work on the First Wars. Anne has been writing some articles on this, and a book by Henry Sophona. We intend sticking firm by the rascals as long as they delight us, which I am glad to say they do at present. I should have mentioned that last summer the school scheme was revived in full vigour. We had prospectusses printed, despatched letters to all acquaintances imparting our plans, and did our little all; but it was found no go. Now I don't desire a school at all, and none of us have any great longing for it. We have cash enough for our present wants, with a prospect of accumulation. We are all in decent health, only that papa has a complaint in his eyes, and with the exception of B., who, I hope, will be better and do better hereafter. I am quite contented for myself: not as idle as formerly, altogether as hearty, and having learnt to make the most of the present and long for the future with the fidgetiness that I cannot do all I wish; seldom or never troubled with nothing to do, and merely desiring that everybody could be as comfortable as myself and as undesponding, and then we should have a very tolerable world of it.

'By mistake I find we have opened the paper on the 31st instead of the 30th. Yesterday was much such a day as this, but the morning was divine.

'Tabby, who was gone in our last paper, is come back, and has lived with us two years and a half, and is in good health. Martha, who also departed, is here too. We have got Flossy; got and lost Tiger; lost the hawk Hero, which, with the geese, was given away, and is doubtless dead, for when I came back from Brussels, I inquired on all hands and could hear nothing of him. Tiger died early last year. Keeper and Flossy are well, also the canary acquired four years since. We are now all at home, and likely to be there some time. Branwell went to Liverpool on Tuesday to stay a week. Tabby has just been teasing me to turn as formerly to "Pilloputate". Anne and I should have picked the black currants if it had been fine and sunshiny. I must hurry off now to my turning and ironing. I have plenty of work on hands, and writing, and am altogether full of business. With best wishes for the whole house till 1848, July 30th, and as much longer as may be, – I conclude. E. J. Brontë.'

The minute available free space on the paper is filled in with one of Emily's lively little scrawls. It is a Parsonage interior, where she or

93

Anne sits inditing her paper, with Keeper at her feet and Flossy in the window-seat.

Anne's paper runs:

'Thursday, July the 31st, 1845. Yesterday was Emily's birthday, and the time when we should have opened our 1841 paper, but by mistake we opened it today instead. How many things have happened since it was written – some pleasant, some far otherwise. Yet I was then at Thorp Green, and now I am only just escaped from it. I was wishing to leave it then, and if I had known that I had four years longer to stay how wretched I should have been; but during my stay I have had some very unpleasant and undreamt-of experience of human nature. Others have seen more changes. Charlotte has left Mr White's, and been twice to Brussels, where she stayed each time nearly a year. Emily has been there too, and stayed nearly a year. Branwell has left Luddenden Foot, and been a tutor at Thorp Green, and had much tribulation and ill health. He was very ill on Thursday, but he went with John Brown to Liverpool, where he now is, I suppose; and we hope he will be better and do better in future. This is a dismal, cloudy, wet evening. We have had so far a very cold, wet summer. Charlotte has lately been to Hathersage, in Derbyshire, on a visit of three weeks to Ellen Nussey. She is now sitting sewing in the dining-room. Emily is ironing upstairs. I am sitting in the dining-room in the rocking-chair before the fire with my feet on the fender. Papa is in the parlour. Tabby and Martha are, I think, in the kitchen. Keeper and Flossy are, I do not know where. Little Dick is hopping in his cage. When the last paper was written we were thinking of setting up a school. The scheme has been dropt, and long after taken up again, and dropt again, because we could not get pupils. Charlotte is thinking about getting another situation. She wishes to go to Paris. Will she go? She has let Flossy in, by-the-by, and he is now lying on the sofa. Emily is engaged in writing the Emperor Julius's Life. She has read some of it, and I want very much to hear the rest. She is writing some poetry, too. I wonder what it is about? I have begun the third volume of *Passages in the Life of an Individual*. I wish I had finished it. This afternoon I began to set about making my grey figured silk frock that was dyed at Keighley. What sort of a hand shall I make of it? E. and I have a great deal of work to do. When shall we sensibly diminish it? I want to get a habit of early rising. Shall I succeed? We have not yet finished our *Gonda Chronicles* that we began three years and a half ago. When will they ·be done? The Gondals are at present in a sad state. The Republicans are uppermost, but the Royalists are not quite overcome. The young sovereigns, with their brothers and sisters, are still at the Palace of Instruction. The Unique Society, about half a year ago, were wrecked on a desert island as they were returning from Gaul. They are still there, but we have not played at them much yet. The Gondals in general are not in first-rate playing condition. Will they improve? I wonder how we shall all be, and where and how situated, on the thirtieth of July 1848, when, if we are all alive, Emily will be just 30. I shall be in my 29th year, Charlotte in her 33rd, and Branwell in his 32nd; and what changes shall we have seen and known; and shall we be much changed ourselves? I hope not, for the worse at least. I for my part cannot well be flatter or older in mind than I am now. Hoping for the best, I conclude. ANNE BRONTË.'

Emily writes in somewhat determined good spirits, like one who means to live her life according to design. It seems she is succeeding pretty well. There is full acceptance of everyday things, but they do not impinge very deeply, not even the débâcle of Branwell. There is just a hint that the writer, having succeeded herself in keeping cheerful, is wondering what the general depression is about. The words concerning the weather are the most vivid and genuine in the paper, as they were in 1841 . . . 'the morning was divine' . . . and at once give us Emily enshrined in the essential natural world. The Gondals still flourish bright as ever.

Anne's spirits could hardly be lower. It is remarkable that she does not even mention the late excursion to York. She is full of doubts and clearly is feeling the effects of the last period at Thorp Green. The letter is dull and drained; the Gondals are not in first-rate playing condition.

This is the last time the sisters mention the Gondals, whose condition reflects the condition of their authors. For fourteen years Gondal has been the place to which Emily and Anne could repair when they wished to lead the creative life or the life of the imagination, where they constructed, invented, wrote bookfuls of history, romance and adventure or simply spoke their own thoughts or prayed their own prayers through the mouths of Gondal characters. Some of the poems on which Emily's fame rests are Gondal poems, and one of Anne's few splendid lines is a description of the imaginary land itself ('To our beloved land I'll flee, Our land of thought and soul').[1] But by the time it comes to the mention of Gondal in this last birthday paper, it is clear that Anne is beginning to lean away. She refers first to 'Passages in the Life of an Individual', which was a draft for *Agnes Grey*, as though that and not Gondal-history was the major literary work she had in hand. Since Anne's writing was to be in the best sense prosaic, perhaps she began to feel now that Sophona and Cordelia Fitzaphnold were in a manner of speaking twice removed from life. However that might be, Gondal had done its work. When the sisters turned deliberately to fiction as understood . . . 'We each set to work on a prose tale' . . . the pens which they took in hand were fully practised.

[1] 'Call me Away.'

VI

BRANWELL'S VICE OR weakness is still referred to in the summer of 1845 as illness, but hopes for him rationally were at an end. By the autumn, Charlotte is calling a spade a spade. 'It is only absolute want of means that acts as any check to him.' 'His health and consequently his temper have been better this last day or two, because he is now *forced* to abstain.' 'Branwell makes no effort to seek a situation and when he is at home I will invite no one to come and share our discomfort. . . . Emily and Anne regret as much as I do that we cannot ask you to Haworth.'

Charlotte has been criticized for her lack of mercy towards Branwell. It has also been said, and no doubt truly, that the fact that she kept her own troubles to herself, while Branwell's were public property, exacerbated her scorn. (On 18 November of that year she was to write the last and most moving of her letters to M. Héger at Brussels.) But Charlotte was disappointed in Branwell in a peculiar way. To him she had never been a little mother. They had been friends, equals and fellow-wits. When she wrote to Southey, Branwell wrote to Wordsworth. Her letters to her brother have their own particular man-to-man tone. We must remember also what it was like for these three delicate women to have Branwell permanently in their midst. In the spring of 1846 Charlotte was to write, 'In his present state it is scarcely possible to stay in the room where he is.' Mr Brontë did his part, and his son slept or failed to sleep in his bedroom, but in 1845 the old man was sixty-eight and his sight had been failing for a long time. Even Emily set her brother down as 'a hopeless being'. So far from censuring Charlotte for her comments we may feel thankful that she had Ellen to whom she could make them, and that Emily and Anne could participate in this relief.

Branwell himself had his periods of hope and activity during which he solicited a friend about employment, arranged for a tablet to be fixed in the church, and wrote. He painted also, and there is a portrait by his hand, evidently part of a family group, that is ascribed to the year 1845. The likeness is most probably of Emily, though it was once thought to be of Anne.

The Reverend Arthur Nicholls, who probably had no special tenderness for the artist, is said to have scrubbed out his wife's portrait and Anne's, as he found them unbearable. Curiously enough, tracings of these portraits have survived, and it is interesting to see in Anne's a certain likeness to a rather ugly picture of Maria Branwell at sixteen, painted by a Mr Tarlin of Penzance.

Anne wrote what might seem a surprising number of poems between June and December 1845. We seem to see her preparing for literary activity when she makes fair copies of five of her earlier compositions and fixes them into a more-than-usually elegant little home-made book. Externally the history of these months consisted largely of the distressing life with the drunkard and drug-addict, and such an atmosphere might not have been generally conducive to the writing of poetry. But Anne was home, after five years; if anyone was used to her brother and his distresses, it was she; Branwell at Haworth, in whatever shape, was probably less nerve-racking than Branwell at Thorp Green. Anne endured; she did not exaggerate; she was well-schooled; Charlotte described her sister as living under a nun-like veil, which she herself notably failed to penetrate; under this veil Anne lived her own life, and in the summer and autumn of 1845 she wrote poems describing her struggles for faith and confidence, in which she was now gaining, and Gondal poems as dissociated and natural as the songs of larks. And in the autumn of 1845 all three sisters began, through an accident, overtly to lead their real lives.

'One day, in the autumn of 1845, I accidentally lighted on a MS. volume of verse in my sister Emily's handwriting. Of course, I was not surprised, knowing that she could and did write verse; I looked it over, and something more than surprise seized me, – a deep conviction that these were not common effusions, nor at all like the poetry women generally write. I thought them condensed and terse, vigorous and genuine. To my ear, they had also a peculiar music – wild, melancholy, and elevating.

'My sister Emily was not a person of demonstrative character, nor one on the recesses of whose mind and feelings, even those nearest and dearest to her could, with impunity intrude unlicensed; it took hours to reconcile her to the discovery I had made, and days to persuade her that such poems merited publication. I knew however that a mind like hers could not be without some latent spark of honourable ambition, and refused to be discouraged in my attempts to fan that spark to flame.

'Meantime, my younger sister quietly produced some of her own compositions, intimating that, since Emily's had given me pleasure, I might like to look at hers. I could not but be a partial judge, yet I thought that these verses, too, had a sweet sincere pathos of their own.

'We had very early cherished the dream of becoming authors. This dream, never relinquished, even when distance and absorbing tasks occupied us, now suddenly acquired strength and consistency; it took the character of a resolve. We agreed to arrange a small selection of our poems, and, if possible, get them printed. Averse to personal publicity, we veiled our own names under those of Currer, Ellis, and Acton Bell; the ambiguous choice being dictated by a sort of conscientious scruple at assuming Christian names positively masculine, while we did not like to declare ourselves women, because – without at that time suspecting that our mode of writing and thinking was not what is called "feminine" – we had a vague impression that authoresses are liable to be looked on with prejudice; we had noticed how critics sometimes use for their chastisement the weapon of personality and for their reward a flattery which is not true praise.'[1]

With characteristic courage and energy Charlotte began the attempt to get the work printed.

The publishing of the Brontës' poems is described to us, in the letters that exist, as tersely and objectively as Branwell's getting money to buy gin or Tabby's slipping on the hill and straining her leg; more tersely and objectively in fact, because we do not read the news in letters to friends, but in letters to printers and publishers, which Charlotte strove to make as brief, sexless, and business-like as possible. Mrs Gaskell observes, 'In the course of this sad autumn of 1845, a new interest came up: faint indeed and often lost sight of in the vivid pain and constant pressure of anxiety respecting their brother . . .', a sanctimonious comment on the publication of their first book which no doubt was the kind of thing that made the sisters prefer not to be known as women-writers.

[1] Biographical Notice of Ellis and Acton Bell.

Yet in spite of Mrs Gaskell and the bald business letters, we are not insensible of what it meant to the sisters to begin to publish their work.

The Brontës were writers, almost literally writers born. They were apprenticed to their craft phenomenally early and they never wavered in its pursuit. There have been writers whose work has finished with the writing, but the sisters were not of this number. They wanted to see themselves in print. This is what Charlotte means by 'cherishing the dream of one day becoming authors', for in all but publication they had been authors almost the whole of their lives.

Even Emily was only superficially averse to the idea. No poet, however desirous of publication, is anything but angry at having his work discovered and read without his permission and at a moment not chosen by himself. But Emily, who could have snuffed out the scheme quite easily if it offended her principles, was persuaded in a few days. Charlotte was right in guessing that the spark of ambition in her breast, though latent, could be made to glow. Anne, it may be noted, always called so shy and retiring, was perfectly realistic on this point and *offered* her poems to Charlotte's eye.

The Brontës turned to their writing when their domestic duties were done. They never mentioned it to their friends nor to anybody except each other. Their attitude towards their work was unaffected to the last degree; yet writing was almost as necessary to them as breathing, and it is a mistake to suppose that it was ever of less than absolutely primary importance. Charlotte tells us this clearly once, in spite of her reticence and the tight hand she keeps on herself.

In the Biographical Notice she describes Currer Bell's attempts to find a publisher for 'The Professor'. 'After many refusals there came a letter which he opened in the dreary expectation of finding two hard hopeless lines, intimating that Messrs Smith Elder & Co "were not disposed to publish the MS." and, instead, he took out a letter of two pages. He read it trembling. . . .' In these four words everything is said.

The Brontës did not delude themselves by supposing that publishers would be found eager to sponsor three unknown women's verses, and the poems were printed at their own expense. The cost was £31 10s. 0d., plus a further £5 for alterations. The book was issued by Messrs Aylott and Jones, who were printers rather than publishers, and there is a stiff little series of communications to them from Charlotte, covering all practical questions – type, paper, number of pages, proofs, review copies, and advertisements, on which an additional £2 and later an additional £10 was laid out. The poems were published at the end of May 1846. The book, in a cover of stamped blue linen, looking like a decent ancient school book, is inscribed

POEMS
by
Currer, Ellis,
and Acton
Bell.
4/-

and the poems are signed Currer, Ellis, Acton (without any surname), as the case may be.

On 15 July Charlotte wrote to the publishers: 'Will you favour me with a line, stating whether *any* or how many copies have yet been sold.' The answer was that two copies had been sold; there were two favourable reviews, in the *Atheneum* and the *Dublin University Magazine*, and a Mr Enoch of Warwick asked the authors for their autographs.

For a private outlay of about £16 Anne had put twenty-one poems before the public. 'In the Atheneum review Currer was placed midway between Ellis and Acton.'[1] 'The bringing out of our little book was hard work,' Charlotte's Notice continued. 'As was to be expected neither we nor our poems were at all wanted; but for this we had been prepared at the outset. . . . The book was printed; it is scarcely known, and all of it that merits to be known are the poems of Ellis Bell. . . . Ill-success failed to crush us; the mere effort to succeed had given a wonderful zest to existence; it must be pursued. We each set to work on a prose tale; Ellis Bell produced *Wuthering Heights*, Acton Bell, *Agnes Grey*. . . .'

Anne is fledged at last. She sits down to prepare for publication the first of the two novels which for more than a hundred years have had a quiet yet determined existence.

Agnes Grey, as we know, was already partly written as 'Passages in the Life of an Individual', and we could almost wish that it had kept that title, so good, so flat, so characteristic. The early part of the book presents Anne in charge of the infant Inghams and the later part presents Thorp Green and was largely written at Thorp Green, which not only supplies the ample country-house background of the

---

[1] *The Shakespeare Head Brontë: The Life and Letters*, Vol. II.

Murrays in the book, but also of the Huntingdons and their circle in *The Tenant of Wildfell Hall.*

In a journal we see the author in a self-portrait; in poems we see the same self-portrait, but stylized; in the autobiographical novel the author is not gazing at her own reflection, but pushing herself out, along with her characters, on to the stage. *Agnes Grey* is a young, spontaneous, naïve autobiography; it is the autobiography written at the beginning and not at the end of the writing-life; the extraneous matter is sufficiently disguised, but there is little attempt to disguise the central figure. Anne offers herself in simplicity, confidence, and without self-conscious handling in juxtaposition to her people and situations; we can learn about her pretty well.

Of course she gives herself a lover and a husband. What else are novels for? Weightman was under the stone, but Weston was to survive and marry Agnes; and here Anne did invent, not her own love, but the man on whom it was bestowed; she had succumbed to Weightman's charm, but a husband must be stable, or must in the end grow stable. So Anne added this requisite and made her curate all that could be needed or desired.

The most inexplicable thing in the whole Brontë saga, or perhaps the only truly inexplicable thing (for about everything else we are free to charm ourselves with our different explanations) is that anybody could ever have supposed (as early critics did) that *Jane Eyre* and *Agnes Grey* were written by men. For, among much else, they are two intensely feminine essays in the art of making heroes, remarkable historically for their outspokenness, and fascinating humanly for the light they throw on their authors. The authors are dissimilar; as are the ideal loves, and out of the mouth of her hero each author woos herself as she desires to be wooed. No more romantic heart than Charlotte's ever beat; the hero who she set to play opposite her, dark, thick-set, saturnine, overpoweringly masculine, is a member of the class of which Tolstoi's Vronsky is the most perfect example.

Anne was not romantic; by nature, and, we guess, by reaction, she was the opposite; hers is a hero if not of understatement at least of very level statement; but he has his charms, and the charm of implying everything and saying almost nothing is perfectly conveyed. In the book, while she is exiled at the Murrays, Agnes's father dies. Nothing so far has passed between her and Weston that is real evidence of his interest in herself. They meet at last. 'How is your mother?' is what he asks her. It is a transport.

Agnes Grey and *Jane Eyre* do well to be read together. Charlotte's is of course the greater book; its intensity is amazing; but its ridiculousness can be amazing also, and there are moments when we turn gratefully to her sister's tale.

As emancipated women, as well as authors, Anne and Charlotte are interesting to compare and contrast. All the Brontës could fairly be called emancipated; their mother in a sense had been emancipated too; she had owned no impropriety in telling her love. . . .

'Neither can I walk our accustomed rounds without thinking on you,' she writes, 'and why should I be ashamed to add, wishing for your presence. If you knew what my feelings were while writing this you would pity me.' And again, 'Jane put into my hand Lord Lyttleton's *Advice to a Lady*. When I read those lines, "Be never cool reserve with passion joined, with caution choose but then be fondly kind", my heart smote me for having in some cases used too much reserve towards you.'

Anne in her turn allows Agnes much frankness. . . . 'Sometimes such thoughts would give me trouble enough, but sometimes I could quiet them with thinking . . . it is not the man, it is his goodness that I love.' And Charlotte makes openness of this sort almost a moral duty.

Anne's emancipation, as we shall discover when we consider *The Tenant of Wildfell Hall*, was remarkable, but there was little about her to suggest it. Charlotte on the other hand was typical – aggressive and courageous in spirit, though shy and awkward in practice; tremendously direct and scorning the womanly arts of diplomacy and compromise, yet longing passionately for love, romance and personal beauty; forbidding to men and debarred by intellectuality from much of what is accessible to the most ordinary of women, a vehement exponent of the sex-war.

'Why,' she demands of Ellen apropos a friend, 'should Mrs Anderton wish her to marry the prig of a curate (as prig I have no doubt he is . . . .'

Anne could never have written such a sentence. Through superior attractiveness she is altogether softer, or perhaps part of her greater attractiveness comes through her being soft. Her emancipation is as it were the continuation of her mother's. She remains womanly and unaggressive, though never, through excuse of her sex, surrendering her independence, principles or judgement in the smallest degree.

Charlotte in fact had the qualities that only particular members of the other sex admire. We hear of Anne, in the single extant description of her by a gentleman's hand, as being 'by no means pretty, yet of a pleasing appearance. Her manner was curiously expressive of a wish for protection and encouragement, a kind of constant appeal which invited sympathy.' Pretty or not, Anne's is a bearing that appeals not only to the few but to the generality of male bosoms. The pity was that she was so extremely shy, too shy, as she herself felt often.

Agnes Grey reminds us of Anne's mother; at times she reminds us of Anne's father too. Agnes knew right from wrong and black from white; the Brontës, through Patrick, were also very clear upon this point. Anne was as clear as any of them. On moral matters she was, at least at the age of twenty-five, naïvely inflexible, and as a result she involved her heroine in quite a little web of moral confusion.

It happens in the book that the frivolous Rosalie Murray is offering encouragement to the worldly Rev. Hatfield at the same time as Agnes Grey is beginning not only to remember the Rev. Weston in her prayers but also to have him much in her daily thoughts. Rosalie, just 'out', and destined by her mother for an important marriage, is developing the habit of walking alone with a book, not in the gardens or the park, but in the outer fields. Mrs Murray asks Miss Grey specifically to keep an eye on the girl and remind her gently that this is not suitable behaviour for a young lady of rank and prospects. Agnes complies, and succeeds in curtailing a tête-à-tête. Three days later, although expressly stating that Rosalie is less indifferent to Hatfield than she protests, she obeys the girl's command to leave her alone and allows herself to be despatched on an errand, which of course turns into an errand of mercy, and on it she meets the Rev. Weston similarly disposed. Meanwhile Hatfield has seized the chance not only to propose to Rosalie but to threaten that he can compromise her reputation.

Now Anne had not been five years at Thorp Green for nothing, and we have not read thus far without knowing that behind her quietness she is a shrewd and intelligent observer of life. The whole chapter is particularly well done and we are left in no doubt at all that Agnes appreciates the episode from the worldly point of view, and understands the necessity for the girl's reputation to remain immaculate. Yet she disregards her employer's request and takes her orders from her charge; and Anne, in the very act of making these things happen, still goes on confidently claiming our sympathy for her heroine. The 'good' ones in fact can do no wrong; the 'bad' ones, such as Rosalie Murray, can cheerfully be left to perish.

Anne in fact allows Agnes to have it both ways. She may enjoy the lovers' meeting with as clear a conscience as if she had a right to it; her visit to the sick cottager is essentially a 'good' errand and her meeting with the Rev. Weston, being entirely fortuitous, is therefore above reproach; Miss Murray had been very exigent and practically forced the duenna from her side. Many a governess indeed would have allowed herself to be persuaded. But never Agnes, if she is all that we have been told she is. That expert on duty, limned in Anne's mirror, would have stuck to her post.

Certainly when we read *Agnes Grey* the legend of the author's passivity goes by the board. Anne is fresh and spirited; she is not vastly humorous, but she is humorous compared with Charlotte, and her humour, as might have been expected, is of the brief and quiet sort. The book is simple and the author is young, but there is evidence of self-knowledge and also of self-acceptance in it, which promise well for Anne's maturity both as a woman and a writer. Like Charlotte, Anne is discovered to be prim. Primness is not a quality that surprises us in Victorians or even in emancipated women; but it was not universal. Mary Taylor's style, in comparison with the Brontës, is startlingly modern, and Charlotte's extant childish letters contrast painfully with one written by Martha Taylor to Ellen Nussey from Roe Head.

The ending of Agnes Grey is brief almost to the point of being inartistic. Agnes marries her curate, but the description of her happiness is cut to the bone. Anne could dwell on love's vicissitudes, but either the attempt to describe fulfilment was still too painful or such joy was beyond even her imagination's ken.

VII

CHARLOTTE'S DOMESTIC correspondence has continued side by side with her letters to Aylott and Jones in London, and in it there have been one or two references to Anne's relationship with Ellen Nussey. 'I send you the drawing and copy, which is Anne's doing,' she writes on 20 April 1846; and on 25 April, 'Anne says it pleases her to think you have kept her little drawing she would rather have done it for you than for a stranger. . . .' On 9 August she writes, 'Anne and I both thank you for your kind invitation and our thanks are not mere words of course . . . but we cannot accept it and I think even you will think our motives for declining valid this time. . . .' Several times we hear of Anne being warmly invited to Brookroyd, though we never hear of her being able to accept the invitation. Along with the bond between Ellen and Charlotte there existed a steady bond between Ellen and Anne. Charlotte's letter continues, 'In a fortnight I hope to go with Papa to Manchester to have his eyes couched . . . Emily and I made a pilgrimage there a week ago to search out an operator and we found one in the person of a Mr Wilson. – He could not tell from description whether the eyes were ready for an operation – Papa must therefore take a journey to Manchester to consult him – if he judges the cataract ripe we shall remain – ' On 21 August she writes from rooms in Manchester. The day of the operation is fixed, she is dreading the arrival of a nurse and is worrying about 'how poor Emily and Anne will get on at home with Branwell'. From this pressure of anxiety and gloom there was one escape for Charlotte and she had the strength to seize it. She began to write *Jane Eyre*.

Anne and Emily were left at home with Branwell for a month, during which we may suppose they were finishing or sending out their prose tales. At the end of September Charlotte and her father were home: the operation had been successful, and shortly afterwards Aylott and Jones sent the *Dublin University Magazine,* which contained a very favourable review of the sisters' book. Anne wrote six poems between May and October 1846. The first, 'Domestic Peace' is a lament for the pass to which Branwell has brought them. Home is no longer blest and desired above all places.

> *The fire is burning in the grate*
> *As redly as it used to burn*
> *But still the hearth is desolate*
> *Till mirth and love with* peace *return.*

The remaining five are Gondal poems, four of which, with their constant theme of love and imprisonment, echo Anne's own longing and deprivation. The winter was particularly hard, and Anne was ill. 'We have all had severe colds and coughs in consequence of the severe weather. Poor Anne has suffered greatly from asthma, but is now, I am glad to say, rather better – she had two nights last week when her cough and difficulty of breathing were painful indeed to hear and witness and must have been most distressing to suffer – she bore it, as she does all affliction, without one complaint – only sighing now and then when nearly worn out – she has an extraordinary heroism of endurance. I admire, but certainly could not imitate her.'

The specific mention of asthma makes us wonder whether the nervous strain to which they were all subjected is causing Anne's weakness to take this form.

In Charlotte's next letter Anne is better.

'Anne is now much better – but Papa has been for near a fortnight far from well with influenza.'

On 1 March comes the surprising announcement that the Robinson girls have resumed writing to Anne. 'The Misses Robinson, who had entirely ceased their correspondence with Anne for half a year after their father's death have lately recommenced it – for a fortnight they sent her a letter almost every day – crammed with warm protestations of endless esteem and gratitude – they speak with great affection too of their mother – and never make any allusion intimating acquaintance with her errors – it is to be hoped they were and always will remain in ignorance on that point – especially since – I think – she has bitterly repented them. We take special care that Branwell does not know of their writing to Anne.'

It sounds as though the ban on communications with Haworth has been lifted suddenly and that the late pupils are effusively making up for lost time. In April the weather is very cold again . . . 'consequently we are all in the full enjoyment of colds; much blowing of noses is heard and much making of gruel goes on in the house.'

Next month, after so long, Ellen is expected on a visit. 'We shall all be glad to see you on the Thursday or the Friday of next week, whichever day will suit you best.' 'Come in black, blue, pink, white or scarlet, as you like. Come shabby or smart; neither the colour nor the condition signifies; provided only the dress contain Ellen Nussey, all will be right.' They have brought themselves at last, for the sake of a breath of air, to expose the skeleton in the cupboard; use and indifference, with Charlotte at least, have succeeded on pain and shame. And from Ellen the skeleton hardly needed concealing. One of twelve children, she was used to the vicissitudes and also to the horrors of family life, for one of her own brothers was insane. 'Branwell is quieter now. . . . You must expect to find him weaker in mind and the complete rake in appearance. I have no apprehension of his being at all uncivil to you; on the contrary, he will be as smooth as oil.' But Ellen's own family affairs obtrude, as so often before, and she does not come. Charlotte is angrily disappointed. 'Dear Ellen, Your letter of yesterday did indeed give me a cruel chill of disappointment. I cannot blame you – for I know it was not your fault – but I must say I do not altogether exempt your sister Ann from reproach – I do not think she considers it of the least consequence whether little people like us of Haworth are disappointed or not, provided great nobs like the Briar Hall gentry are accommodated. . . .' We may be sure that Anne, in her quieter fashion, was deeply disappointed too.

In April 1847, when William Weightman had been dead five years, Anne wrote 'Severed and Gone', her longest and most moving poem in his memory.

About a year after the publication of *Poems by Currer, Ellis and Acton Bell*, Charlotte sent copies of the little book to Wordsworth, Tennyson, Lockhart and De Quincey. As impresario she has all our gratitude, and we know that the letter to accompany the poems could not have been easy to write; but the semi-facetiousness to which she is driven strikes us as strange cover for Emily and Anne.

'Sir' (she wrote the same letter to them all), 'My relatives, Ellis and Acton Bell, and myself, heedless of the repeated warnings of various respectable publishers, have committed the rash act of printing a volume of poems. . . . In the space of a year our publishers have disposed but of two copies, and by what painful efforts have succeeded in getting rid of these two, himself only knows. . . .'

If the recipients offered any criticism, it has not survived.

Currer Bell, Charlotte tells us, wrote a narrative in one volume at the same time as her sisters were writing *Agnes Grey* and *Wuthering Heights*. This was *The Professor*. 'These MSS were perseveringly obtruded upon various publishers for the space of a year and a half,' accompanied by the following letter:

'SIR, I request permission to send for your inspection the MS of a work of fiction in 3 vols. It consists of three tales, each occupying a volume and capable of being published together or separately, as thought most advisable. The authors of these tales have already appeared before the public.

'Should you consent to examine the work, would you, in your reply, state at what period, after transmission of the MS to you the authors may expect to receive your decision upon its merits. I am Sir, Yours respectfully, C. BELL,

'Address Mr Currer Bell.

'The Parsonage. Haworth. Bradford. Yorks.'[1]

Like a strong-minded businesswoman Charlotte cites the family credits – Poems by Currer, Ellis and Acton Bell, 2 copies sold. Like a frail author she begs to know how long the agonizing interval will be between getting the package out of the house and receiving a pronouncement. 'Usually,' the Biographical Notice continues, 'the fate of the MSS was an ignominious and abrupt dismissal. At last *Wuthering Heights* and *Agnes Grey* were accepted on terms somewhat impoverishing to the two authors; Currer Bell's book found acceptance nowhere. . . . As a forlorn hope he tried one publishing house more . . . Messrs Smith, Elder and Co. . . .'

The Professor had been received by Smith, Elder about the middle of August 1847. The book had not been accepted, but it had been declined with such a useful and courteous letter of criticism that 'this very refusal cheered the author better than a vulgarly-expressed letter of acceptance would have done. It was added that a work in three volumes would meet with careful attention.[2] The work in three

---

[1] Dr Charles A. Huguenin, 'Bronteana at Princeton University,' *Brontë Society Transactions*, Vol. XII, No. 5, pp. 391–400.

[2] Biographical Notice.

volumes was now ready, and *Jane Eyre* was dispatched to Smith, Elder on 24 August and appeared on 16 October.

When *Wuthering Heights* and *Agnes Grey* were accepted we do not know, but it was some months before. The publisher was Thomas Cautley Newby of Mortimer Street, at whose hands Emily and Anne suffered a very different fate from that of Charlotte with Smith, Elder. *Jane Eyre* had a lightning acceptance and passage through the press. Clearly its publishers had no doubt that they had been offered a best-selling novel and they were handsomely corroborated by events. Newby, who is said to have been greatly shocked by *Wuthering Heights*,[1] required Emily and Anne to pay part of the costs of the publication of their works. He had the books set up, but he made no attempt to issue them, and they did not see the light until *Jane Eyre* had been proved a success. He then gave out to the book-trade that Currer, Ellis and Acton Bell were a single writer.

On 10 November Charlotte wrote to W. S. Williams, her discoverer, and the literary adviser to Smith, Elder, with whom she was now in frequent correspondence: 'A prose work by Ellis and Acton, will soon appear; it should have been out indeed long since for the first proof sheets were already in the press at the commencement of last August, before Currer Bell had placed the MS of *Jane Eyre* in your hands. Mr Newby however does not do business like Messers Smith and Elder; a different spirit seems to preside at 172 Mortimer Street to that which guides the helm at Cornhill. Mr Newby shuffles, gives his word and breaks it. . . . My relatives have suffered from exhausting delay and procrastination. . . . I should like to know if Mr Newby often acts as he has done to my relatives. . . . Do you know, and can you tell me anything about him?'

On 17 November she wrote, 'Ellis and Acton beg to thank you for the kind offer of your services with Mr Newby, but as the last of the proof-sheets has at length been sent down for correction, they deem it useless to trouble you on the subject, trusting that the publication of the work cannot now be delayed much longer.' On 14 December she continues, '*Wuthering Heights* is, I suppose, at length published, at least Mr Newby has sent the authors their six copies. I wonder how it will be received. I should say it merits the epithet "vigorous" and "original" much more than *Jane Eyre* did. *Agnes Grey* should please such critics as Mr Lewes, for it is "true" and "unexaggerated" enough. The books are not well got up. On a former occasion I expressed

---

[1] Mrs Gaskell.

myself with perhaps too little reserve regarding Mr Newby, yet I cannot but feel, and feel painfully, that Ellis and Acton have not had the justice at his hands that I have had at the hands of Messers Smith and Elder.'

Wuthering Heights and *Agnes Grey* were published together as a three-volume novel in December 1847. '*Agnes Grey*. A Novel, by Acton Bell' formed by itself the last volume of the three. By this time Haworth Parsonage, through the tremendous success of *Jane Eyre*, had become a focus of literary life – secretly, of course, which must have added to the sisters' enjoyment. On 15 October Charlotte had written Ellen one of her routine domestic letters, the points of interest being the misfortunes of her friend's family, Branwell, and the un-pleasingness of Mr Nicholls the curate. 'We are getting on here much as usual,' she remarks. Next day *Jane Eyre* was published; a week later her idol Thackeray was writing of it that he had 'lost (or won if you like) a whole day in reading it' and that 'some of the love passages made me cry'; it was speedily reviewed by all the papers that mattered and the Bank-bill which Charlotte received on 11 December was of a size to make her 'glad and proud'. 'There are moments when I can hardly credit that anything I have done should be found worthy to give even transitory pleasure to such men as Mr Thackeray, Sir John Henschel, Mr Fonblanque, Leigh Hunt and Mr Lewes', she had joyously confided to Williams. The same pen had written with the utmost smoothness a fortnight earlier, 'Dear Ellen, The old pangs of fearing you should fancy I forget you drives me to write to you, – though Heaven knows I have precious little to say. . . .'

Charlotte and Ellen were close, but Ellen had never set foot in the world that Charlotte inhabited with Branwell, Emily, and Anne. There she and her family were almost unimaginably close; and, just as long ago she had confessed to Southey, as though it were the most natural thing in the world, that she had showed his 'dose of cooling admonition' to her father, brother, and sisters, so now Emily and Anne must have shared and rejoiced with her in every detail of her fabulous success.

Nothing comparable awaited them, however, when at last their book emerged, and there was no interchange of complimentary letters and of Bank-bills between them and their publishers. But Charlotte's publisher, who had by now also become her friend, was greatly inter-ested, and his estimate of her sisters' work was much the same as her own. 'You are not far wrong in your judgement respecting *Wuthering*

Heights and *Agnes Grey*', she writes. 'Ellis has a strong original mind full of strange though sombre power. . . . *Agnes Grey* is the mirror of the mind of the writer. The orthography and punctuation of the books are mortifying to a degree: almost all the errors that were corrected in the proof sheets appear intact in what should have been the fair copies.' On their chagrin at seeing themselves defaced Anne and Emily once again are silent, but Charlotte's reference to it tells us that it was keen.

The first week of the New Year yields a surprise in the form of a letter to Ellen from Anne. Anne has written to her also in the previous October, a dull letter, it must be confessed, in which the most important news was the cessation of the east wind, which was indeed of crucial importance to the writer. 'I suffered from it in some degree, as I always do, more or less; but this time it brought no reinforcements of coughs and colds, which is what I dread the most.'

In January Anne is much more cheerful. Despite her modesty, she is delightfully confident in Ellen's affection and quite ready to be accepted by Ellen's friend.

'Haworth, January 4th, '48.

'MY DEAR MISS NUSSEY, – I am not going to give you a "nice *long* letter" – on the contrary, I mean to content myself with a shabby little note, to be engulphed in a letter of Charlotte's, which will, of course, be infinitely more acceptable to you than any production of mine, though I do not question your friendly regard for me, or the indulgent welcome you would accord to a missive of mine even without a more agreeable companion to back it; but you must know there is a lamentable deficiency in my organ of language, which makes me almost as bad a hand at writing as talking unless I have something particular to say. I have now, however, to thank you and your friend Miss Ringrose for your kind letter and her pretty watch-guards, which I am sure we shall all of us value the more for being the work of her own hands. . . . You do not tell us how *you* bear the present unfavourable weather. We are all cut up by this cruel east wind, most of us, i.e. Charlotte, Emily, and I have had the influenza, or a bad cold instead, twice over within the space of a few weeks. Papa has had it once. Tabby has escaped it altogether. I have no news to tell you, for we have been nowhere, seen no one, and done nothing (to *speak* of) since you were here – and yet we contrive to be busy from morning to night. Flossy is fatter than ever, but still active enough to relish a sheep hunt. I hope you and your circle have been more fortunate in the matter of colds than we have.

'With kind regards to all, I remain, dear Miss Nussey, yours ever affectionately, ANNE BRONTË.'

The strictly accurate description of the Parsonage authors busy on their next books, 'We have done nothing (to *speak* of) since you were here . . .' pleases us almost as much as it must have pleased Anne.

The year 1847, which witnessed so much literary activity, saw also a homely but important operation on the other side of the house. 'I got the well cleaned by a pump-sucker – and two men – for five shillings. The water was tinged yellow – by eight tin cans in a state of decomposition. It had not been cleaned for twenty years, before.'

This entry, signed B., comes from a diary or pocket-book of Mr Brontë's, another little home-made book of the most touching sort, consisting of a few leaves fixed together into a leather cover with three long stitches of brown thread. The crooked little book seems to bear the signs of Mr Brontë's own manufacture, and the arrangement and writing of the items suggest that the old man's sight was very bad.

During the early spring we wait for news of *Agnes Grey*. The volume was reviewed – containing *Wuthering Heights*, it could hardly fail to be noticed – but Emily's masterpiece naturally overshadowed her sister's book. The *Atlas* critic, however, at least described it by comparison as 'level and sunny'. *Britannia* allowed that some characters and scenes were nicely sketched in and *Douglas Jerrold's Weekly* found it 'a tale well worth the telling'.

On 22 January we hear that the confusion as to which sister (or brother) has written which book is increasing, and in some quarters this is reckoned good publicity. 'I see I was mistaken in my idea that the *Atheneum* and others wished to ascribe the authorship of *Wuthering Heights* to Currer Bell,' writes Charlotte to her publisher; 'the contrary is the case; *Jane Eyre* is given to Ellis Bell, and Mr Newby, it appears, thinks it expedient so to frame his advertisements as to favour the misapprehension. If Mr Newby had much sagacity, he would see that Ellis Bell is strong enough to stand without being propped by Currer Bell – and would have disdained what Ellis himself of all things disdains – recourse to trickery. However Ellis, Acton, and Currer care nothing for the matter personally. . . .'

Charlotte's letter of 28 January, to Ellen, seems to be the one Anne promised more than three weeks ago. The references to her sister, and Charlotte's inability to see her as a full-size being (except in illness) irritate us, though as usual we understand them, and, giving her the benefit of the doubt, allow that Charlotte is amazed because the Robinson girls are constant, rather than because their constancy should be inspired by Anne.

'It is kind in you to continue to write occasionally to Anne – for I think your letters do her good and give her pleasure. The Robinsons still amaze me by the continued frequency and constancy of their correspondence. Poor girls! they still continue to complain of their mother's proceedings; that woman is a hopeless being, calculated to bring a curse wherever she goes. . . . We all thank you for the tasteful watch-guards you sent; the steel beads glitter like diamonds by candle-light. We chose them by lot. I got the single bead. Anne the double, Emily the treble.' In February we hear that *Wuthering Heights* is selling, and as *Agnes Grey* was bound up with it, *Agnes Grey* was selling too. 'I am glad to hear that the second edition [of *Jane Eyre*] is selling. *Wuthering Heights* it appears is selling too, and consequently Mr Newby is getting into marvellous good tune with his authors.'

The purchasers of *Wuthering Heights* had value for their money. Novels, a hundred years ago, were required to be written in three volumes, and readers might expect perhaps two volumes of pith to one volume of padding. Nobody suffered more, or surrendered more in this fashion than Charlotte's adored master Thackeray, but between the covers of *Wuthering Heights* there was not one book and padding; there were two books.

The only evidence we have of Mr Newby being in good tune or indeed of his being in any communication with his authors is in a single letter by his hand. It is dated 15 February 1848, and runs:

'Dear Sir, I am much obliged by your kind note and shall have great pleasure in making arrangements for your next novel. I would not hurry its completion for I think you are quite right not to let it go before the world until well satisfied with it, for much depends on your next work. If it be an improvement on your first you will have established yourself as a first rate novelist, but if it fall short the critics will be too apt to say that you have expended your talent in your first novel. I shall therefore have pleasure in accepting it upon the understanding that its completion be at your own time. Believe me, my dear Sir, sincerely, T. C. Newby.'

The letter, we are told, was found in Emily's desk, and an envelope inscribed in the same hand 'Ellis Bell Esq,' was found with it. The letter fitted the envelope exactly but was not inside it. Does this mean that they belonged together or that the letter belonged to a similar envelope addressed to Anne? And is the book mentioned therefore *The Tenant of Wildfell Hall*, or a second book by Emily of which there is no trace? The suggestion that the author's book had met with some success points to Emily; the fact that the second book was in existence and that it was discussed before it was actually finished points rather to Anne.

Whatever book is referred to, Anne was at work on and had probably almost finished her second novel, for it was to be published in a few months. Her success with *Agnes Grey* had been less than that of either of her sisters, which is not surprising when the books they had produced were *Jane Eyre* and *Wuthering Heights*; yet if we think of Anne as a separate figure and compare her position at the end of 1847 with that of 1845, we see that here too there has been a spectacular advance. In the summer of 1845 she was a governess, and a very wretched governess, in Yorkshire. By the summer of 1847 she had had a book accepted by a London publisher. The two years had covered much distress – the sorrow of her father's all-but-blindness and the fear that he would become totally blind were added to the misery of existence with Branwell – but in this period her own private life had come to fruition – and manifestly. We hear of her confessing on a certain occasion, with a gentle smile of pleasure, that *Chambers Magazine* contained a poem by her pen.[1] Withdrawn, mild, seemingly passive, modest to the last degree, the acceptance of her book and the license to devote herself to writing spelt the same satisfaction for Anne as it would for any other nature – perhaps a greater satisfaction, by virtue of her very modesty and the small apparent likelihood that she would ever be heard of in the world.

If by August 1847 the three first prose tales had been finished and on offer for eighteen months, Anne must have been engaged on *The Tenant of Wildfell Hall* for about two years. Attaining the requisite length by itself, it is a considerable book. We may suppose that Anne, on her return from Thorp Green, finished her saga of governess-ship, which was almost entirely autobiographical, and in due course embarked

---

[1] Mrs Gaskell, in her *Life of Charlotte Brontë*; no poem by Anne has been found in *Chambers Magazine* and it is thought that the incident refers to the publication of 'The Three Guides' in *Frazer's Magazine* in August 1848.

upon the natural second novel, in which invention and actual experience combine. (Charlotte had done much the same thing in *The Professor* and *Jane Eyre*.) Mr Williams, like an appreciative publisher's reader and a good man of business, made a bid to secure for his list the 'relatives' of his hen that laid the golden eggs, but they were or considered themselves pledged to Newby.

'Dear Sir,' wrote Charlotte on 17 February,[1] 'I have received your letter and its enclosure – Bank-bill for 100*l* – for which I thank you. Your conduct to me has been such that you cannot doubt my relatives would have been most happy to avail themselves of your proposal respecting the publication of their future works, but their present engagements to Mr Newby are such as to prevent their consulting freely their own inclinations and interests. . . .'

On 6 March Charlotte, in a letter to Ellen, makes a strange and serious mention of a past illness of Anne's. 'The symptoms you mention seem to indicate the presence of a constant low fever in the system – a bad sign often accompanying scrofulous habits – Anne suffered from much the same ailment, except that constant thirst, I recollect, was one of her peculiarities. . . .'

We know that Anne has only another year to live. Everything concerning her health is of deep interest. What does Charlotte mean? And does she refer to that very serious long-ago illness at Roe Head or to one which Anne has suffered more lately?

On 11 March we have another reference to the plot that is thickening around the sisters' identity. 'I have just received the copy of the second edition [of *Jane Eyre*] and will look over it and send the corrections as soon as possible. I will also, since you think it advisable avail myself of the opportunity of a third edition to correct the mistake concerning the authorship of *Wuthering Heights*, and *Agnes Grey*.' Charlotte is beginning to suspect that the anonymity or the assumption of pen-names may not be so satisfactory after all. On 28 April there is the suggestion that the subject may be giving rise to conjectures nearer home. 'Write another letter and explain that last note of yours distinctly,' she commands Ellen. 'If your allusions are to myself, which I suppose they are – understand this – I have given no one a right to gossip about me and am not to be judged by frivolous conjecture emanating from any quarter whatever. Let me know what you heard and from whom you heard it.' Five days later Ellen receives the full broadside.

[1] To George Smith of Smith, Elder.

'May 3rd, 1848.

'DEAR ELLEN, – All I can say to you about a certain matter is this: the report – if report there be – and if the lady, who seems to have been rather mystified, had not dreamt what she fancied had been told to her – must have had its origin in some absurd misunderstanding. I have given *no one* a right either to affirm, or hint, in the most distant manner, that I am "publishing" – (humbug!) Whoever has said it – if any one has, which I doubt – is no friend of mine. Though twenty books were ascribed to me, I should own none. I scout the idea utterly. Whoever, after I have distinctly rejected the charge, urges it upon me, will do an unkind and an ill-bred thing. The most profound obscurity is infinitely preferable to vulgar notoriety; and that notoriety I neither seek nor will have. If then any Birstallian or Gomersallian should presume to bore you on the subject, – to ask you what "novel" Miss Brontë has been "publishing", – you can just say, with the distinct firmness of which you are perfect mistress, when you choose, that you are authorized by Miss Brontë to say, that she repels and disowns every accusation of this kind. You may add, if you please, that if any one has her confidence, you believe you have, and she has made no drivelling confessions to you on the subject.'

Charlotte stands confessed, perhaps condemned, out of her own mouth. But if she is condemned, she had her excuses. For twenty years, while always conscious of her own and her family's powers, she had striven, without outward rebellion, to cram herself into the mould of the needy parson's eldest daughter. In her life, apart from her brother and sisters, she had encountered one mind of calibre, and she had flung herself upon its owner hungrily. For the rest, she brought herself to the level of the people about her. Of these Ellen Nussey was the best and in that life her level was the highest. She was a steady, sensible, affectionate, and utterly loyal friend. But Charlotte at this moment had emerged into another life. The horrid asperity of the letter denotes not only annoyance and perhaps a touch of anxiety, but the magnitude of Charlotte's resentment against all that the Brontës had had to be.

VIII

‎———=⟫◈⟪=‎———

THE SECRET WAS out in Yorkshire; Anne's second novel was shortly to force it out in London too. 'You will perhaps have observed', wrote Charlotte to Williams on 22 June, 'that Mr Newby has announced a new work by Acton Bell. The advertisement has, as usual, a certain tricky turn to its working which I do not admire.' Charlotte was right about Newby. Up till now we may have felt that his trickery was not quite proven; we may have thought also that perhaps Emily and Anne stuck to him because he was their own publisher and not Charlotte's, and that, having been the first to put up money for the Brontës, if only part of the money, he deserved that they should. Be that as it might, Newby published *The Tenant of Wildfell Hall* at the end of June or the beginning of July 1848 and immediately reported it to a firm of American publishers as a new work by Currer Bell, asserting that to the best of his belief all the four Brontë novels were by the same hand. This, nine months after the publication of *Jane Eyre* and all that had followed, could be nothing but a plain lie. As soon as Smith, Elder heard of Newby's deception they reported it to Charlotte.

[1]'Presently after came another missive from Smith and Elder; their American correspondent had written to them complaining that the first sheets of a new work by Currer Bell had been already received, and not by their house, but by a rival publisher, and asking the meaning of such false play; it enclosed an extract from a letter from Mr Newby (A. and E. Bell's publisher) affirming that to the best of his belief *Jane Eyre*, *Wuthering Heights*, and *Agnes Grey*, and *The Tenant of Wildfell Hall* (the new work) were all the production of one author.

'This was a *lie*, as Newby had been told repeatedly that they were the production of three different authors, but the fact was he

[1] Charlotte to Mary Taylor in New Zealand (4 September).

118

wanted to make a dishonest move in the game to make the public and the trade believe that he had got hold of Currer Bell, and thus cheat Smith and Elder by securing the American publisher's bid.'

It is interesting, in parenthesis, to see how Newby went to work. Opposite the title page of Volume 1, of *The Tenant of Wildfell Hall* he printed the following

Opinions of the Press

On Mr Bell's First Novel [the opinions actually referred to *Wuthering Heights*]

"*Jane Eyre* it will be reflected was edited by Mr Currer Bell. Here are two tales so nearly related to *Jane Eyre* in cast of thought, incident, and language as to excite curiosity. All these might be the work of one hand." *Atheneum.*

"The work has affinity to *Jane Eyre.*" *Spectator.*

"Written with considerable ability." *John Bull.*

"A work of very great merit." *Examiner.*

"The work is strongly original. It reminds us of Jane Eyre . . ." *Britannia.*

"We strongly recommend all our readers who love novelty to get this story, for we can promise them they never read anything like it before. It is like *Jane Eyre.*" *Douglas Jerrold.*

"It is a colossal performance." *Atlas.*

The brew could hardly have been stirred more thoroughly. And *Wildfell Hall* was actually first published by Harper Brothers, in America as '*The Tenant of Wildfell Hall*, by Acton Bell. Author of *Wuthering Heights.*'

'The upshot of it was,' Charlotte continues, 'that on the very day I received Smith and Elder's letter, Anne and I packed up a small box, sent it down to Keighley, set out ourselves after tea, walked through a snowstorm to the station, got to Leeds, and whirled up by the night train to London with the view of proving our separate identify to Smith and Elder, and confronting Newby with his *lie*. We arrived at the Chapter Coffee-House[1] (our old place, Polly, we did not well know where else to go) about eight o'clock in the

---

[1] The Chapter Coffee-House at the west corner of Paul's Alley, Paternoster Row, had literary associations with critics, publishers, and poets reaching as far back as Chatterton. It was altered in 1858. The sisters had stayed there with their father on the way to Brussels.

morning. We washed ourselves, had some breakfast, sat a few minutes, and then set off in queer inward excitement to 65 Cornhill. Neither Mr Smith nor Mr Williams knew we were coming – they had never seen us – they did not know whether we were men or women, but had always written to us as men.

'We found 65 to be a large bookseller's shop, in a street almost as bustling as the Strand. We went in, walked up to the counter. There were a great many young men and lads here and there; I said to the first I could accost: "May I see Mr Smith?" He hesitated, looked a little surprised. We sat down and waited a while looking at some books on the counter, publications of theirs well known to us, of many of which they had sent us copies as presents. At last we were shown up to Mr Smith. "Is it Mr Smith?" I said looking up through my spectacles at a tall young man. "It is." I then put his letter into his hand directed to Currer Bell. He looked at it and then at me again. "Where did you get this?" he said. I laughed at his perplexity – a recognition took place. I gave my real name: Miss Brontë. We were in a small room – ceiled with a great skylight – and there explanations were rapidly gone into; Mr Newby being anathematized, I fear, with undue vehemence. Mr Smith hurried out and returned quickly with one whom he introduced as Mr Williams, a pale, mild, stooping man of fifty, very much like a faded Tom Dixon. Another recognition, and a long nervous shaking of hands. Then followed talk; – talk – talk Mr Williams being silent, Mr Smith loquacious.

'Mr Smith said we must come and stay at his house, but we were not prepared for a long stay and declined this also; as we took our leave he told us he should bring his sisters to call on us that evening. We returned to our inn, and I paid for the excitement of the interview by a thundering headache and harassing sickness. Towards evening, as I got no better and expected the Smiths to call, I took a strong dose of sal-volatile. It roused me a little; still, I was in grievous bodily case when they were announced. They came in, two elegant young ladies, in full dress, prepared for the Opera – Mr Smith himself in evening costume, white gloves, etc. We had by no means understood that it was settled we were to go to the Opera, and were not ready. Moreover, we had no fine, elegant dresses with us, or in the world. However, on brief rumination I thought it would be wise to make no objections – I put my headache in my pocket, we attired ourselves in the plain, high-made country garments we possessed, and went with them to their carriage, where we found Mr Williams. They must have thought us queer, quizzical-looking beings, especially me with my spectacles. I smiled inwardly at the contrast, which must have been apparent, between me and Mr Smith as I walked with him up the crimson-carpeted staircase of the Opera House and stood amongst a brilliant throng at the box door, which was not yet open. Fine ladies and gentlemen glanced at us with a slight, graceful superciliousness quite warranted by the circumstances.[1] Still I felt pleasantly excited in spite of headache and sickness and conscious clownishness, and I saw Anne was calm and gentle, which she always is.

'The performance was Rossini's opera of the *Barber of Seville*, very brilliant, though I fancy there are things I should like better. We got home after one o'clock; we had never been in bed the night before, and had been in constant excitement for twenty-four hours. You may imagine we were tired.

'The next day, Sunday, Mr Williams came early and took us to church. He was so quiet, but so sincere in his attentions, one could not but have a most friendly leaning towards him. He has a nervous hesitation in speech, and a difficulty in finding appropriate language in which to express himself, which throws him into the background in conversation; but I had been his correspondent and therefore knew with what intelligence he could write, so that I was not in danger of undervaluing him. In the afternoon Mr Smith came in his carriage with his mother, to take us to his house to dine. Mr Smith's residence is at Bayswater, six miles from Cornhill; the rooms, the drawing-room epecially, looked splendid to us. There was no company – only his mother, his two grown-up sisters, and his brother, a lad of twelve or thirteen, and a little sister, the youngest of the family, very like himself. They are all dark-eyed, dark-haired, and have clear, pale faces. The mother is a portly,

[1] They took the pseudonym of 'Brown' when introduced to Mr Smith's friends. 'All this time,' says Mrs Gaskell, 'those who came in contact with the "Miss Browns" seem only to have regarded them as shy and reserved little countrywomen, with not much to say.' Mr Williams said that on the night when he accompanied the party to the Opera, as Charlotte ascended the flight of stairs leading from the grand entrance up to the lobby of the first tier of boxes, she was so much struck with the architectural effect of the splendid decorations of that vestibule and saloon, that involuntarily she slightly pressed his arm and whispered, 'You know I am not accustomed to this sort of thing.'

handsome woman of her age, and all the children more or less well-looking – one of the daughters decidedly pretty. We had a fine dinner, which neither Anne nor I had appetite to eat, and were glad when it was over. I always feel under an awkward constraint at table. Dining out would be hideous to me.

'Mr Smith made himself very pleasant. He is a *practical* man. I wish Mr Williams were more so, but he is altogether of the contemplative, theorizing order. Mr Williams has too many abstractions.

'On Monday we went to the Exhibition of the Royal Academy and the National Gallery, dined again at Mr Smith's, then went home with Mr Williams to tea and saw his comparatively humble but neat residence and his fine family of eight children. A daughter of Leigh Hunt's was there. She sang some little Italian airs which she had picked up among the peasantry in Tuscany, in a manner that charmed me.

'On Tuesday morning we left London laden with books which Mr Smith had given us, and got safely home. A more jaded wretch than I looked when I returned it would be difficult to conceive. I was thin when I went, but was meagre indeed when I returned; my face looked grey and very old, with strange, deep lines ploughed in it; my eyes stared unnaturally. I was weak and yet restless. In a while, however, the bad effects of excitement went off and I regained my normal condition. We saw Mr Newby, but of him more another time. Good-bye. God bless you. Write. C.B.'

The meeting in Smith, Elder's parlour is historic and the whole trip to London one of the minor dramas of literary history. Nobody could improve on Charlotte's relation of it . . . only we may pause here and there to let imagination fill it out a little . . . the swell of generous and indignant emotion that impelled the sisters' whirlwind departure and bore them on through the sympathetic elements to Keighley in the wake of their little box, the night express to London and then the capital itself. We like to think that Anne's one trip to Town, though classically exhausting, was exciting, typical, and glorious, and we bless the good fortune that included Covent Garden, and a lodging almost touching St Paul's, and Leigh Hunt's daughter singing Italian airs in one impromptu week-end.

Anne, playing the second role, but by no means second fiddle, was perhaps less exhausted than Charlotte. Charlotte talked; she vibrated with feeling and action; Anne no doubt was content to be carried along. We see her as she was in George Smith's description, calm even in the awful embarrassment of having nothing to wear for the Opera, and, since she was nowhere the protagonist, quietly absorbing the new acquaintances and scenes. It is interesting that Charlotte mentions almost with gratitude that Anne was calm and gentle, in fact clearly a considerable support, and there is not a word about her being shy.

Charlotte noted the expenses of the London trip in a little pocket-book, which has survived.

Expenses of Journey
July 7th 1848

Carriage of box		1s.	6d.
Ticket 2nd class to Leeds		5s.	
Box porter		1s.	
Tea		4s.	
Box porter	0		4d.
Ticket 1st Class	4	9s.	0
Cab hire	0	3	0
Gloves 2 ps	0	5	0
2 parasols	0	16	0
Cab hire	0	4	0
Cab hire	0	1	6
Do.	0	4	0

The second page continues:

	l	*s.*	*d.*
Exhibition	0	2	0
—C.C.H.	2	5	0
(Chapter Coffee House)			
Tennyson's poems	0	12	0
Books for M and T	0	4	0
Cab to Eus. Sq.	0	2	6
Tickets 2nd Class	3	4	0
Porter	0	0	6
Leeds	0	9	6
Boots	0	0	2
Tickets from L.K.O.		5	0
Porter	0	2	6
	7	8	8

Charlotte also wrote down directions for reaching the Smiths' house. 'Few doors on the other side of the bridge over the great Western.' The house was in Westbourne Place. We learn from this little Account that it was hot in London, that Charlotte and Anne had gone to the Academy (then in Trafalgar Square), that they bought Tennyson's poems as a present for Emily and that, as many a traveller has done before and since, they drew in their horns on the return journey and came home second class.

London virtually excluded from the map, Charlotte resumes her correspondence with Ellen Nussey. A large portion of her first letter since her return refers to Anne in her domestic aspect.

On 28 July she wrote:

'. . . Anne continues to hear constantly, almost daily, from her old pupils, the Robinsons. They are both now engaged to different gentlemen, and if they do not change their minds, which they have done two or three times, will probably be married in a few months. Not one spark of love does either of them profess for her future husband, one of them declares that interest alone guides her, the other, poor thing! is acting according to her mother's wish, and is utterly indifferent herself to the man chosen for her. The lighter headed of the two sisters takes pleasure in the spectacle of her fine wedding-dresses and costly wedding-presents; the more thoughtful can derive no gratification from these things and is much depressed at the contemplation of her future lot. Anne does her best to cheer and counsel her, and she seems to cling to her quiet, former governess, as her only true friend. Of their mother I have not patience to speak. . . .

'Branwell is the same in conduct as ever; his constitution seems shattered. Papa, and sometimes all of us, have sad nights with him, he sleeps most of the day, and consequently will lie awake at night. But has not every house its trial?

'Write to me very soon, dear Nell, and believe me,

Yours sincerely, C. Brontë.'

The first topic of Charlotte's literary correspondence is naturally Anne's book.

'You will have seen some of the notices of *Wildfell Hall*,' she writes to W. S. Williams on 31st July. 'I wish my sister felt the unfavourable ones less keenly. She does not *say* much, for she is of a remarkably taciturn, still, thoughtful nature, reserved even with her nearest of kin, but I cannot avoid seeing that her spirits are depressed sometimes. The fact is, neither she nor any of us expected that view to be taken of the book which has been taken by some critics.

'Permit me to caution you not to speak of my sisters when you write to me. I mean, do not use the word in the plural. Ellis Bell will not endure to be alluded to under any other appellation than the *nom de plume*. I committed a grand error in betraying his identity to you and Mr Smith. It was inadvertent – the words "we are three sisters" escaped me before I was aware. I regretted the avowal the moment I had made it; I regret it bitterly now, for I find it is against every feeling and intention of Ellis Bell.

'I was greatly amused to see in the *Examiner* of this week one of Newby's little cobwebs neatly swept away by some dextrous brush. If Newby is not too old to profit by experience, such an exposure ought to teach him that "Honesty is indeed the best policy".

'Your letter has just been brought to me. I must not pause to thank you, I should say too much. Our life is, and always has been, one of few pleasures, as you seem in part to guess, and for that reason we feel what passages of enjoyment come in our way very keenly; and I think if you knew *how* pleased I am to get a long letter from you, you would laugh at me.

'In return, however, I smile at you for the earnestness with which you urge on us the propriety of seeing something of London society. There would be an advantage in it – a great advantage; yet it is one that no power on earth could induce Ellis Bell, for instance, to avail himself of. And even for Acton and Currer, the experiment of an introduction to society would be more formidable than you, probably, can well imagine. An existence of absolute seclusion and unvarying monotony, such as we have long – I may say, indeed, ever – been habituated to, tends, I fear, to unfit the mind for lively and exciting scenes, to destroy the capacity for social enjoyment.'

Anne herself must undoubtedly have hoped great things for *Wildfell Hall*. With *Agnes Grey* she had achieved publication and a mild success. Her second book was longer, weightier, and more ambitious. It was to be her *Jane Eyre* or *Wuthering Heights*. The reception of the book was amazing. It was noticed and it was treated as a performance, but the critics, with few exceptions, declared it to be brutal and coarse.

This, for Anne, was a moment when action was necessary, and she did not hesitate to take action. On 22 July she sent her publisher a Preface to the second edition, which had followed rapidly upon the first. At once she made haste to clear up Newby's deception by pointing out that she and neither of her sisters was responsible for the book; then she took up her own defence.

The subject matter of *Wildfell Hall* which Charlotte had pontifically found Anne unfitted to handle, was profligacy, Arthur Huntingdon, an important character in the book, being a dissolute young man with dissolute friends; 'a specimen' as Charlotte herself admirably says 'of the naturally selfish, sensual, superficial man, whose merit of a joyous temperament only avails him while he is young and healthy, whose best days are his earliest, who never profits by experience, who is sure to grow worse as he grows older.' Anne took it upon herself to point out that it was the treatment of the subject rather than the subject itself that mattered.

'While I acknowledge the success of the present work to have been greater than I anticipated,' she writes, 'and the praises it has elicited from a few kind critics to have been greater than it deserved, I must also admit that from some other quarters it has been censured with an asperity which I was as little prepared to expect, and which my judgement as well as my feelings assure me is more bitter than just. It is scarcely the province of an author to refute the arguments of his censors and vindicate his own productions, but I may be allowed to make here a few observations. . . .'

Anne did not like adverse criticism. Particularly she did not like criticism that was mistaken as well as adverse. She bore it in silence, or at least, she did not discuss it with Charlotte. But her defence, when she made it, was hardly that of a drooping spirit. 'An asperity . . . which my judgement as well as my feelings assures me is more bitter than just.' Her words are not highly-coloured, but they are shrewd. 'I find myself censured,' she continues, 'for depicting *con amore* a morbid love of the coarse. . . . If I can gain the public ear at all, I would rather whisper a few humble truths therein than much soft nonsense.'

With *Jane Eyre* Charlotte had had an enormous and richly deserved success. She was sorry for Anne, naturally enough. And as she did not care for her sister's book she could not offer any real support. We are interested in what she says about *Wildfell Hall* and we believe in her sincerity. But the pathetic and silent figure is the younger sister seen, once again, through the elder's eyes. For our part we see Anne going

into a second edition within the month, receiving more praise as well
as more blame for her novel than she expected, and when convinced of
the necessity of taking action, taking it with an independent firmness.
After all she was only twenty-eight and there is no doubt that she was
modest. She could not have failed to feel that, sisters or no sisters, she
had made some kind of mark.

Eight days after the writing of the Preface, the Birthday Papers
of 1845 were due to be opened and new ones due to be indited.
Whether these things were ever done, or whether they were neglected
in face of more important literary matters we can only guess.

Williams's letters were shared with Emily and Anne, and Anne's
life and tastes and habits, as well as her own, are described in Charlotte's answers to him.

By the middle of August Anne has made up her mind definitely to
repudiate Newby and to reward Williams's kindness and interest
by promising Smith, Elder the refusal of her next book. But the
first paragraph of the letter that contains this intelligence slightly
startles us.

'My dear Sir, – My sister Anne thanks you, as well as myself,
for your just critique on *Wildfell Hall*. It appears to me that your
observations exactly hit both the strong and weak points of the book,
and the advice which accompanies them is worthy of, and shall receive
our most careful attention.' It sounds as though Mr Williams has
given Anne advice and that Charlotte is going to see that she swallows
it, though in a later letter it appears that Williams had given advice to
them both. 'Your own comments also demand our best thanks. . . .
Defects there are both in *Jane Eyre* and *Wildfell Hall* which it will
be the authors' wisdom and duty to endeavour to avoid in future. . . .'
'You say,' the letter of 14 August continues, 'that Mr Huntingdon
reminds you of Mr Rochester.' Charlotte then proceeds to point out
that this is a misapprehension and to distinguish between Huntingdon,
Heathcliff, and her own hero. 'I must not forget to thank you,' she
concludes, 'for the *Examiner* and *Atlas* newspapers. Poor Mr Newby!
It is not enough that the *Examiner* nails him by both ears to the pillory,
but the *Atlas* brands a token of disgrace on his forehead. This is a
deplorable plight, and he makes all matters worse by his foolish little
answers to his assailants. It is a pity that he has no kind friend to
suggest to him that he had better not bandy words with the *Examiner*.
His plea about the "printer" was too ludicrous, and his second note is
pitiable. I only regret that the names of Ellis and Acton Bell should

perforce be mixed up with his proceedings. My sister Anne wishes me to say that should she ever write another work, Mr Smith will certainly have the first offer of the copyright.'

Anne made £50 out of *Wildfell Hall* and she made nothing at all out of *Agnes Grey*, in fact she lost £25 pounds over it. These facts emerged when Charlotte agreed to a reprint of *Wuthering Heights* and *Agnes Grey* by Smith and Elder in 1850 and sought to discover what contracts had been made between Newby and Ellis and Acton Bell and how far they had been honoured. She found that they had not been honoured and tried to pin Newby down, even going so far as to decide that if Anne and Emily's dues were ever settled, half of them should go, through Smith, Elder, to the writer Miss Kavanagh for her next work. But Newby was 'needy as well as tricky'. Charlotte decided not to distress him, even for her sisters' rights.

We hear again of the wretched Robinson girls, whom Anne had inspired to some kind of faithfulness, on 18 August. 'The Robinsons are not married yet, but expect to be, in the course of a few months. The unhappy Lady Scott is dead, after long suffering. . . . Mrs Robinson is anxious to get her daughters husbands of any kind, that they may be off her hands and that she may be free to marry Sir Edward Scott.'

The Bells or Brontës were now somebody, and would, a publisher might hope, be more important people still, and Smith, Elder took over the *Poems* from Aylott and Jones in September. Charlotte was glad. 'I should feel unmixed pleasure in the chance of its being brought under respectable auspices before the public,' she wrote of the book, 'were Currer Bell's share of its contents absent.' Of Ellis Bell's work she declares, 'I know no woman that ever lived ever wrote such poetry before.' Of Anne's she makes no mention.

IX

In 1847 Branwell thought that he would live a long time. He had written to his friend J. B. Leyland in the beginning of that year, 'I know that it is time for me to be something when I am nothing. That my father cannot have long to live and that when he dies, my evening, which is already twilight, will become night – that I shall then have a constitution still so strong that it will keep me years in torture and despair. . . .' It is interesting that in his decline he turned to the older generation; we remember, after his early debauches, with what affection he spoke of his aunt. Branwell felt, it would seem, that his sisters had done with him, and we guess that in the main he was right. The attitude of each of them towards her brother seems to have been different. Charlotte, so painfully positive, who had loved him most, seems in his ruin almost to have hated him. Of course no whisper of the family's literary successes was reported to him – it would have been madness to trust him with the incognito; but in Charlotte's references he is utterly forgotten as a person to whom this could ever have been communicated; he is only a sot; at some point he has been put beyond the pale.

Emily's attitude towards human beings was both greater and less than the normal. On the ordinary level she was self-schooled by now to have little need of them; therefore in general she suffered from them less. She felt now no sense of either the family or herself being degraded or betrayed by Branwell, and in 'The Wanderer from the Fold' she wrote a lament or elegy for him, perhaps before his death, in which her detachment lends to her affection and grief a divinely limpid and unjudging quality.

> *How few of all the hearts that loved*
> *Are grieving for thee now;*
> *And why should mine to-night be moved*
> *With such a sense of woe?*

Too often thus, when left alone
Where none my thoughts can see,
Comes back a word, a passing tone
From thy strange history.

As for Anne, Branwell was in some degree her theme. For though he was not the model for Arthur Huntingdon in character, he was undoubtedly the model for Arthur Huntingdon in drunken and dissolute behaviour. She looked at him both as a sister and a writer. He had in fact forced her from a sister to become a writer, by the painful intensity of the experience which he had thrust upon her.

In this dual relation to her brother Anne's feelings must have been strange and mixed. As an actor in his own drama, in which he had involved her, she must have felt pity for him, but also resentment and censure, possibly worse. When he became her theme he had done his worst to her; he had as it were passed through her and emerged altered, sublimated, or transformed; in this aspect she would feel for him love, of a certain distinct kind, the love one feels for what serves one's purpose. But Branwell was there, still in the flesh, in the next room. He was still there as a fearful incubus and a brother ruined by his own hand. No doubt her heroic powers of silent endurance served Anne here too.

Branwell's constitution after all was not so strong as he feared, though none of his sisters, in the summer of 1848, suspected how ill he was, or rather calculated how little resistance he would have when the time came. For though they dealt with him perforce, his was not an ailment that roused the tender solicitude of women, and his looks must have been ghastly for a long time.

'DEAR JOHN, – I shall feel very much obliged to you if [you] can contrive to get me Five pence worth of Gin in a proper measure. Should it be speedily got I could perhaps take it from you or Billy at the lane top, or, what would be quite as well, sent out for, to you.

'I anxiously ask the favour because I know the good it will do me *Punctually* at Half past Nine in the morning you will be paid the 5d out of a shilling given me then.

Yours, P.B.B.'

The writer of this letter, addressed to John Brown the sexton, was what the brother had become. They had in a sense got used to it. 'Papa is harassed night and day – we have little peace – he is always sick,

130

has two or three times fallen down in fits – what will be the ultimate end God knows.' So Charlotte had written in the beginning of 1848. There is a brief mention of Branwell in July in a letter to Ellen, and less than two months after that he is dead.

'The past three weeks have been a dark interval in our humble home,' wrote Charlotte to her friend on 9 October. 'Branwell's constitution had been failing fast all the summer, but still neither the doctor nor himself thought him so near his end as he was. He was entirely confined to his bed but for one single day, and was in the village two days before his death. The end came after twenty minutes struggle on Sunday morning, 24th September. He was perfectly conscious till the last agony came on. His mind had undergone the peculiar change which frequently precedes death. Two days previously the calm of better feelings filled it. . . .

'Papa was acutely distressed at first, but on the whole he has borne the event well. Emily and Anne are pretty well, though Anne is always delicate and Emily has a cough and a cold at present. . . .'

In two letters to Williams, Charlotte conveyed the 'bitterness of pity for his (Branwell's) life and death' that pervaded the house, as well as the father's grief.

'My poor father naturally thought more of his *only* son than of his daughters, and, much and long as he had suffered on his account he cried out for his loss like David for that of Absalom – my son! my son! – and refused at first to be comforted. And then, when I ought to have been able to collect my strength and support him, I fell ill with an illness whose approaches I had felt for some time previously, and of which the crisis was hastened by the awe and trouble of the death-scene – the first I had ever witnessed. . . .'

(It had been for Emily and Anne, who had also witnessed the death-scene, to support their father).

'I looked on the noble face and forehead of my dead brother – and asked myself what had made him go ever wrong, tend ever down-wards, when he had so many gifts. . . . When the struggle was over – and a marble calm began to succeed the last dread agony – I felt as I had never felt before that there was peace and forgiveness for him in Heaven. All his errors – to speak plainly – all his vices seemed nothing to me in that moment. . . .'

Charlotte, who was driven to assume the role of strength, always moves us to pity in her weaker moments, as when she begs Aunt Branwell for a loan that would spell life for them all, or prays her rigid professor for a sign, or falls sick of grief and shock and remorse after her brother's death. For clearly Charlotte felt remorse; we can read it in her sententious phrases; she confessed also that not even after the deaths of Emily and Anne did she have such nights as she had after the death of Branwell.

Anne had no reason to feel remorse, but she was a frail subject to support the grief and shock. All the same it was her hand that took control during the period of immediate mourning. From her sick-bed Charlotte had been concerned about letters from Williams which remained unanswered, and on 29 September Anne had written to him for her.

'DEAR SIR, – My sister wishes me to thank you for your two letters, the receipt of which gave her much pleasure, though coming in a season of severe domestic affliction, which has so wrought upon her too delicate constitution as to induce a rather serious indisposition, that renders her unfit for the slightest exertion. Even the light task of writing to a friend is at present too much for her, though, I am happy to inform you, she is now recovering; and I trust, ere long, she will be able to give you her own sentiments upon the contents of your letters. Meantime, she desires her kindest regards to you, and participates with me in sincere pleasure at the happy effects of Mrs Williams's seaside residence. – I am, dear Sir,

Yours sincerely, A. BRONTË.'

What with anxiety about a proper tone from Charlotte's sister to Charlotte's literary friend, and Branwell scarcely dead, and the need for politeness to rise above private affliction, it turns out a stiff little letter, with just one simple phrase characteristic of Anne, 'even the light task of writing to a friend is at present too much for her.'

Branwell had written to J. B. Leyland in June of 'five months of violent cough'. His friend Francis Grundy, of railroad days (with whom most likely he was in the village two days before his death) came to Haworth to see him and sent to 'the great square cold-looking rectory' for Branwell to dine with him at the Black Bull. He describes Branwell's terrible appearance . . . 'all told the sad tale but too surely'. . . . After two glasses of brandy and a little food he had rallied. 'I never knew his intellect clearer. He described himself as waiting anxiously for death, indeed longing for it, and happy, in these his sane moments, to think it was so near. He once again declared that death would be due to the story I knew, and to nothing else.'

Branwell thought that he died of love for Mrs Robinson. What did Grundy think? Did he realize that consumption, as well as gin and opium had killed his friend? And did Charlotte realize it? It seems strange that she never hints at it in relation to Branwell, or, up till now, in relation to Emily. Coughs, colds, and influenza are the constant burden of her letters. Emily made a determined use of the word 'hearty', but clearly the family did not regard themselves as strong. Anne, Charlotte always spoke of specifically as delicate. She remembered 'the constant low fever in the system – a bad sign'. To us, in retrospect, consumption seems to have been in the very air of Haworth Parsonage. Not only was it the general scourge; it had been the cause of the unforgotten deaths of the two little elder sisters; part of the churchyard was above the Parsonage and drained down into it; the slight over-sensitive figures of the Brontës emerged to get soaked on the moors. Mr Brontë seems to have looked upon consumption as the enemy against which it was useless to struggle. Perhaps deep in their own consciousness the sisters never thought of any other end for themselves.

X

EMILY SICKENED immediately after Branwell's funeral. She never left the Parsonage again and in less than three months she was dead. This unmitigated suddenness strikes us, even as mere readers of history, with a strange shock. Her illness and death were a chapter of inexpressible pain. Emily's creed was to confront and be equal to what was before her and to accept it not in submission, but face to face. Accordingly she would have no medical advice; her illness was not acknowledged and she would scarcely have it referred to until she died.

Charlotte writes to Ellen on 29 October in response to enquiries after her own health: 'I feel much more uneasy about my sisters than myself just now. Emily's cold and cough are very obstinate. I fear she has pain in the chest and I sometimes catch a shortness in her breathing, when she has moved at all quickly. She looks very, very thin and pale. Her reserved nature occasions me great uneasiness of mind. It is useless to question her; you get no answers. It is useless to suggest remedies. . . . Nor can I shut my eyes to Anne's great delicacy of constitution. . . . The weather has been most unfavourable to invalids of late; sudden changes of temperature and cold penetrating winds have been frequent here.'

Once again we feel the pathos of the Brontë prayers to the English weather, of which they were such devotees.

By 2 November Charlotte is calling Emily's illness a 'kind of slow inflammation of the lungs'. We follow its progress in her letters to W. S. Williams, George Smith, and Ellen Nussey. Her friends in London did their utmost by writing, sending parcels of books, which constituted one of Emily's last pleasures, and suggesting medical advice. Charlotte did actually go so far as to consult one London doctor by letter on her sister's behalf ten days before she died.

They also sent reviews of books, including the new issue of the *Poems* which had also been published in America. The reading aloud of a criticism in the *North American Review* gives us our last picture of the three sisters together in character. 'The *North American Review* is worth reading; there is no mincing the matter there. What a bad set the Bells must be! What appalling books they write! Today, as Emily appeared a little easier, I thought the *Review* would amuse her, so I read it aloud to her and Anne. As I sat between them at our quiet but now somewhat melancholy fireside, I studied the two ferocious authors. Ellis, the "man of uncommon talents, but dogged, brutal, and morose", sat leaning back in his easy-chair drawing his impeded breath as best he could, and looking, alas! piteously pale and wasted; it is not his wont to laugh, but he smiled half-amused and half in scorn as he listened. Acton was sewing, no emotion ever stirs him to loquacity, so he only smiled too, dropping at the same time a single word of calm amazement to hear his character so darkly portrayed. I wonder what the reviewer would have thought of his own sagacity could he have beheld the pair as I did.'

The last week of November and the first week of December go by. To Ellen Charlotte confesses that she must envisage the possibility of Emily's death; Mrs Robinson and one of her daughters are reported married; Anne and Charlotte sadly renounce the idea they have entertained that a visit from Ellen might do Emily good; Charlotte acknowledges a book on homeopathy from Williams which Emily reads but which interests her no farther. There is also the astonishing announcement that Newby is still giving out that he is to publish another work by Ellis and Acton Bell, and Aylott and Jones forward £24 0s. 6d. paid over by Smith, Elder for the poems.

Now Charlotte's anxieties for Anne as well as Emily are mounting. 'Anne, with the best will in the world to be useful, is too delicate to do or bear much. She too at present has frequent pains in the side.' In the same letter she reports, 'The Robinsons were here about a week ago. They are attractive and stylish-looking girls. They seemed overjoyed to see Anne; when I went into the room they were clinging round her like two children – she meanwhile looking perfectly quiet and passive.' Such, exactly, is Anne's passivity, and Charlotte at last unconsciously gives us the true picture of Anne.

On the 19th she writes, 'Dear Ellen, I should have written to you before if I had had one word of hope to say; but I had not. She grows daily weaker. The physician's opinion was expressed too obscurely to be of use. He sent some medicine which she would not take. Moments so dark as these I have never known.'

This was the day on which Emily died. It is said that she died on her feet, as Branwell also had desired to do. At least she did not die in bed, having by her own efforts dressed and descended to the parlour where her sisters were, Anne sewing and Charlotte writing a letter, no doubt the actual letter to Ellen.

'She is gone, after a hard short conflict. She died on Tuesday the very day I wrote to you. . . . Yesterday we put her poor wasted mortal frame quietly under the church pavement. We are very calm at present. . . .'

The pain of the last months had been inexpressible, but Charlotte had attempted to express it. She had two correspondents, in Ellen and W. S. Williams, whom she was bound to keep posted; her nature was to speak, and so she got herself some measure of relief. Emily and Anne over Branwell, then Anne alone over Emily suffered in silence. The silence of each of them, so different, seems at the end to take on a fatal quality. Emily, with her lack of attachment to the human race in general, was attached to Life itself with mighty and peculiar ties.

> *Life that in me hast rest*
> *As I, undying Life, have power in thee* . . .

and whatever she had schooled herself to think and to become, the inalienable attachment to her family still existed. It is difficult not to feel that Branwell's actual death was in part responsible for Emily's, and that Emily's death on top of Branwell's was largely responsible for Anne's.

'My sister Emily first declined. The details of her illness are deep-branded in my memory, but to dwell on them, either in thought or narrative, is not in my power. Never in all her life had she lingered over any task that lay before her, and she did not linger now. She sank rapidly. She made haste to leave us. Yet, while physically she perished, mentally she grew stronger than we had yet known her. Day by day, when I saw with what a front she met suffering, I looked on her with an anguish of wonder and love. I have seen nothing like it; but, indeed, I have never seen her parallel in anything. Stronger than a man, simpler than a child, her nature stood alone. The awful point was, that while full of ruth for others, on herself she had no pity; the spirit was inexorable to the flesh; from the trembling hand, the unnerved limbs, the faded eyes, the same service was exacted as they had rendered in health. To stand

by and witness this, and not dare to remonstrate, was a pain no
words can render.'[1]

All that Charlotte recorded, Anne experienced. Emily, when she
died, was the dearest thing on earth to Charlotte. She loved her as a
Brontë could love a sister; her admiration of Emily's character and
powers amounted to awe; she appreciated Emily's work as well as it
has ever been appreciated and indeed directed posterity how to think
of it. What remained of Emily, over and above all this, Charlotte, it is
little wonder, did not understand. She could not quite accept the
obverse of the medal. She wished Emily tractable; in short, even she,
with her extreme enlightenment, suffered some of the troubles of
living with a genius.

What did Anne and Anne alone experience as she watched her
sister die? She must have experienced an inexpressible feeling *with*
Emily, quite different from anything Charlotte could entertain.
Though self-sufficiency was Emily's creed at the end of her life, the
bond between her and Anne had been peculiarly close. It was what
Ellen Nussey returned to when asked by Mrs Gaskell to recall and
describe Emily. Anne had shared Emily's tremendous life. 'She, and
gentle Anne, were often seen twined together as united statues, of
power and humility.' 'Anne and Emily were always together,' she
repeats, 'and in unison like dearly attached twins.' 'The two dogs
Keeper and Flossy were always in quiet waiting by the side of Emily
and Anne during their Scotch breakfast of oatmeal and milk and
always had a share handed down to them at the close of the meal.'
The Birthday Papers, and Gondal, kept alive so long, bespeak an
extraordinary closeness. We visualize Emily and Anne, as they grow
older, still twined together at the roots, yet accepting their profound
differences and not seeking to follow each other into the territory
where they branched apart. We cannot imagine any pursuit of Emily
by Anne. Charlotte and Emily were nearer in temperament – both
were natures of passion, scorn, and afflatus, of hyperbole in a word.
But Anne's was an elemental attachment. Charlotte speaks of her
'very still but deep sorrow'. 'Anne Brontë drooped and sickened more
rapidly from that time,' says Mrs Gaskell, speaking of the day of
Emily's funeral. 'And so ended the year 1848.'

Nevertheless Anne wished to live and frankly attempted to procure help for herself and avail herself of such help as her friends could

[1] Biographical Notice of Ellis and Acton Bell.

procure. For the remainder of her life she and Charlotte seem like two people making brave and rational attempts to escape from a rising tide. Charlotte's letters and one from Anne herself and an account by Ellen Nussey tell the story.

The letters to Ellen, everlastingly signed 'Yours faithfully, C. Brontë', have read a little hard and chill during the period of Charlotte's leap to fame and Ellen's attempt to pin authorship upon her. But Ellen was a lifelong friend, and in one sense Charlotte was twined with her. 'I am not acquainted with anyone whose influence is at once so tranquil and so genial.' This she had written of Ellen at the end of 1847, and in affliction the old friend came back into her own. To write to Ellen was a natural act and relief to Charlotte, even when she was near extremity. In all her sister's letters now Anne is almost the exclusive topic. To W. S. Williams, on 2 January 1849 Charlotte writes: '. . . My sister Anne sends the accompanying answer to the letter received through you the other day; will you be kind enough to post it? She is not well yet, nor is papa, both are suffering under severe influenza colds. . . .'

Ellen had gone to her friends soon after Emily's death and had stayed on over the New Year. Early in January Mr Brontë sought an outside medical opinion on Anne's case and Ellen wrote to W. S. Williams to give him the doctor's report. 'I found the family wonderfully calm and sustained, but anxious respecting Anne. Mr Brontë enquired for the best doctor in Leeds. Mr Teale was recommended; and came to Haworth. Anne was looking sweetly pretty and flushed, and in capital spirits for an invalid. While consultations were going on in Mr Brontë's study, Anne was very lively in conversation, walking round the room supported by me. Mr Brontë joined us after Mr Teale's departure, and, seating himself on the couch, he drew Anne towards him and said, "My *dear* little Anne." That was all – but it was understood. Charlotte afterwards told me that Mr Teale said – The disease of consumption had progressed too far for cure; and he thought so seriously of the case, he took the trouble to acquaint my friends and urge them to call me home from my visit.'

The occasion on which Anne received her sentence is almost the only one on which we hear of her in high spirits. She sees it as one of her occasions, and no weakness will prevent her rising to it. Therefore we see her so uncharacteristically chattering on, flushed with excitement and fever and the determination to keep up. But she understood in her heart that it was her sentence that she had received, however the doctor may have disguised his conclusions. Hers was a flattering malady, as Charlotte said, and she continued to hope, but in her last poem, begun a few days after Mr Teale's visit, she faces the fact.

> *A dreadful darkness closes in*
> *On my bewildered mind.*
> *Oh, let me suffer and not sin*
> *Be tortured, yet resigned.*

Charlotte printed eight only of the twelve stanzas of this poem when she collected her sisters' work. Her examination of their papers was a labour of piety and anguish, and this last poem of Anne's must have been one of the most agonizing of all for Charlotte to read, but her gross editing of it is proof that she did not understand Anne and was not able to present her picture to the world. For this assumption of authority, however well-meaning, the knowing what is best for others and best to be written in their names, is, in itself, misunderstanding.

Ellen went home the day after Anne began her poem and Charlotte wrote constantly to keep her posted. The bulletin of 10 January was:

'Anne had a very tolerable day and a pretty quiet night last night though she did not sleep much — Mr Wheelhouse[1] ordered the blister to be put on again — she bore it without sickness — and she is risen and come downstairs — she looks somewhat pale and sickly — She has had one dose of Cod-liver oil — it smells and tastes like train oil.'

On 15 January Charlotte wrote:

'I can scarcely say Anne is worse, nor can I say she is better. She varies often in the course of a day, yet each day is passed pretty much the same. The morning is usually the best time; the afternoon and evening the most feverish. Her cough is the most troublesome at night, but it is rarely violent. The pain in her arm still disturbs her. She takes the cod-liver oil and carbonate of iron regularly; she finds them both nauseous, but especially the oil. Her appetite is small indeed. Do not feel that I shall relax in my care of her. She is too precious to me not to be cherished with all the fostering strength I have. . . .

'As to your queries about myself . . . I have not yet got rid of the pains in my back and chest . . . but I combat them steadily with pitch plasters and bran tea.'

[1] The local doctor at Haworth.

Not the least harrowing details of this last period are blisters and cod-liver oil, pitch plasters and bran tea. It is a crumb of general comfort that the care of Anne was felt to be shared by Ellen.

Charlotte seeks a little relief in a long letter to W. S. Williams, dated 18 January:

'In sitting down to write to you I feel as if I were doing a wrong and selfish thing. . . . But the fact is, sometimes I feel it absolutely necessary to unburden my mind. To papa I must only speak cheeringly, to Anne only encouragingly, to you I may give some hint of the dreary truth.

'Anne and I sit alone and in seclusion as you fancy us, but we do not study; Anne cannot study now, she can scarcely read; she occupies Emily's chair – she does not get well. A week ago we sent for a Medical Man of skill and experience from Leeds to see her; he examined her with the stethoscope; his report I forbear to dwell on for the present; even skilful physicians have often been mistaken in their conjectures.

'My first impulse was to hasten her away to a warmer climate, but this was forbidden – she must not travel – she is not to stir from this house this winter – the temperature of her room is to be kept constantly equal.

'Had leave been given to try change of air and scene, I should hardly have known how to act – I could not possibly leave papa – and when I mentioned his accompanying us the bare thought distressed him too much to be dwelt upon. Papa is now upwards of seventy years of age, his habits for nearly thirty years have been those of absolute retirement – any change in them is most repugnant to him and probably could not at this time especially – when the hand of God is so heavy upon his old age, be ventured upon without danger.

'When we lost Emily I thought we had drained the very dregs of our cup of trial, but now when I hear Anne cough as Emily coughed, I tremble lest there should be exquisite bitterness yet to taste. . . .

'Anne is very patient in her illness – as patient as Emily was unflinching. I recall one sister and look at the other with a sort of reverence as well as affection – under the test of suffering neither have faltered.

'All the days of this winter have gone by darkly and heavily like a funeral train; since September sickness has not quitted the house – it is strange – it did not use to be so – but I suspect now all this had been coming on for years: unused any of us to the possession of robust health, we have not noticed the gradual approaches of decay; we did not know its symptoms; the little cough, the small appetite, the tendency to take cold at every variation of atmosphere have been regarded as things of course – I see them in another light now.'

The visit of the doctor from Leeds seems to have brought home to Charlotte at last that consumption had been in their midst for a long time.

Mr Smith of Smith, Elder hopes, meanwhile, that the Brontës will let him send a doctor from London to see Anne. Charlotte answers him on 22 January:

'MÝ DEAR SIR, – I think it is to yourself I should address what I have to say respecting a suggestion conveyed through Mr Williams on the subject of your friend, Dr Forbes.

'The proposal was one which I felt it advisable to mention to my Father, and it is his reply which I would now beg to convey to you.

'I am enjoined, in the first place, to express my Father's sense of the friendly and generous feeling which prompted the suggestion, and in the second place to assure you that did he think any really useful end could be answered by a visit from Dr Forbes he would, notwithstanding his habitual reluctance to place himself under obligations, unhesitatingly accept an offer so delicately made. He is, however, convinced that whatever aid human skill and the resources of science can yield my sister is already furnished her in the person of her present medical attendant, in whom my Father has reason to repose perfect confidence, and he conceives that to bring down a Physician from London would be to impose trouble in quarters where we have no claim, without securing any adequate result.

'Still – having reported my Father's reply – I would beg to add a request of my own, compliance with which would – it appears to me – secure us many of the advantages of your proposal without subjecting yourself or Dr Forbes to its inconveniences. I would state Mr Teale's opinion of my sister's case, the course of treatment he has recommended to be adopted – and should be most happy to obtain, through you, Dr Forbes's opinion on the *régime* prescribed.

'Mr. Teale said it was a case of tubercular consumption, with congestion of the lungs – yet he intimated that the malady had not yet reached so advanced a stage as to cut off all hope; he held out a prospect that a truce and even an arrest of disease might yet be procured; till such truce or arrest could be brought about he forbade the excitement of travelling, enjoined strict care, and prescribed the use of cod-liver oil and carbonate of iron. It would be a satisfaction to know whether Dr Forbes approves these remedies – or whether there are others he would recommend in preference.

'To be indebted to you for information on these points would be felt as no burden either by my sister or myself; your kindness is of an order which will not admit of entire rejection from any motives; where there cannot be full acceptance there must be at least considerate compromise. – Believe me, my dear Sir, Yours sincerely,'

Ellen hears on the same day:

'Anne really did seem to be a little better during some mild days last week but today she looks very pale and languid again – her cough is very teazing at night – she has on the whole less pain and fever than when you were here – she perseveres with the cod-liver oil but still finds it nauseous.

'She is truly obliged to you for the soles and finds them extremely comfortable. I am to commission you to get her just such a respirator as Mrs Heald had – and about the same price – she would not object to give a higher price if you thought it better. If it is not too much trouble you may likewise get me a pair of soles – you can send them and the respirator when you send the box – you must put down the price of all and we will pay you in a Post-Office Order.'

On 30 January Charlotte writes:

'Anne has decided to take the 30/- respirator. I enclose a Post-Office Order for payment. My cork soles I find extremely comfortable. Dear Ellen, *let* me have the comfort of thanking you for your kindness.

'During the mild weather Anne really seemed something better. I began to flatter myself she was gathering strength. But the change to frost has told upon her; she suffers more of late. Still her illness had none of the fearful, rapid symptoms which appalled in Emily's case. Could she only get over spring, I hope summer may do much for her, and then an early removal to a warmer locality for the winter might, at least, prolong her life. Could we only reckon upon another year, I should be thankful; but can we do this even for the healthy? A few days ago I wrote to have Dr Forbes' opinion. He is editor of the *Medical Review* and one of the first authorities in England on consumptive cases. I stated Mr Teale's report of her state and the system of treatment prescribed. Dr Forbes said he knows Mr Teale well, and thinks highly of his skill. The remedies were precisely those he would have recommended himself. He warned us against entertaining sanguine hopes of recovery. The cod-liver oil he considers a peculiarly efficacious medicine. He, too, disapproved of the change of residence for the present. There is some feeble consolation in thinking we are doing the very best that can be done. The agony of forced, total neglect, is not now felt, as during Emily's illness.'

Charlotte's letter to Williams, written two days later, describes the fluctuations of hope.

'MY DEAR SIR, — Anne seems so tranquil this morning, so free from pain and fever, and looks and speaks so like herself in health, that I too feel relieved, and I take advantage of the respite to write to you, hoping that my letter may reflect something of the comparative peace I feel.

'Whether my hopes are quite fallacious or not, I do not know; but sometimes I fancy that the remedies prescribed by Mr Teale, and approved – as I was glad to learn – by Dr Forbes, are working a good result. Consumption, I am aware, is a flattering malady, but certainly Anne's illness has of late assumed a less alarming character than it had in the beginning: the hectic is allayed; the cough gives a more frequent reprieve. Could I but believe she would live two years – a year longer, I should be thankful: I dreaded the terrors of the swift messenger which snatched Emily from us, as it seemed, in a few days.

'The parcel came yesterday. You and Mr Smith do nothing by halves. Neither of you care for being thanked, so I will keep my gratitude in my own mind. The choice of books is perfect. Papa is at this moment reading Macaulay's *History*, which he had wished to see. Anne is engaged with one of Frederika Bremer's tales.'

The London friend hears again on 4 February:

'. . . Anne continues a little better: the mild weather suits her. At times – I hear the renewal of Hope's whisper – but I dare not listen too fondly – she deceived me cruelly before. A sudden change to cold would be the test – I dread such change but must not anticipate. Spring lies before us – and then summer – surely we may hope a little.

'Anne expresses a wish to see the notices of the poems – you had better therefore send them. We shall expect to find painful allusions to one now above blame and beyond praise – but these must be borne. For ourselves – we are almost indifferent to censure.'

Charlotte claimed for herself and Anne, as almost all artists do at times, that they were superior to adverse criticism. We remember, however, how she wished that Anne had felt the reviewers' condemnation of *Wildfell Hall* less keenly, and we have still before us what she had written to G. H. Lewes when he proposed to review *Jane Eyre*.

'You will be severe; your last letter taught me as much. Well, I shall try to extract good out of your severity; and besides, though I am now sure you are a just, discriminating man, yet being mortal, you must be fallible; and if any part of your censure galls me too keenly to the quick – gives me deadly pain – I shall for the present disbelieve it, and put it quite aside, till such time as I feel able to receive it without torture.'

On 16 February hope seems to recede again.

'DEAR ELLEN, – We received the box and its contents safely today. The pen-wipers are very pretty and we are much obliged to you for them. I hope the respirator will be useful to Anne in case she should ever be well enough to go out again.

'She continues very much in the same state – I trust not greatly worse – though she is becoming very thin – I fear it would be only self-delusion to fancy her better – What effect the advancing season may have on her I know not – perhaps the return of really warm weather may give nature a happy stimulus – I tremble at the thought of any change to cold wind or frost – would that March were well over – Her mind seems generally serene and her sufferings hitherto are nothing like Emily's. The thought of what may be to come grows more familiar to my mind. . . . Anne sends her thanks and kind love to you. . . .'

To W. S. Williams, Charlotte writes on 2 March 1849:

'MY DEAR SIR, – My sister still continues better: she has less languor and weakness; her spirits are improved. This change gives cause, I think, both for gratitude and hope.'

To Ellen she writes on 8 March:

'DEAR ELLEN, – Anne's state has apparently varied very little during the last fortnight or three weeks. I wish I could say she gains either flesh, strength or appetite, but there is no progress on these points, nor I hope, as far as regards the two last at least, any falling off; she is piteously thin. Her cough, and the pain in her side continue the same. . . .'

There is a letter to W. S. Williams again on 11 March:

'MY DEAR SIR, – My sister has been something worse since I wrote last. We have had nearly a week of frost, and the change has tried her, as I feared it would do, though not so severely as former experience had led me to apprehend. I am thankful to say she is now again a little better. Her state of mind is usually placid, and her chief sufferings consist in the harassing cough and a sense of languor.'

March is proving a trying month, as we learn on the 16th.

'DEAR ELLEN, – I must write a line in acknowledgment of your last letter and to tell you how Anne is getting on.

'We have found the past week a somewhat trying one – it has not been cold – but still there have been changes of temperature whose effect Anne has felt unfavourably – She is not I trust seriously worse but her cough is at times very hard and painful – and her strength rather diminished than improved. I wish the month of March was well over. . . .

'. . . The pain of my position is not one likely to lessen with habit – its solitude and isolation are oppressive circumstances. Yet I do not wish for any friend to stay with me; I could not do with any one – not even *you* to share the sadness of the house – it would rack me intolerably. Meantime judgement is still blent with mercy – Anne's sufferings continue mild.'

Now the quality of Ellen's friendship and the kindness of her family is shown by an invitation to Anne to Brookroyd.

'Dear Ellen,' Charlotte answers, 'I read your kind note to Anne and she wishes me to thank you sincerely for your friendly proposal. She feels, of course, that it would not do to take advantage of it by quartering an invalid upon the inmates of Brookroyd – but she intimates that there is another way in which you might serve her perhaps with some benefit to yourself as well as her. Should it, a month or two hence, be deemed advisable that she should go either to the seaside or to some inland watering place – and should papa still be disinclined to move – and I – consequently – be obliged to remain at home – she asks could you be her companion? Of course I need not add that in case of such an arrangement being made you would be put to no expense.'

Anne, all the year, had longed to get away. Not only was the seaside generally thought good for her complaint, but if ever change was healthy, it must have seemed healthy to be removed from the sick, dark atmosphere that had prevailed at Haworth for so long.

'This, dear Ellen, is Anne's proposal', the letter continues, 'I make it to comply with her wish – but for my own part – I must add that I see serious objections to your accepting it – objections I cannot name to her. She continues to vary – is sometimes worse and sometimes better, as the weather changes – but on the whole I fear she loses strength. Papa says her state is most precarious – she may be spared for some time – or a sudden alteration might remove her ere we are aware – were such an alteration to take place while she was far from home and alone with you – it would be too terrible – the idea of it distresses me inexpressibly, and I tremble whenever she alludes to the project of a journey. In short I wish we could gain time and see how she gets on – if she leaves home, it certainly should not be in the capricious month of May which is proverbially trying to the weak – June would be a safer month – if we could reach June – I should have good hopes of her getting through the summer.

'Write such an answer to this note as I can shew Anne – you can write any additional remarks to me on a separate piece of paper – '

To W. S. Williams Charlotte wrote on 2 April:

'... When I *can* write – the book I have in hand must claim all my attention. – Oh if Anne were well – if the void Death has left were a little closed up – if the dreary word *nevermore* would cease sounding in my ears – I think I could yet do something.'

When Charlotte had strength, during this dark period, she was writing *Shirley*, and had sent part of it to her publishers.

On 5 April Anne herself wrote to Ellen. The letter remains as modest and gentle a plea as could ever be transcribed on what was to the writer a matter of life and death. It is written on a whole black-bordered double sheet of note-paper, such as the family no doubt thought fitting to indulge in after their bereavements. Anne's delicate handwriting – the handwriting of the period and also the handwriting of the Brontës, but in her case a little sharper and more pointed – remains fairly firm. The writing is crossed into symmetrical squares but it remains entirely legible.

'My dear Miss Nussey,' Anne writes. 'I thank you greatly for your kind letter, and your ready compliance with my proposal as far as the *will* can go at least. I see, however, that your friends are unwilling that you should take the responsibility of accompanying me under present circumstances. But I do not think there would be any great responsibility in the matter. I know, and everybody knows, that you would be as kind and helpful as any one could possibly be, and I hope I should not be very troublesome. It would be as a companion, not as a nurse, that I should wish for your company; otherwise I should not venture to ask it. As for your kind and often repeated invitation to Brookroyd, pray give my sincere thanks to your mother and sisters, but tell them I could not think of inflicting my presence on them as I now am. It is very kind of them to make so light of the trouble, but still there must be more or less, and certainly no pleasure, from the society of a silent invalid stranger. I hope, however, that Charlotte will by some means make it possible to accompany me after all. She is certainly very delicate, and greatly needs a change of air and scene to renovate her constitution. And then your going with me before the end of May is apparently out of the question, unless you are disappointed in your visitors; but I should be reluctant to wait till then if the weather would at all permit an earlier departure. You say May is a trying month, and so say others. The early part is often cold enough, I acknowledge, but according to my experience, we are almost certain of some fine warm days in the latter half, when the laburnums and lilacs are in bloom; whereas June is often cold, and July generally wet. But I have a more serious reason than this for my impatience of delay. The doctors say that change of air or removal to a better climate would hardly ever fail of success in consumptive cases, if the remedy be taken *in time*; but the reason why there are so many disappointments is that it is generally deferred till it is too late. Now I would not commit this error; and, to say the truth, though I suffer much less from pain and fever than I did when you were with us, I am decidedly weaker, and very much thinner. My cough still troubles me a good deal, especially in the night, and, what seems worse than all, I am subject to great shortness of breath on going up stairs or any slight exertion. Under these circumstances, I think there is no time to be lost. I have no horror of death; if I thought it inevitable, I think I could quietly resign myself to the prospect, in the hope that you, dear Miss Nussey, would give as much of your company as you possibly could to Charlotte, and be a sister to her in my stead. But I wish it would please God to spare me not only for papa's and Charlotte's sakes; but because I long to do some good in the world before I leave it. I have many schemes in my head for future practice, humble and limited indeed, but still I should not like them all to come to nothing, and myself to have lived to so little purpose. But God's will be done. Remember me respectfully to your mother and sisters, and believe me, dear Miss Nussey, yours most affectionately, ANNE BRONTË.'

The natural warmth of the conclusion strikes our ear with relief. Charlotte wrote to Williams on the same day:

'. . . I am not going to complain. Anne has indeed suffered much at intervals since I last wrote you – frost and east wind have had their effect. She has passed nights of sleeplessness and pain, and days of depression and languor which nothing could cheer – but still, with the return of genial weather she revives. I cannot perceive that she is feebler now than she was a month ago, though that is not saying much. It proves, however, that no rapid process of destruction is going on in her frame, and keeps alive a hope that with the renovating aid of summer she may yet be spared a long time. . . .

'The Cornhill books are still our welcome and congenial resource when Anne is well enough to enjoy reading. . . . Anne thanks you sincerely for the kind interest you take in her welfare, and both she and I beg to express our sense of Mrs Williams's good wishes, which you mentioned in a former letter. We are grateful, too, to Mr Smith and to all who offer us the sympathy of friendship.'

The cold spring still forbids Anne's advisers and friends to allow her to try the longed-for change of air and of scene, and she has to continue to suffer from their apparent tardiness.

'Dear Ellen,' Charlotte writes on 12 April, 'I read Anne's letter to you; it was touching enough – as you say. If there were no hope beyond this world – no eternity – no life to come – Emily's fate and that which threatens Anne would be heart-breaking. I cannot forget Emily's death-day; it becomes a more fixed – a darker, a more frequently recurring idea in my mind than ever: it was very terrible, she was torn conscious, panting, reluctant though resolute out of a happy life. But it *will not do* to dwell on these things – I am glad your friends object to your going with Anne – it would never do: to speak truth – even if your Mother and Sisters had consented I never could – it is not that there is any laborious attention to pay her – she requires and will accept but little nursing – but there would be hazard and anxiety of mind beyond what you ought to be subjected to.

'If a month or six weeks hence, she continues to wish for a change as much as she does now – I shall – D.V. – go with her myself – It will certainly be my paramount duty – other care must be made subservient to that – I have consulted Mr Teale – he does not object and recommends Scarbro' which was Anne's own choice. I trust affairs may be so ordered that you may be able to be with us at least part of the time.

'When the Miss Cockhills went alone do you know whether they went to a boarding-house or took lodgings. I wonder which would be the best plan. – Anne is rather in favour of a boarding-house – but do you think it would suit an invalid? I know nothing about them myself – she thinks it would be more lively. Whether in lodgings or not – I should wish to be boarded – Providing oneself is – I think – an insupportable nuisance – I don't like keeping provisions in a cupboard, locking up, being pillaged, and all that. . . .'

W. S. Williams's assiduous kindness received a reply on 16 April:

'MY DEAR SIR, – Your kind advice on the subject of Homeopathy deserves and has our best thanks. We find ourselves, however, urged from more than one quarter to try different systems and medicines, and I fear we have already given offence by not listening to all. The fact is, were we in every instance compliant, my dear sister would

be harassed by continual changes. Cod-liver oil and carbonate of
iron were first strongly recommended. Anne took them as long as
she could, but at last she was obliged to give them up; the oil
yielded her no nutriment, it did not arrest the progress of emaciation,
and as it kept her always sick, she was prevented from taking food
of any sort. Hydropathy was then strongly advised. She is now
trying Gobold's Vegetable Balsam; she thinks it does her some
good; and as it is the first medicine which has had that effect, she
would wish to persevere with it for a time. She is also looking hopefully forward to deriving benefit from change of air.
We have obtained Mr Teale's permission to go to the seaside in
the course of six or eight weeks. At first I felt torn between two
duties – that of staying with papa and going with Anne; but as it is
papa's own most kindly expressed wish that I should adopt the latter
plan, and as, besides, he is now, thank God! in tolerable health
I hope to be spared the pain of resigning the care of my sister to
other hands, however friendly. We wish to keep together as long as
we can. I hope, too, to derive from the change some renewal of
physical strength and mental composure (in neither of which points
am I what I ought or wish to be) to make me a better and more
cheery nurse.'

Two things emerge from the foregoing letter, first the fact that
hope could still rise high in Anne, inasmuch as she suggested staying at
a boarding-house, and second, the strength of Charlotte's unresentful
sense of filial duty. Throughout Anne's illness we have striven to
assess her chances and have been left wrestling with Mr Brontë, Mr
Teale, Mr Forbes, and the longing for Anne to have the benefit of a
change before it is absolutely hopeless. Mr Brontë, at over seventy,
had 'a sort of chronic cough' as his only complaint and two servants to
look after him, one of them active, although the other was old; yet
he still had first claim on Charlotte's attention. With regard to medical
advice in Anne's illness he was satisfied that she had had the best,
and if Mr Brontë was satisfied, that was the end of the matter. To
put himself under an obligation, fruitlessly, for a daughter's sake, even
for a dying daughter's sake, was quite beyond his ken, and it was
equally beyond Charlotte's ken to impose such an action on her father.

XI

Charlotte wrote to Ellen on 1 May:

'Dear Ellen, — I am glad to hear that when we go to Scarboro', you will be at liberty to go with us; but the journey and its consequences still continue a source of great anxiety to me; I must try to put it off two or three weeks longer if I can; perhaps by that time the milder season may have given Anne more strength, perhaps it will be otherwise; I cannot tell. The change to fine weather has not proved beneficial to her so far. She has sometimes been so weak, and suffered so much pain in the side, during the last few days, that I have not known what to think. She may rally again, and be much better, but there must be *some* improvement before I can feel justified in taking her away from home. Yet to delay is painful; for, as is *always* the case, I believe, under the circumstances, she seems herself but half conscious of the necessity for such delay. She wonders, I believe, why I don't talk more about the journey: it grieves me to think she may even be hurt by my seeming tardiness. She is very much emaciated, far more so than when you were with us; her arms are no thicker than a little child's. The least exertion brings a shortage of breath. She goes out a little every day, but we creep rather than walk. Papa continues pretty well, and I have had better health myself, during the last two or three weeks, than I had a month ago. *I trust* I shall be enabled to bear up. . . .

'If Anne seems at all better or even worse in a week or two I will let you know.'

W. S. Williams received a letter a week later:

'. . . That fine spring weather of which you speak did not bring such happiness to us in its sunshine as I trust it did to you and thousands besides – the change proved trying to my sister. For a week or ten days I did not know what to think, she became so weak, and suffered so much from the increased pain in the side, and aggravated cough. The last few days have been much colder, yet, strange to say, during their continuance she has appeared rather to revive than sink. She not unfrequently shows the very same symptoms which were apparent in Emily only a few days before she died – fever in the evenings, sleepless nights, and a sort of lethargy in the morning hours; this creates acute anxiety – then comes an improvement, which reassures. In about three weeks, should the weather be genial and her strength continue at all equal to the journey, we hope to go to Scarboro'. It is not without misgiving that I contemplate a departure from home under such circumstances; but since she herself earnestly wishes the experiment to be tried, I think it ought not to be neglected. We are in God's hands and must trust the result to Him. An old schoolfellow of mine, a tried and faithful friend, has volunteered to accompany us. I shall have the satisfaction of leaving Papa to the attentions of two servants equally tried and faithful. One of them is indeed now old and infirm, and unfit to stir much from her chair by the kitchen fireside; but the other is young and active, and even she has lived with us seven years. I have reason, therefore, you see, to be thankful amidst sorrow, especially as Papa still possesses every faculty unimpaired, and though not robust, has good general health – a sort of chronic cough is his sole complaint.'

Four days later Ellen hears that Anne is to be moved at last and that arrangements for lodgings have been made. Miss Wooler, who remained deeply interested in her old pupils, had offered them her house at Scarborough, but its position was thought to be too exposed.

'. . . Anne was worse during the warm weather we had about a week ago. She grew weaker, and both the pain in her side and her cough were worse; strange to say, since it is cooler, she had appeared rather to revive, than sink. I still hope that if she gets over May she may last a long time.

'We have engaged lodgings at Scarbro'. We stipulated for a good-sized sitting-room and an airy double-bedded lodging-room, with a sea view, and if not deceived, have obtained these desiderata at No. 2 Cliff. Anne says it is one of the best situations in the place. It would not have done to have taken lodgings either in the town or on the bleak steep coast, where Miss Wooler's house is situated. If Anne is to get any good she must have every advantage. Miss Outhwaite left her in her will a legacy of £200, and she cannot employ her money better than in obtaining what may prolong existence, if it does not restore health. We hope to leave home on the 23rd, and I think it will be advisable to rest at York, and stay all night there. I hope this arrangement will suit you. We reckon on your society, dear Ellen, as a real privilege and pleasure. We shall take little luggage, and shall have to buy bonnets and dresses and several other things either at York or Scarbro'; which place do you think would be best? I wish it seemed less like a dreary mockery in us to talk of buying bonnets, etc.

'Anne was very ill yesterday. She had difficulty in breathing all day, even when sitting perfectly still. Today she seems better again. I long for the moment to come when the experiment of the sea air will be tried. Will it do her good? I cannot tell; I can only wish. O, if it would please God to strengthen and revive Anne, how happy we might be together!'

To Miss Margaret Wooler Charlotte wrote on 16 May:

'MY DEAR MISS WOOLER, – I will lose no time in thanking you for your letter and kind offer of assistance. We have, however, already engaged lodgings. I am not myself acquainted with Scarbro' but Anne knows it well – having been there three or four times – she had a particular preference for the situation of some lodgings (No. 2 Cliff).[1] We wrote and, finding them disengaged, took them at 30s. per week. Your information is notwithstanding valuable – should we find this place in any respect ineligible – it is a satisfaction to be provided with directions for future use.

'Next Wednesday is the day fixed for our departure; Ellen Nussey accompanies us at her own kind and friendly wish.[2] I would not refuse her society but I dared not urge her to go, for I have little hope that the excursion will be one of pleasure or benefit to those engaged in it. Anne is extremely weak. She herself, has a fixed impression that the sea-air will give her a chance of regaining strength – that chance therefore we must have.

[1] The houses called 'The Cliff' have been pulled down. The Royal Hotel stands on the site.

[2] Opposite this, in the original letter, Miss Wooler has added a pencil note: 'Anne had implored E. to accompany her but I did not know it.'

'Having resolved to try the experiment – misgivings are useless – and yet – when I look at her – misgivings will rise. She is more emaciated than Emily was at the very last – her breath scarcely serves her to mount the stairs however slowly. She sleeps very little at night – and often passes most of the forenoon in a semi-lethargic state. Still she is up all day – and even goes out a little when it is fine – fresh air usually acts as a stimulus – but its reviving power diminishes. . . .'

On the same day Ellen hears the date and the details of the proposed journey.

'DEAR ELLEN, – We have now made our arrangements for the journey. We shall leave Keighley about ½ 10 'clock and expect to reach Leeds soon after two – Wednesday 23rd that is next week.

'It is with a heavy heart I prepare – and earnestly do I wish the fatigue of the journey were well over – it may be borne better than I expect – for temporary stimulus often does much – but when I see the daily increasing weakness – I know not what to think.

'I fear you will be shocked when you see Anne – but be on your guard – dear Ellen – not to express your feelings – indeed I can trust both your self-possession and your kindness.

'I wish my judgement sanctioned this step of going to Scarboro' more fully than it does.

'You ask have I arranged about leaving papa – I could make no special arrangement – he wishes me to go with Anne – and would not hear of Mr Nicholls coming – or anything of that kind – so I do what I believe is for the best and leave the result to Providence.'

They had planned to go on the 23rd, but Anne was not well enough, and their departure had to be postponed till the next day. Ellen could not be informed and waited in vain for them several hours on the station at Leeds.

The journey was difficult. It had to be made by carriage from Haworth to Keighley and thence by train to York, with a tiresome change at Leeds. Ellen, made acutely anxious by the non-appearance of the Brontës at the junction, had gone to Haworth the next day and arrived just in time to see Anne being lifted, half-fainting, as she told Mrs Gaskell, into a chaise that stood at the Parsonage gate at the top of the steep ramp. She too entered, and the journey as far as York was achieved. By a second benevolent stroke of fate, which has preserved so few traces of Anne, Ellen's diary for 1849 has survived, a little leather-covered Christian Remembrancer, given to her by one of her sisters. Under 23 May is the entry '*To Scarborough with C.B. and A.B.*' This is crossed out and below is written '*To Leeds.*' For 24 May the entry is, '*To Minster at York. The George Hotel.*'

Charlotte's pocket-book, which contained a list of expenses for the trip to London the summer before, contained a similar note for the journey to Scarborough. First comes a short list of articles to be bought – Bonnet, Corsets, stockings – black silk dress, gloves, ribbon for neck – and then the following items:

	L.	s.	d.
3 Tickets for Leeds	0 –	10 –	0
3 ditto to York	0 –	16 –	6
Cocoa	0 –	0 –	6
Coach hire	0 –	1 –	0
Bonnets	2 –	14 –	6
Chair	0 –	1 –	6

A pencil line suggests that this was the end of 24 May. Four pages of Ellen's little diary give us 'a short account of the last days of dear Anne', which account she afterwards filled out and sent to Mrs Gaskell – 'Through the trials and fatigues of the journey', Ellen says of the 24th and 25th, 'she evinced the pious courage and fortitude of a martyr – dependence and helplessness were with her a far sorer trial than hard and racking endurance. Her visit to Y. Minster was an overwhelming pleasure not for its imposing and impressive grandeur only, but because it brought before her susceptible nature a vital sense of the greatness of our divine architect.'

Anne knew York. She went there with the Robinsons, and had taken Emily there on their little trip of 1845. We picture her, immensely fragile and wearing the new bonnet, being wheeled about the Cathedral in a chair; and we imagine how wonderful York must have seemed to them all, in their heightened state of sensibility – not only the Minster and its perfect precincts, but the many-coloured, warm, ungrimed, Georgian brick, the rich, low, narrow streets and the lovely bow-fronted windows of the luxurious little shops.

Charlotte's list of expenses continues:

	L.	s.	d.
Coach hire	0 –	1 –	0
Y. Biscuits	0 –	0 –	6

	L.	s.	d.
Inn Bill	2 —	0 —	6
Ticket to S	1 —	10 —	0
Dandelion coffee		2 —	0
Tortoise Shell Comb		2 —	5
Lemonade		0 —	3
3 Tickets for Bridge		. 7 —	6
Oranges ½ doz.		0 —	4
Carriage boxes		3 —	9

They have entrained, furnished with all necessities and assuagements for the invalid's thirst, traversed the calm pastoral stretch between York and Scarborough, reached the low line of downs that edges it and at last seen the sea.

On 27 May Charlotte wrote to W. S. Williams of their journey and safe arrival.

'No. 2 Cliff, Scarboro'

'MY DEAR SIR, – The date above will inform you why I have not answered your last letter more promptly. I have been busy with preparations for departure and with the journey. I am thankful to say we reached our destination safely, having rested one night at York. We found assistance wherever we needed it; there was always an arm ready to do for my sister what I was not quite strong enough to do; lift her in and out of the carriages, carry her across the line, etc.

'It made her happy to see both York and its Minster, and Scarboro' and its bay once more. There is yet no revival of bodily strength – I fear indeed the slow ebb continues. People who see her tell me I must not expect her to last long – but it is something to cheer her mind.

'Our lodgings are pleasant. As Anne sits at the window she can look down on the sea, which this morning is calm as glass. She says if she could breathe more freely she would be comfortable at this moment – but she cannot breathe freely.

'My friend Ellen is with us. I find her presence a solace. She is a calm, steady girl – not brilliant, but good and true. She suits and has always suited me well. I like her, with her phlegm, repose, sense, and sincerity, better than I should like the most talented without these qualifications. . . . Write to me. In this strange place your letters will come like the visits of a friend.'

Emily would not accept treatment; Anne accepted the current treatment eagerly, but the results were the same. We watch her rising, walking, performing her toilet, visiting York Minster, prodigally consuming what the disease had left unconsumed.

The lodgings were beautifully situated and perhaps had been used by the Robinsons, who were accustomed to the good things of life. The house stood half-way up the cliff and sheltered by it, above the centre of the bay. To the left was the old town, with fishing and boating activities, lighthouse and jetty, and the headland above, crowned with its ruined castle. To the right was the curve of the shore, bordered by low green cliffs.

Ellen Nussey's account continues:

'Her weakness was great but her fortitude was greater after an exertion such as walking to her bedroom she would clasp her hands and raise her eyes in silent gratitude ere she prepared for rest and she did this not to the exclusion of wonted prayer for that too was performed on bended knee. On the 26 she drove on the sands for an hour and lest the poor donkey should be urged by its driver to a greater speed than her tender heart thought right she took the reins and drove herself – when she was joined by a friend after bathing time she was charging the boy master of the donkey to treat the poor animal well. She was ever fond of dumb things and would give up her own comfort for them – On Sunday she wished to go to the church and her eye brightened with the thought of once more worshipping her God among her fellow creatures but her friends thought it prudent to dissuade her from the attempt – she submitted without an objection though it was plain her heart was longing for the performance of such worship – she walked a little in the afternoon and meeting with a comfortable seat near the beach she begged her companions would leave her and enjoy the various scenes within their reach for the place and its attractions was new to them.'

Dying as she is, Anne does the honours of Scarborough, gently subduing the donkey-boy and taking the reins into her own hands. They must have hired the little carriage from near the fishing-boats and driven across to where, among rocky pools, in past holidays, she had found the cornelians. Turning, they looked back at the ruined tower of the Castle and the square tower of St Mary's Church, repeating its shape on the skyline a little below. On Sunday Anne insists on being left alone in her sheltered seat while her friends explore some of the beauties to which she has directed them. She actually accompanied them to the Bridge – 'A.B. and C.B. and E.N. on Scarbro' bridge', Ellen wrote in her diary on Sunday 27th. The Bridge, an early-Victorian iron structure which still stands, spans a break or a little ravine between the low cliffs that surround the bay. The expenditure of seven shillings and sixpence tells us that Anne, knowledgeable again, had directed the purchase of season tickets – a mockery no less than the new bonnets purchased at York.

'The evening closed in,' says Ellen's later account, 'with the most glorious sunset ever witnessed. The castle on the cliff stood in proud glory, gilded by the rays of the declining sun. The distant ships glittered like burnished gold; the little boats near the beach heaved on the ebbing tide, inviting occupants. The view was grand beyond description. Anne was drawn in her easy chair to the window, to enjoy the scene with us. Her face became illumined almost as much as the glorious scene she gazed upon. Little was said, for it was plain that her thoughts were driven by the imposing view before her to penetrate forwards to the regions of unfading glory. She again thought of public worship, and wished us to leave her, and join those who were assembled at the house of God. We declined, gently urging the duty and pleasure of staying with her, who was now so dear and so feeble. On returning to her place near the fire she conversed with her sister upon the propriety of returning to their home. She did not wish it for her own sake, she said; she was fearing others might suffer more if her decease occurred where she was. She probably thought the task of accompanying her lifeless remains on a long journey was more than her sister could bear – more than the bereaved father could bear, were she borne home another and a third tenant of the family vault in the short space of nine months.

'The night was passed without any apparent accession of illness. She rose at seven o'clock, and performed most of her toilet herself, by her expressed wish. Her sister always yielded such points, believing it was the truest kindness not to press inability when it was not acknowledged. Nothing occurred to excite alarm till about 11 a.m. She then spoke of feeling a change. "She believed she had not long to live. Could she reach home alive, if we prepared immediately for departure?" A physician was sent for. Her address to him was made with perfect composure. She begged him to say "how long he though she might live — not to fear speaking the truth, for she was not afraid to die". The doctor reluctantly admitted that the angel of death was already arrived and that life was ebbing fast. She thanked him for his truthfulness, and he departed to come again very soon. She still occupied her easy chair, looking so serene, so reliant: there was no opening for grief as yet, though all knew the separation was at hand. She clasped her hands, and reverently invoked a blessing from on high; first upon her sister, then upon her friend, to whom she said, "Be a sister in my stead. Give Charlotte as much of your company as you can." She then thanked each for her kindness and attention.

'Ere long the restlessness of approaching death appeared, and she was borne to the sofa. On being asked if she were easier she looked gratefully at her questioner, and said, "It is not *you* who can give me ease, but soon all will be well through the merits of our Redeemer." Shortly after this, seeing that her sister could hardly restrain her grief, she said, "Take courage, Charlotte; take courage." Her faith never failed, and her eye never dimmed till about two o'clock, when she calmly, and without a sigh, passed from the temporal to the eternal. So still and so hallowed were her last hours and moments. There was no thought of assistance or of dread. The doctor came and went two or three times. The hostess knew that death was near, yet so little was the house disturbed by the presence of the dying, and the sorrow of those so nearly bereaved, that dinner was announced as ready, through the half-opened door, as the living sister was closing the eyes of the dead one. She could now no more stay the welled-up grief of her sister with her emphatic and dying "Take courage", and it burst forth in brief but agonizing strength. Charlotte's affection, however, had another channel, and there it turned in thought, in care, and in tenderness. There was bereavement, but there was not solitude; sympathy was at hand, and it was accepted. With calmness came the consideration of the removal of the dear remains to their home resting-place. This melancholy task, however, was never performed; for the afflicted sister decided to lay the flower in the place where it had fallen. She believed that to do so would accord with the wishes of the departed. She had no preference for place. She thought not of the grave, for that is but the body's goal but of all that is beyond it.'

The word 'passive' comes to mind once again. In one sense we are all passive when it comes to dying; in another sense Anne is almost awesomely in command. She rises supremely to her last occasion, and as long as she is conscious, she directs it.

'Anne died on the Monday,' Mrs Gaskell added. 'On the Tuesday Charlotte wrote to her father, but knowing that his presence was required for some annual Church solemnity at Haworth, she informed him that she had made all necessary arrangements for the interment and that the funeral would take place so soon that he could hardly arrive in time for it. The surgeon who had visited Anne on the day of her death, offered his attendance, but it was respectfully declined.'

Ellen herself concluded. 'A lady from the same neighbourhood as E—— was staying at Scarborough at this time, she too kindly offered sympathy and assistance; and when that solitary pair of mourners (the sister and the friend) arrived at the Church, this lady was there, in unobtrusive presence, not the less kind because unobtrusive.'

There are three entries, for Monday, Tuesday, and Wednesday, in the Christian Remembrancer –

'M 28   Whit Monday   Anne Brontë died at Scarborough.
T 29   A walk with C. on the sands.
W 30   A.B. interred at Scarbro' '

Writing to the servant, Martha Brown, and thinking only of the simple woman and of Anne, Charlotte divests herself of all stiffness and composes a little letter perfectly in tune with her subject:

'DEAR MARTHA, – I was very much pleased with your note and glad to hear that all at home are getting on pretty well. It will still be a week or ten days before I return and you must not tire yourself too much with the cleaning.

'My sister Anne's death could not be otherwise than a great trouble to me, though I have known for many weeks that she could not get better. She died very calmly and gently – she was quite sensible to the last – about three minutes before she died she said she was very happy and believed she was passing out of earth into heaven. It was not her custom to talk much about religion but she was very good and I am certain she is now in a far better place

than any this world contains. . . . Give my best love to Tabby. —
I am — dear Martha, Your sincere friend,

C. BRONTË.'

To Williams she had written the day before:

'. . . You have been informed of my dear sister Anne's death. Let
me now add that she died without severe struggle, resigned, trusting
in God — thankful for release from a suffering life — deeply assured
that a better existence lay before her. She believed, she hoped — and
declared her belief and hope with her last breath. Her quiet,
Christian death did not rend my heart as Emily's stern simple,
undemonstrative end did. I let Anne go to God, and felt He had a
right to her. I could hardly let Emily go. I wanted to hold her back
then, and I want her back now. Anne, from her childhood, seemed
preparing for an early death. Emily's spirit seemed strong enough
to bear her to fulness of years. . . .

'For the present Anne's ashes rest apart from the others. I have
buried her here at Scarbro' to save Papa the anguish of the return
and a third funeral. . . .

'I have heard from Papa. He and the servants knew when they
parted from Anne they would see her no more. All tried to be
resigned. I knew it likewise, and I wanted her to die where she
would be happiest. She loved Scarbro'. A peaceful sun gilded her
evening.'

We know that the sea at Scarborough made Anne happy, for she
tells us so in her own voice:

'. . . I was dressed and out when the church clock struck a quarter
to six. There was a feeling of freshness and vigour in the very
streets, and when I got free of the town, when my foot was on the
sands and my face towards the broad, bright bay, no language can
describe the effect of the deep clear azure of the sky and ocean, the
bright morning sunshine on the semicircular barrier of craggy
cliffs surmounted by green swelling hills, and on the smooth wide
sands and the low rocks out to sea, looking, with their clothing of
weeds and moss, like little grass-grown islands, and, above all, on
the brilliant sparkling waves. And then the unspeakable purity and
freshness of the air ! . . . My footsteps were the first to press the
firm unbroken sands. Nothing before had trampled them since
last night's flowing tide had obliterated the deepest marks of

yesterday and left it fair and even, except where the subsiding water had left behind it the traces of dimpled pools and little running streams.

'Refreshed, delighted and invigorated, I walked along, forgetting all my cares, feeling as if I had wings to my feet. . . . About half-past six, however, the grooms began to come down to air their masters' horses – first one, and then another, till there were some dozen horses and five or six riders. But that need not trouble me, for they would not come as far as the low rocks which I was now approaching. When I had reached these, and walked over the moist, slippery seaweed at the risk of floundering into one of the numerous pools of clear salt water that lay between them to a little mossy promontory with the sea splashing round it, I looked back again to see who next was stirring. Still there were only the early grooms with their horses, and one gentleman with a little dark speck of a dog running before him, and one water-cart coming out of the town to get water for the baths. In another minute or two the distant bathing machines would begin to move. . . .

'But the tide was coming in; the water was rising; the gulfs and lakes were filling; the straits were widening. It was time to seek some safer footing; so I walked, skipped and stumbled back to the smooth wide sands. . . .'[1]

*　　　　*　　　　*

The pilgrim or the stranger follows in the footsteps of Charlotte, Ellen, and the unobtrusive friend up to the church of St Mary, on the hill, where Anne is buried. He climbs by the steep little streets and alleys of the old town to the foot of Church Stairs Street, where he pauses, struck by the likeness between this last stretch and the slope between Haworth Church and the Parsonage – only this is a stair, too steep for wheels, and the church is at the top. Gaining the stairhead, he looks over a wall to the left into a disused churchyard, and stands rooted to the spot with a sense of shock. Black decayed tombstones, not blackened, but absolutely black, stick up crookedly at sparse intervals out of rank grass and weeds. It is a desolation beside which Haworth churchyard is a smiling prospect. Can Anne lie here?

Nerving himself to go on, the stranger reaches the church and masters the lie of the land. The church, which is low and square-towered, stands at the top of the ridge that rises to the Castle headland.

[1] *Agnes Grey*.

Graves are widely scattered round it; among them is a ruin, a fragment of an abbey or an outlying fragment of the Castle perhaps. To extend the churchyard, the uneven plateau of the hill-top has been taken in as needed with wide-flung irregular reaches of brick wall.

Anne lies in the plot almost under the headland. On her tombstone, below a draped urn supported on two books, in the manner of the period, is the inscription:

'Here lie the remains of Anne Brontë, daughter of the Rev. P Brontë, Incumbent of Haworth, Yorkshire. She died, aged 28, May 28th, 1849.'[1]

Her grave is kept up, but the greater part of the surrounding stones are ragged, hollow, and black, ruined not by soot, for there is none, but perhaps by some particular action on the stone of the salt air. Once again the pilgrim stands and looks about him. Above Anne is the Castle, rising over a thin glade of trees. Below her is the sea. The hill-top wind blows, the clouds drive, sun and storm move on the water, the crazy black stones and the ruins jut from the brilliant grass. It is dramatic and romantic, the perfect Brontë site. . . . All at once a throng of words and images invade the pilgrim's mind – Heathcliff and Catherine, Zamorna, Rochester, black moors and snow, the Byronic genesis of Gondal, the Pruntys by a stroke of wild magniloquence become Sicilian Brontës. . . . By a strange contradiction, or perhaps by poetic justice, it is the grave of quiet Anne that is the focus. All their beginnings seem to crowd into her end.

[1] The age is incorrect. Anne was twenty-nine.

Part Two

ANNE BRONTË:
HER WORK

by Derek Stanford

NOTE

I have placed my chapter on Anne Brontë as Poet before that on Anne as Novelist, which procedure might be thought to stand in need of explanation.

Anne, with justice, is more commonly remembered as the author of *Agnes Grey* and *The Tenant of Wildfell Hall* than as the author of some hundred odd poems, none of which – for all their modest graces – have entered the popular memory.

My reason, then, for treating Anne's poetry first is that it constitutes a sort of inner autobiography, so that an account of it follows quite naturally upon Miss Harrison's account of Anne's outward life-story.

As touching the quotation of source-material – passages from letters, novels, or poems – I have sometimes reappropriated such to my own purpose and comment. I hope such reduplication of the text, after Miss Harrison's presentation of it, will not appear uncalled for. It seemed better, however, to give the reader a chance to keep his eye upon the object (even at the cost of some repetition) than to speak with the evidence not present to hand. Where there has been any diversity of comment, I have indicated in a footnote the corresponding page in Miss Harrison's portion of the book.

The passages from *Conversation in Ebury Street* by George Moore are quoted by kind permission of Mr C. D. Medley.

D. S.

ANNE BRONTË AS POET

XII

The Poet's Mind

THE POETRY OF ANNE BRONTË is largely autobiographical. This it is that guarantees its interest, while at the same time limiting its range.

Apart from less than a dozen excursions into the world of the Gondal myth (an imaginative game which the younger sister shared with Emily, who took the lead in it), Anne had a way of sticking close to her own experience in the poetry she wrote; in other words, her imagination was reflective rather than creative; it functioned by working back over the events and impressions of her actual daily living, instead of inventing and elaborating a set of fictions. But this is not to suggest that her imaginative faculty was defective. In his book, *English Prose Style*, Sir Herbert Read observes a nice distinction between the terms 'imagination' and 'invention'. It is this latter he takes to be the fiction-making ability. Too often, it would seem, the terms are confused, and the under-development of the one is taken for an absence of the other.

If we dwell upon the matter a moment, we see that Sir Herbert is not just making an abstract differentiation between words, but is describing a normal thinking process. Without reflecting about its nature, we readily allow Wordsworth's *Prelude* to be a poem of great imagination; yet here, as with the bulk of Anne's poems, the subject is not fictional. Like Anne's poetry, *The Prelude* deals with the given substance of the poet's life. In saying that both are examples of auto-biographical composition, we imply, of course, that they are not *imaginary*. To call them *unimaginative* would be a very different matter.

The comparison of Anne's poems with *The Prelude* is naturally one of kind. Wordsworth's masterpiece is possessed of vastly higher literary and spiritual merits. Even as a mode of autobiography, *The*

Prelude is far in advance of Anne's work – it is conscious in intention, sequential in development, and sustained in purpose and treatment. Beside this poem, and considered as a form of life-story, Anne's poetry is fragmentary and unequal, a broken series of lyrical confessions. But after all these elementary discrepancies are noted, the comparison remains useful. Different as *The Prelude* is in having a conscious *working-plan*, it is one with Anne's poems in being the product of the same *working force.* This force I shall call the *reflective imagination* – an habitual power of mind playing backwards and forwards over past experience, re-creating scenes and situations, not as objective history, but as the material of personal feelings, discovering their meaning in the light of later experience, and passing judgement on them in accordance with this knowledge.

When I say, then, that Anne's poetry is largely autobiographical, I am really thinking of two claims it has upon us. The first is the simple claim arousing our interest by acquainting us with the course of her life viewed from the inside. This biographical interest is one every poet possesses whose work records or reflects his existence. Regarding Anne, it is indeed the keener in as much as it feeds our curiosity concerning the Brontë circle as a whole. How Anne reacted to her sisters and her brother; how far she was prepared to take her cue from Emily in the game of Gondal myth-making; what she thought and felt about the fall of Branwell; and what were her sentiments towards the Reverend Weightman – we seek enlightenment on these points and are grateful for what the poems can tell us.

But the second claim upon our interest, still of an autobiographical order, is one that is special and proper to Anne, and derives from the nature of her talent. That talent, in poetical matters, I have already defined as the power of reflective imagination; and it is this power of first recollecting and then assessing past experience, which leaves in Anne's poetry not a mere record of the emotional happenings of her life, but a scrupulous stock-taking of them. Much of Anne's poetry is in fact didactic, a term to which current usage has imparted a certain chill. But Anne is a teacher with a difference, for she is concerned not so much in instructing others as in discovering what is right for herself. Her desire is to refine her own moral education. It is herself and her own problems which she examines, and herself whom she exhorts. She does not address her thoughts to the solution of wrong or evil in the abstract; nor does she universalize her own predicaments, although in themselves they are universal issues. What we recognize in reading Anne's poems is the impress of experience. We feel and can trace her susceptibility to various sensations, we mark the inroads which impressions make, we see reflection at work, and sense the pressure of conscience. As didactic compositions these poems resemble, not the general demonstration of a theorem, but its application to a particular case.

A plausible argument might be made out for calling Anne a pragmatist in moral affairs. Keeping always close to the outline of experience as it presented itself to her, she did not attempt to legislate for others. Her own troubles and dilemmas absorbed her moral energies completely; and if she was rigorous towards herself, she was liberal and forbearing to everybody else.

But part of Anne's essential experience was certainly of a religious order. It was not, it is true, the type of experience such as one often finds in religious mysticism, which takes place, as it were, on a separate plane. Between her religious thoughts and feelings, and the thoughts and feelings arising in Anne from other kinds of experience, there was no divorce or separation. Indeed, we may say that her religious experience was largely quickened and called into play by the pressure of other experience upon her, and the need to adapt herself to its tension. Just how far Anne employed her religion to organize her difficult experience, and just how far she knew of her need for faith, is probably impossible to assess. Here, I want briefly to suggest that we look at Anne's poetry as a species of what we have come to call existential thinking.

In choosing this term I am not referring to the thought of any one philosophic school. I am not attempting to show that Anne believed, as Sartre does, that existence precedes essence[1] (which as a Christian she would never have accepted). All I imply is, that in Anne's poems, and particularly in their didactic passages, the thought is not of an abstract kind but is moulded and compelled by direct experience.

From Charlotte's words on her sister an image of the younger Brontë has been formed that does small credit to Anne as an artist, and under-rates her status as a person. Taking Charlotte's portrait on trust, we think of Anne as gentle, ineffectual, devout, obedient, and conventional – a mind with scant personal features of its own. And when, with such preconceptions as these, we come to Anne's poems and cursorily mark the moral occupation in them, we assume

[1] i.e. that the ends and ideals of human existence are not inherent in it.

that it proves her conventional nature, and very probably close the book.

Our tacit equation between the moral and the conventional is often shown to be false. It is certainly mistaken when applied to Anne. But we must be alive to another danger for though the morality in Anne's poetry is not the expression of mere convention, it squares at most points with traditional teaching,[1] and 'the traditional', like 'the conventional', to many modern readers is suspect.

If we are to lay ourselves open to Anne's poems and appreciate her strangely personal moral experience, we must make some small concessions. We must be prepared to admit that the tenets of a traditional morality can be held and practised with enthusiasm, and that the dictates of such a morality need not impose themselves on the individual as an external tyranny, but be welcomed as consolidating his own experience. If we allow ourselves to entertain these two 'old-fashioned' hypotheses, we shall read Anne's poetry in a different light, and discover in the place of respectable pieties, a record of the growth of a moral intelligence, earnest, self-questioning, and sincere.

The poems, then, may be said to constitute a moral autobiography which, like all such autobiographies contains other than moral matters; for it is not until we are hemmed in by the congestion of experience that morality becomes a passionate business. Thus, there are the records of other elements in these poems besides the moral interest: fantasies of love, and its actual impact, and later still the lament for love bereaved; thoughts of friendship, and feelings of home-sickness; and brief but genuine enjoyment of nature. But none of these experiences in themselves seemed to hold the key to their own solution. Regarded separately, each distinct experience inveigled Anne in its trammels. As ways and aspects of life, they did not make sense; did not add up to a single clear meaning.

So it is that the moral reflection in Anne's poems increased in force as she grew older and the insufficiency and non-coherence of different experiences were borne in upon her. The more that life appeared to disappoint her, to break its promises and ruin her chances, the more firmly she held to the one interpretation that saved her will from disintegrating. This interpretation was simple enough. Twenty-five years odd before her, Keats had discovered it for himself when he

---

[1] There are some important exceptions to this: one of which is touched on in the study on her novels, and the other observed later in this essay.

spoke of the world as 'a Vale of Soul-making'. Anne, rather more bleakly declared 'Life was for labour, not for joy'.

But what is morally significant in Anne's poetry is not the enunciation of any general principle of living, so much as the constant presence and pressure of conscience and reflection.

It is in this sense that her poems are most rewardingly autobiographical.

XIII

Poetic Fiction

ANNE'S GONDAL POEMS are eight in number; and these, together with one or two other pseudonymous pieces, constitute the sum of her 'imaginary' compositions. For the rest,[1] her poems are concerned with the happenings of her physical existence and the commentary of her spirit upon them.

We may glance first at the 'imaginary' poems.

Anne began writing verse in 1836; and although Gondal poems follow at intervals during the period of the next ten years, the greater number of her 'imaginary' pieces were composed between 1836 and 1840.

These poems are more buoyant in spirit, more unreserved in their expression of hope and expectation, than those which follow after. There are probably many reasons for this. Anne's powers of make-believe had not as yet discovered their range and limitation. Stimulated, perhaps, for the first time by the Gondal game which was started in 1831, Anne's desire and ability to invent a world of her own were probably strongest in the years between 1836 and 1840.

Not leaving home until 1839, to take her initial 'situation', Anne had still to taste, as Charlotte said, 'the cup of life as it is mixed for the class termed "Governesses" '. This cup was particularly disagreeable to her; but it was not the bitterest she was to know. She was not yet sensible of the shadow of death. The anticipation of love had not been thwarted. Branwell's touch of genius had not proved ineffectual and his moral character had not yet collapsed. In short, Anne had not yet been hauled down to earth by the weight and drag of experience. Her fate had hardly begun to form itself, and her destiny and death had not looked her in the face.

---

[1] The one important exception is her poem 'The Three Guides', a moral allegory.

Some of these poems, it is true, deal with partings and unrequited love; but these are the traditional stock-in-trade of younger poets who have still to discover their own feelings, and while these are lying partly dormant exercise their emotions on the sorrows of others. In any case, the theme of grief in these poems is handled in a light melodious manner. They are graceful 'tasks', lacking that graver note which results from Anne's fuller acquaintance with her lot.

Prisons – one of Emily's favourite imaginary purlieus – figure in three of these poems ('A voice from the Dungeon', 'The Captain's Dream', and 'The North Wind'), but a love- and nature-interest are present also; and there is little of that abnormal sadistic-masochistic gloating which Emily imparted to poems of a similar theme.

The third of these pieces is filled with a blithe natural excitement. The movement of the wind seems to billow out the poem, contracting it suddenly and filling it again, through a sequence of changing stanzas and rhythms. The conclusion, in which the prisoner bewails her captivity, but asks the wind to continue blowing so that she may hear it and feel the less captive, lacks the vivid impress of the earlier portion. We can see that Anne, in her present state, found it easier to identify herself with the vital unshackled wind than with the gloom-worn prisoner:

> *That wind is from the North: I know it well;*
> *No other breeze could have so wild a swell*
> *Now deep and loud it thunders round my cell,*
> *Then faintly dies, and softly sighs,*
> *And moans and murmurs mournfully.*
> *I know its language: thus it speaks to me:*
>
> *'I have passed over thy own mountains dear,*
> *Thy northern mountains, and they still are free;*
> *Still lonely, wild, majestic, bleak, and drear,*
> *And stern, and lovely, as they used to be*
>
> *'When thou, a young enthusiast,*
> *As wild and free as they,*
> *O'er rocks, and glens, and snowy heights,*
> *Didst often love to stray.*
>
> *'I've blown the pure, untrodden snows*
> *In whirling eddies from their brows;*

And I have howled in caverns wild,
Where thou, a joyous mountain-child,
   Didst dearly love to be.
The sweet world is not changed, but thou
Art pining in a dungeon now,
   Where thou must ever be.

'No voice but mine can reach thy ear,
And Heaven has kindly sent me here
   To mourn and sigh with thee,
And tell thee of the cherished land
   Of thy nativity.'

Blow on, wild wind; thy solemn voice,
   However sad and drear,
Is nothing to the gloomy silence
   I have had to bear.

Hot tears are streaming from my eyes,
   But these are better far
Than that dull, gnawing, tearless time,
   The stupor of despair.

Confined and hopeless as I am,
   Oh, speak of liberty!
Oh, tell me of my mountain home,
   And I will welcome thee!

The grief and anxiety of love in absence is the theme of the two poems entitled 'The Parting'. But this composition (in two parts) cannot be said to concern itself in any real fashion with the feelings of desertion. It is not an analysis or explication of the emotion of bereavement, but a straightforward study of romantic story-telling in the form of the romantic ballad. When we compare these swift tripping lines, and their unreflecting felicity of expression, with the slower graver measure of her later poems, we feel the greater weight of experience in the latter.

But now the lustre of her eye
   Is dimmed with many a tear;
Her footstep's elasticity
   Is timed with grief and fear.
The rose has left her hollow cheeks;
In low and mournful tones she speaks,

describes what has happened to the lonely heroine ('The lady of Abyerno's hall') in purely external terms. The limits and workings of her sorrow are presented to us by means of a formula long associated with narrative verse. The outward symptoms of change are noted, but there is no indwelling stress in this description. It is not experience in itself, but the signs of transition from one state of experience to another, that Anne is concerned with in this poem. Very different is the account of the effects of time and change in her poem 'Self-Communion', written in 1848, some ten years later.

> God *alters not; but Time on me*
>   *A wide and wondrous change has wrought:*
> *And in these parted years I see*
>   *Cause for grave care and saddening thought.*
> *I see that time, and toil, and truth*
>   *An inward hardness can impart, –*
> *Can freeze the generous blood of youth,*
>   *And steel full fast the tender heart.*

The inner 'wasting power of time' is clearly manifest in these verses. Action and incident, at this stage, have added up for Anne to that compound phenomenon which, in a special sense, we call 'experience'; and 'experience', here, has the further been refined by reflection. This is a quality in Anne's thought and expression which will not be found in her earlier pieces.

But apart from the absence of the pressure of experience, which reveals itself negatively, so to speak, in Anne's 'imaginary' poetry, giving even to those poems which deal with grief an almost truant or holiday air, her buoyancy and anticipation make themselves felt more positively in devising a story with a happy ending. 'Alexander and Zenobia' (1837) treats of the plight of lovers who are separated but manage to come together at last. Another aspect of optimism about this poem is its youthfulness of feeling.

This choice of innocent undefiled characters makes a pleasant change from the torrid type of hero – seared with the lightning of tempestuous experience – which Emily took over wholesale from Byron.[1]

---

[1] Anne did not escape the infection wholly. Emily, no doubt through her powerful enthusiasm, communicated it to her younger sister who, fortunately, did not take it too badly. Her early poem 'The Captain's Dream' acquaints us with the all-too-well-known physiognomy of the Byronic type: 'woe-worn

The two young people of this poem appeal to our sympathy, even if only at a surface level. The presentation of these lovers, and the charm they exert upon us, is admittedly of a conventional order. It is generally the fashion for critics to speak of Anne's moral poems as conventional pieces, but if by that adjective we imply that which is artificial rather than real, imitative rather than first-hand, it is these early and 'imaginary' poems which more properly deserve the term.

For instance, the moral element in these poems is always correct; nay, more – exemplary. Unlike Emily in her Gondal poems, Anne shows no enthusiasm for the ideas of revenge and return to power. But the impeccable renunciations of the opportunity to persecute and torture, which Anne's 'imaginary' characters make, do not bear the mark of experience. As Anne presents them, they have only the force of conventionally noble gestures (and fictitious gestures, at that). In one poem entitled 'Song' (1845), she makes a leader of the Republican party muse upon the victory of their cause over the Royalist faction:

> *We have their princely homes, and they*
> *To our wild haunts are chased away,*
>   *Dark woods and desert caves;*
> *And we can range from hill to hill,*
> *And chase our vanquished victors still,*
> *Small respite will they find, until*
>   *They slumber in their graves.*

> *But I would rather be the hare*
> *That, crouching in its sheltered lair,*
>   *Must start at every sound;*
> *That, forced from cornfields waving wide,*
> *Is driven to seek the bare hillside,*
> *Or in the tangled copse-wood hide,*
>   *Than be the hunter's hound!*

And in another piece, with the same title, written the very next day,[1] the pomps of power and the emptiness of triumph, as well as the

cheek', 'ashy lips', 'haggard eyes', and grief-imprinted brow. The image, however, clearly did not mean the same for Anne as it did for Emily; and her verse, for the most part, is singularly free of these monotonous imitation figures.

[1] A third poem bearing the same date, 4 September 1845, which carries no hint of being a Gondal composition, cogitates upon the vanity of things. This piece, 'Vanitas Vanitatum. Omnia Vanitas' is very much a conventional

risk of mortal danger which the soul runs in conflicts of this kind, form the substance of meditation :

> *It may be pleasant to recall the death*
> *Of those beneath whose sheltering roof you lie;*
> *But I would rather press the mountain-heath*
> *With nought to shield me from the starry sky.*
> *And dream of yet untasted victory —*
> *A distant hope — and feel that I am free!*
>
> *Oh, happy life! To range the mountains wild,*
> *The waving woods, — or ocean's heaving breast,*
> *With limbs unfettered, conscience undefiled,*
> *And choosing where to wander, where to rest!*
> *Hunted, opposed, but ever strong to cope*
> *With toils and perils; ever full of hope!*
>
> *'Our flower is budding.' When that word was heard*
> *On desert shore, or breezy mountain's brow;*
> *Wherever said, what glorious thoughts it stirred!*
> *'Twas budding then; say, 'Has it blossomed now'*
> *Is* this *the end we struggled to obtain?*
> *Oh, for the wandering Outlaw's life again!*

What is important about these poems is not their conventional moral statement, but the light which these statements throw upon the temperament of the poet. For if they fail to convince us that they are the fruits of reflective experience, they do at least tell us about certain virtues inherent in Anne's disposition. These are the gifts of charity, and mercy, of humbleness, forgiveness, and simplicity. By simplicity, in this context, I mean the quality which fits its possessor for a quiet retired life in accordance with nature, away from the stress and intrigue of a competitive existence and position :

> *Oh, happy life! To range the mountains wild,*
> *The waving woods, — or ocean's heaving breast,*
> *With limbs unfettered, conscience undefiled,*
> *And choosing where to wander, where to rest!*

abstract of the course to which all life's pleasures tend. 'Toil', 'Vanity', 'Wealth', and 'Fame' (replete with capitals, as in other of Anne's poems), are here merely moral and literary ciphers; not as they so often are with this poet — the shorthand compounds of personal experience. But the poem, taken in conjunction with the other pieces written on the same day, shows the way in which Anne's mind was working.

These virtues, which I shall call indigenous, would have fitted her for the natural life, for an existence such as Rousseau had in mind – an ideal of loyal unpretentious living. But this elementary instinctive happiness was denied her. Anne was led by the pressure of experience – by the thumb-screws of frustration and renunciation – to acquire a new set of qualities, more conscious and meaningful in their working. Of these I shall be speaking later.

But among Anne's 'imaginary' poems there is one ('I Dreamt Last Night' (1846)) which passes beyond a display of conventional thought and feeling. This piece – the last of her compositions to be signed with a pseudonym – deals with the memory of early friendship which political passions have divided. The poignancy of such estrangement, which Coleridge expressed in 'Christabel', is augmented in this poem by the fact that one of the friends has killed the other in order to advance the cause he espouses.

Some of the passages are not so well handled, but the dream which revisits the older of the friends (some time after his act of killing) is vivid, tender, and strangely authentic. He dreams he is with his young friend, in boyhood days before their separation:

> *It was a well-known mountain scene,*
> *Wild steeps, with rugged glens between,*
> *I should have thirsted to explore*
> *Had I not trod them oft before;*
>
> *A younger boy was with me there,*
> *His hand upon my shoulder leant;*
> *His heart, like mine, was free from care,*
> *His breath with sportive toil was spent;*
>
> *For my rough pastimes he would share,*
> *And equal dangers loved to dare,*
> *Though seldom I would care to vie*
> *In learning's keen pursuit with him; –*
> *I loved the free and open sky*
> *Better than books and tutors grim;*
>
> *And we had wandered far that day*
> *O'er that forbidden ground away:*
> *Ground, to our rebel feet how dear, –*
> *Danger and freedom both were there! –*
> *Had climbed the steep and coursed the dale,*
> *Until his strength began to fail.*

He bade me pause and breathe awhile,
But spoke it with a happy smile;
His lips were parted to inhale
The breeze that swept the ferny dale,

And chased the clouds across the sky
And waved his locks in passing by,
And fanned my cheek — so real did seem
This strange, untrue, but truth-like dream.

And as we stood, I laughed to see
   His fair young cheek so brightly glow;
He turned his sparkling eyes to me
   With looks no painter's art could show,

Nor words portray, but earnest mirth,
   And truthful love I there descried,
And, while I thought upon his worth,
   My bosom glowed with joy and pride.

I could have kissed his forehead fair,
   I could have clasped him to my heart,
But tenderness with me was rare,
   And I must take a rougher part;

I seized him in my boisterous mirth,
I bore him struggling to the earth,
And grappling, strength for strength, we strove,
He half in wrath, I all for love.

But I gave o'er that strife at length,
Ashamed of my superior strength,
The rather that I marked his eye
Kindle as if a change were nigh.

We paused to breathe a little space,
   Reclining on the heather-brae;
But still I gazed upon his face,
   To watch the shadow pass away.

I grasped his hand, and it had fled:
A smile, a laugh, and all was well;
Upon my breast he leant his head,
And into graver talk we fell, –

The insight into the physical tenderness which the older boy feels for the younger in this powerful platonic relationship (in Plato's own original sense) is an unusual achievement for a young woman poet. Certainly the understanding which she shows for the trial of strength between the two friends (an archetypal form of communion exclusive almost to the male) marks a rare triumph for the feminine author. The constituent motives and feelings of this contest – high animal spirits, boyish aggressiveness, the urge to power, and physical affection too shy to show itself save in mock combat – have all been exquisitely identified by Anne.

Even the elder's sense of guilt at having abused his more adult strength, the feeling that in his physical coercion he may have acted the bully, has not escaped Anne's inward observation. Neither has the way in which the older boy anxiously watches the face of the younger, like a lover looking intently at his mistress for signs of unhappiness or displeasure. Consummately, delicately, Anne has caught all this.

This poem is of particular importance because it reveals spontaneously – in a way that an unimaginary piece might find itself too inhibited to do – the tender instincts of Anne's nature. And here it is necessary to distinguish between the idea of tenderness and the idea of sentimentality, and to recognize that in this poem what we have is a genuine expression of the former. If we agree with Sir Herbert Read that the term 'sentimental' best describes 'extreme cases of emotional deliquescence'[1] – a degree of feeling disproportionate to the facts of the situation – and decide to reserve the word 'tender' for a ready natural warmth of heart, then the aptness with which we may fit it to Anne assists us in approaching her love-poetry.

One of the attributes of Anne's tenderness is to be seen in the manner in which she identified herself with the young. This is a factor more strongly present in Anne than in either of her sisters. The affection and grief of the virgin lovers in 'Alexander and Zenobia' gives an early indication of this. The gentle intuition of the deep boyhood friendship in 'I Dreamt last Night' gives us another. A third

---

[1] See his essay on Sterne in *The Sense of Glory* (1929).

poem 'The Lover' (1846), written some time after Branwell's dismissal from his post at Thorp Green, and which may possibly refer to his condition, sympathizes with the unhappy suitor:

> *But such wild, such bitter, grieving*
> *Fits not slender boys like thee;*
> *Those deep sighs should not be heaving*
> *Breasts so young as thine must be.*

The Poetry of Love

This constitutional kindness of Anne towards the young was part of a nature which longed for children. Unlike Charlotte, whose lack of partiality for children has been noted,[1] Anne – even in her trying career as a governess, showed a natural affection for them.[2]

So whereas we may say that in Charlotte's wish for love, the desire for a man was the strongest factor, in Anne this natural need was augmented by a very definite desire for children. In Anne's poetry, references to this maternal urge are vividly present: in Charlotte's, they are absent.

When we come to examine Anne's longer and more reflective pieces, with those in which we can feel the moral and religious elements working, it is all the more necessary to remember the two-sided nature of Anne's wish for love. Recalling it here, we are able to gauge the measure of her deep frustration, and the better able therefore to estimate her strenuous efforts to accept this state.

Anne admitted to her longings for a child in more than one of her poems. 'Dreams' (1845) contains the frankest expression of want:

> *While on my lonely couch I lie,*
> *I seldom feel myself alone,*
> *For fancy fills my dreaming eye*
> *With scenes and pleasures of its own.*

> *Then I may cherish at my breast*
> *An infant's form beloved and fair;*
> *May smile and soothe it into rest,*
> *With all a mother's fondest care.*

[1] By Swinburne and Augustine Birrell and George Henry Lewes.
[2] See the example quoted on pages 59-61.

How sweet to feel its helpless form
  Depending thus on me alone;
And while I hold it safe and warm,
  What bliss to think it is my own!

And glances then may meet my eyes
  That daylight never showed to me;
What raptures in my bosom rise
  Those earnest looks of love to see!

To feel my hand so kindly prest,
  To know myself beloved at last;
To think my heart has found a rest,
  My life of solitude is past!

But then to wake and find it flown,
  The dream of happiness destroyed;
To find myself unloved, alone,
  What tongue can speak the dreary void!

A heart whence warm affections flow,
  Creator, Thou hast given to me;
And am I only thus to know
  How sweet the joys of love would be?

Quite the most poignant thought in this poem is the one contained in the last stanza; namely, that far from being really unsuited to domestic love, she had a special faculty for it, a talent which she felt was given her by God; so that more than her physical birthright was denied her in its frustration. We note, too, that in the original MS this last stanza has been lightly cancelled, as if Anne could not bear to contemplate what she had so clearly stated; and yet could not bring herself, too harshly, to cancel it outright. The extent of her self-knowledge was a danger to her.

Anne's poetic imagination had long been dwelling on a child, for as early as 1837, again in dream-form, we are given the image of a mother and her baby, to which – on this occasion – is added the figure of the father. Another poem, entitled 'Verses to a Child' (1838) reveals the same natural preoccupation. This time the mother has been left with a child, whose father has deserted her. The love between mother and child is strangely paralleled by the early love between her and her husband when they were children. Here we meet with another instance of Anne's tender feelings for the young, with whom she easily identified herself. It is possible that this interest in child or adolescent lovers tells us something of Anne's idea of love. Nowhere in Anne's work, in verse or in prose (save in the figure of the young farmer Gilbert Markham, in her novel *The Tenant of Wildfell Hall*) do we have a personification of passion.[1] Shared experience, sympathy, affection, and loyalty, together with the thought of raising children: these seem to constitute the 'notes' of love as Anne conceived it in her poems.

Few or none of Anne's love-poems contain a hint of hope or joy. It seems to have been her cross to endure

> *All the pain and all the sorrow*
> *That attend the steps of love.*
> ('The Lover', 1846)

Briefly, the course of her emotions – as far as her poems reveal them – seems to have been something like this: initial excitement, absence, and despair, followed by the death of the beloved. The poems that record these are followed by pieces (and most of her love-poetry belongs to this group) in which the image of the loved one is called up by memory, and praised. It is in these latter compositions that we get Anne's best handling of the subject, as they are largely the fruits of what I have termed her leading talent, that is, her reflective imagination.

Whether Mr Weightman, her father's curate, whom Anne was known to be fond of, is the subject of these poems does not concern my purpose directly. Most of the evidence points that way, for he died in the October of 1842; and all the love-poems which speak of their subject as being dead are dated later. One only of these poems

---

[1] Huntingdon's affair with Arabella, in the same novel, can hardly be dignified with the title of a passionate love. Hot and uncontrolled as his feeling for her is, it lacks all the exalting psychological symptoms which generally accompany ardent romantic passion. At its best, it is a coarse passionate lust. Stendhal, it is true, would have included it within his category of 'sensual love'. But then, Stendhal in his famous division of love into four kinds would not have found a place for Anne's notion of this feeling. Perhaps it might be argued in defence of this lack, that Anne worked only from imagination, whereas Stendhal wrote from experience. None the less, Stendhal's neglect of married love as a type on its own may be considered as a serious omission. His preoccupation with 'affairs', with intrigues, with adulteries, and short-lived flirtations give to his general pronouncements a somewhat limited Gallic flavour.

by Anne ('Oh, they have robbed me of the hope') appears to imply that the loved one is still living, but its import is by no means clear. The editors of the Shakespeare Head Brontë Poems, Thomas J. Wise and J. Alex Symington, place it as '*circa* 1845', but the original MS is undated.[1]

What remains relevant to the present line of inquiry is that most of the facts appear to establish some connexion between 'real' experience and the love-life recounted in Anne's poems. In other words, the voice of experience – the voice of Anne's reflective imagination which we hear increasingly in these poems – seems to be speaking about substantial happenings; and because of this, we incline to trust its tone of authenticity the more.

The excitement of love is found once only in these poems. That perhaps is because Anne recognized that she had little chance of prospering in this field. Anne was attractive (clearly more so than either of her sisters), but then she was poor, often away from home in a humble dependent position, and lacked that boldness which can serve in place of luck. There was also Charlotte to contend with, who liked to make decisions for others; and perhaps the family as a whole were apt to prove an obstacle.

> *Oh, they have robbed me of the hope*
> *My spirit held so dear;*
> *They will not let me hear the voice*
> *My soul delights to hear.*

She wrote, ambiguously, in an undated poem. It is possible that Anne was here referring to that compulsory family security which Victorian maidens must so often have found galling.

The only excitement in Anne's love-poetry is the excitement of concealment. 'Self-Congratulations' (a pseudonymous poem, signed 'Olivia Vernon' and dated 1 January 1840), tells how a young girl listens to the foot-steps of the man she loves passing by outside the house:

> *There was no trembling in my voice,*
> *No blush upon my cheek,*
> *No lustrous sparkle in my eyes,*
> *Of hope, or joy, to speak;*

[1] See Miss Harrison's interpretation of the background to this poem, pages 78-79.

> *But, oh! my spirit burned within,*
> *My heart beat full and fast!*
> *He came not nigh — he went away —*
> *And then my joy was past.*
>
> *And yet my comrades marked it not:*
> *My voice was still the same;*
> *They saw me smile, and o'er my face*
> *No signs of sadness came.*
> *They little knew my hidden thoughts;*
> *And they will* never *know*
> *The aching anguish of my heart,*
> *The bitter burning woe!*

This initial expectancy quickly yielded to a passion of despair. In 1841 (away from home, at her post as governess), she is writing the poem 'Appeal':[1]

> *O! I am very weary,*
> *Though tears no longer flow;*
> *My eyes are tired of weeping,*
> *My heart is sick of woe;*
>
> *My life is very lonely,*
> *My days pass heavily,*
> *I'm weary of repining,*
> *Wilt thou not come to me?*
>
> *Oh, didst thou know my longings*
> *For thee, from day to day,*
> *My hopes, so often blighted,*
> *Thou wouldst not thus delay!*

With the exception of one piece already quoted, the following poems deal with love in the past: not with the death of love, but with love after death. 'Night' (1845) promises to the bereft the slender consolation of dreams; but the three other pieces struggle to reach a higher plane of acceptance.

Anne's strange compensating reflection, which rescues all thoughts of the loved one's death from a blind and bitter nihilism, reverberates in each poem. This is not to say that the grief dies down, for lament is present in all of them. But in each one the note of lament is followed

[1] In the original MS entitled 'Lines written at Thorp Green'.

by the note of praise. 'A Reminiscence' (1844), like all of these three, begins with the fact of loss and absence, but hints at a clue to endurance in the last two stanzas:

> *Yet, though I cannot see thee more,*
> *'Tis still a comfort to have seen;*
> *And though thy transient life is o'er,*
> *'Tis sweet to think that thou hast been;*

> *To think a soul so near divine,*
> *Within a form so angel fair,*
> *United to a heart like thine,*
> *Has gladdened once our humble sphere.*

'Severed and Gone' (1847) carries the exploration of absence and loss a stage farther. From thinking of the body in its tomb, Anne passes on to consider the higher but more distant residence of its spirit. And the thought of Heaven, in this context, offers no comfort because it accentuates the sense of separation. Then, Laodamia-like she prays to be given a vision of the lost one. The prayer is not answered, not granted directly in physical fashion, as in Wordsworth's poem on this theme; but consolation is granted in the form of a thought. In a way we can say that Anne's poem is the kinder of the two; for Wordsworth's Laodamia is given the sight of her husband only to have him taken away with counsels of self-restraint on his lips. What consoles Anne is the thought of the imperishability of her lover's essence. This has its origin in her memory of him:

> *Thou breathest in my bosom yet,*
> *And dwellest in my beating heart;*
> *And while I cannot quite forget,*
> *Thou, darling, canst not quite depart.*

But this memory assumes the properties of vision. Because of her loved one's existence in the past, the present and the future have been changed. What his existence has come to mean to her is a revelation of possibility:

> *Life seems more sweet that thou didst live,*
> *And men more true that thou wert one;*
> *Nothing is lost that thou didst give,*
> *Nothing destroyed that thou hast done.*

So even after death has separated them, Anne can bring herself to write:

> *And while I cannot quite forget,*
> *Thou, darling, canst not quite depart.*

This is what we may term a creative use of grief, creative in the change it works upon our whole psychological approach. Instead of bitter emptiness, instead of dull passivity of damped-down feeling, Anne has understood how necessity can be received in a positive fashion. Her acceptance has become constructive.

Part of the process of this creative grief consists in a deed of self-transcendence, by which a personal sorrow is forgotten in the gesture of celebrating another. The lament is absorbed in an act of tribute; a passion to commemorate transcends the sense of grief.

'Farewell to Thee! but not Farewell' (1847), Anne's last love-poem, speaks of the perpetuity of the presence of the loved one active in her. This essence she feels to be working like a yeast in the otherwise uninspired present – a force that has power to raise her flagging spirits:

> *Farewell to thee! but not farewell*
> *To all my fondest thoughts of thee:*
> *Within my heart they still shall dwell;*
> *And they shall cheer and comfort me.*
>
> *O beautiful, and full of grace!*
> *If thou hadst never met mine eye,*
> *I had not dreamed a living face*
> *Could fancied charms so far outvie.*
>
> *If I may ne'er behold again*
> *That form and face so dear to me,*
> *Nor hear thy voice, still would I fain*
> *Preserve for aye their memory.*
>
> *That voice, the magic of whose tone*
> *Could wake an echo in my breast,*
> *Creating feelings that, alone,*
> *Could make my tranced spirit blest.*

So the story of Anne's love-life, as reflected in her poetry, comes to an end. In material terms, it could be said that all she experienced was hunger and loss. But hunger and loss were the raw substances which reflection and imagination transmuted. Love, which the world tends to understand as a form of possessiveness, or – at best – possession, came – through struggle – to be understood by Anne as an affection of acceptance. Her unfortunate experience of human love brought her nearer to a love for God, and made her acceptance of hardship and frustration (which she took to be the work of the Divine Will) the deeper.

The Didactic Poems

In one sense, the greater part of Anne's poetry is didactic; but in the more limited meaning of the word, the didactic pieces (wherein the concern is wholly moral matters) number only half a dozen. But of these, five constitute the most vigorous and interesting section of Anne's verse as a vehicle of her thought. This section contains the longest poems she wrote, and most of them belong to her later years.

In them, we have the spectacle of one who in youth was shy but hopeful and is now no longer hopeful but still retiring, bringing to bear an honesty and maturity of mind on the problems of her existence. Courage (not defiance) and clarity of approach characterize this scrutiny of hers.

'Fluctuations' (1844) is the record, in the form of analogy, of Anne's attempts to keep her spirits up. And the means she uses are not Emily's for she sounds no note of truculent challenge. Anne's effort to retain a stout heart (something she was seldom able to do) depended on two factors: her own moral will, and her prayers for grace. And even the first of these resources, the moral will, she knew to be dependent upon her access to grace. Not that her will was feeble. In fact, both from her life and from her novels, we know that Anne could generally be relied on to *do* the right thing, or to *assert* it by word or thought. Towards the outside world, in her attitude or conduct, we feel that her will was largely irreproachable. But what was beyond its power was to keep her spirits raised. 'Without the resources of joy' (a poignant phrase that Coleridge uses), her spirits often became despondent; and she had not the vigour to restore them. Then it was that grace seemed imperative to her, and the search for it became one of her most consistent preoccupations. Often in her poems (the religious pieces), she deals with this quest directly. At other times, as here, in this descriptively entitled composition, she looks for it in terms of analogy:

What though the Sun had left my sky;
To save me from despair
The blessed Moon arose on high,
And shone serenely there.

The light (of grace) is followed in the poem through its alternate shinings and dowsings. First it is the sun, and then the moon that gives light; after that the clouds obscure the sky, and all is gloomy until a star shines forth. This, in its turn, is extinguished; but is followed by a meteor. And when this last is plunged out of sight, the darkness is shortly relieved again by the moon, which makes a second appearance. And that this returning of the light is not felt to be a mere accident of nature, is suggested to us by the last stanza:

Kind Heaven! increase that silvery gleam,
And bid these clouds depart,
And let her soft celestial beams
Restore my fainting heart.

In the original MS of the poem, the divine intervention, symbolized by the moon's re-emergence is more plainly stated. 'And let her kind and holy beam . . .' is poetically inferior to '. . . . her soft celestial beam', but it makes Anne's meaning plainer.

It is possible, too, that the Sun and the Moon in this poem are symbols, respectively, of love and faith – 'The greatest blessings life can show', as Anne was later to describe them.

Love, like the sun, never shone again for Anne; and faith, like the moon, was her guiding light hereafter. This suggestion in nowise runs counter to our first reading of the poem. It does not change, but adds to, its meaning; and may therefore be permitted.

When we speak of 'Views of Life' (1845) as a Johnsonian poem, a poem somewhat on the lines of 'The Vanity of Human Wishes', we imply its type and tone rather than its status. But if it lacks the concentrated force, the compactness of judgement and statement, of Johnson's poem, it does at least aspire towards a similar effect. The grave reflective beat of the poem is the same;[1] and there is the same exploration of the vanity of things beneath their appearances – a searching moral scrutiny which takes us to the cliff-edge of scepticism and pulls back, surely, and just in time.

The poem is divided into two parts, and takes the form of an argument. In the first part, Anne defends her position from those who

[1] Though not written in the same rhyme or metre.

accuse her of morbidity. She understands their attitude, she says, for she too, once believed life was all promise. Life has disproved this notion, she says – for time has a way of revealing the truth. It is with life as it shows itself, 'chilled by the damps of truth', that she must now deal.

The second part of the poem sets out the claims of 'Youth' and 'Experience', and 'Hope' as the chief ally of 'Youth'. In the form of an allegory of the seasons, 'Experience' urges that the promises of 'Hope' were always being made but never honoured.

> *When in the time of early Spring,*
> *Too chill the winds that o'er me passed,*
> *She said, each coming day would bring*
> *A fairer heaven, a gentler blast.*
>
> *And when the sun too seldom beamed,*
> *The sky, o'ercast, too darkly frowned,*
> *The soaking rain too constant streamed,*
> *And mists too dreary gathered round;*
>
> *She told me, Summer's glorious ray*
> *Would chase those vapours all away,*
> *And scatter glories round;*
> *With sweetest music fill the trees,*
> *Load with rich scent the gentle breeze,*
> *And strew with flowers the ground.*

The poem concludes with the poet intervening in this debate between 'Youth' and 'Experience', by taking up the argument on behalf of 'Hope'. Anne knows the limits of its hope, but can still appreciate its operations. Nor does she see it as inimical to a religious view of life; it is the temporary consoler of the human heart whose final consolation lies in God, and can be viewed therefore as an agent of Providence:

> *Yet hope* itself *a brightness throws*
> *O'er all our labours and our woes;*
> *While dark foreboding Care*
> *A thousand ills will oft portend,*
> *That Providence may ne'er intend*
> *The trembling heart to bear.*

Psychologically, the poem is important for the light it throws on Anne's attitude to the youthful hopes and aspirations of others. The illusions of youth, which experience destroys, and which Anne had come to recognize as illusions by the time she reached her twenty-sixth year, were not spurned by her because of their brevity. Melancholy as was her experience in all those renunciatory thoughts which religion assisted her in formulating, there was nothing puritanical about it. She did not rejoice for herself or for others in the yielding-up of joys and pleasures. Necessity and wisdom imposed this course upon her, and she accepted it in humility of spirit. But in this acceptance there was no perversion. Unlike Emily, Anne was neither masochistic nor sadistic; and her attitude to early pleasures was never prohibitive or vindictive, but always gentle and sympathetic. In Anne's approach to these matters, we shall find no trace of the hedonist *manqué*.

> *Because the road is rough and long,*
> *Shall we despise the skylark's song,*
> *That cheers the wanderer's way?*
> *Or trample down, with reckless feet,*
> *The smiling flowerets, bright and sweet,*
> *Because they soon decay?*

The same feelings of thankfulness for those comforts that still remain inform the last stanzas of her poem '*Vanitas Vanitatum, Omnia Vanitas*' (1845):

> *What, then, remains for wretched man?*
> *To use life's comforts while he can,*
>
> *Enjoy the blessings Heaven bestows,*
> *Assist his friends, forgive his foes;*
> *Trust God, and keep his statutes still;*
> *Upright and firm, through good and ill;*
>
> *Thankful for all that God has given,*
> *Fixing his firmest hopes on Heaven;*
> *Knowing that earthly joys decay,*
> *But hoping through the darkest day.*

Anne was never eager to impose the same strictures of acceptance which she herself endured upon others.

In 1847, less than two years before her death, Anne wrote 'The Three Guides', perhaps her most important poem. It is a sustained moral allegory in which three great genii – the Spirits of Earth, Reason, and Faith – are questioned as to the best course of life, and advance their claims one after another. The seeker finally concludes that the 'Spirit of Faith' alone offers wisdom, and the apostrophe to this daimon has all the fervent lyricism of a good hymn.[1]

It has been remarked that the three Spirits – of Earth, Pride, and Faith – form a curious trio; for two of these are personifications of abstract qualities, while Earth – the third – is a concrete conception.

Muriel Spark has suggested that in the Spirit of Pride Anne was possibly guying Emily, whose Byronic arrogance she would have had good chance to study in her sister's Gondal poems.[2] If this is correct, it is also possible that Anne inclined to identify Charlotte with the Spirit of Earth, and herself with the Spirit of Faith. Such a supposition would account for her choice of three rather incongruous elements; but it would be a deal harder to distinguish the qualities of Charlotte's thought in the attributes of the Spirit of Earth, than those of Emily or Anne in the characteristics of Pride and Faith.[3] The hypothesis is fascinating nevertheless.

My own reading equates the Spirit of Earth and the forces of materialism, the popular morality of 'the main-chance', and the current utilitarian outlook.[4] The Spirit of Pride I take to stand for gnosticism and the antinomian approach (for all those systems of knowledge and behaviour that stem from an excess of spiritual self-confidence). The Spirit of Faith is self-explanatory: it represents the humble submission of the mind to deity. It is Christian, but with no particular theological bias; unless it be that the absence of dogma, and a sense of direct communication with God, can be said to give it a Protestant slant.

The real achievement of the poem lies in the manner in which Anne has succeeded in creating a kind of multiple image to describe

[1] Twenty-four lines from this passage were extracted by Dr James Martineau and Dr Hunter to make a hymn.

[2] *Emily Brontë: Her Life and Work* by Muriel Spark and Derek Stanford (1953).

[3] In Charlotte's own character, rather than in her works, there was a powerful strain of prudence.

> *Firm is my tread, and sure though slow:*
> *My footsteps never slide*
> *And he that follows me shall know*
> *I am the surest guide.*

might be taken as referring to this aspect of the eldest sister; but the rest of the description of the Spirit of Earth does not readily bear this out.

[4] Hazlitt informs us that he was told 'that self-interest, or the *main-chance*, is the unvarying loadstar of our affections'.

the attributes of the first two powers. Partly implicit in the image, and partly present in a commentary upon it, we get Anne's assessment of these forces of conduct. Her picture of the Spirit of Pride is a psychological portrait and judgement upon the whole Byronic 'left-wing' of the Romantic Movement:

> *Yes, I have seen thy votaries oft,*
> *Upheld by thee their guide,*
> *In strength and courage mount aloft*
> *The steepy mountain-side;*
> *I've seen them stand against the sky,*
> *And gazing from below,*
> *Beheld thy lightning in their eye,*
> *Thy triumph on their brow.*
>
> *Oh, I have felt what glory then,*
> *What transport must be theirs!*
> *So far above their fellow men,*
> *Above their toils and cares;*
> *Inhaling Nature's purest breath,*
> *Her riches round them spread,*
> *The wide expanse of earth beneath,*
> *Heaven's glories overhead!*
>
> *But I have seen them helpless, dashed*
> *Down to a bloody grave,*
> *And still thy ruthless eye has flashed,*
> *Thy strong hand did not save;*
> *I've seen some o'er the mountains's brow*
> *Sustained awhile by thee,*
> *O'er rocks of ice, and hills of snow,*
> *Bound fearless, wild, and free.*
>
> *Bold and exultant was their mien,*
> *While thou didst cheer them on;*
> *But evening fell, — and then, I ween,*
> *Their faithless guide was gone.*
> *Alas! how fared thy favourites then —*
> *Lone, helpless, weary, cold?*
> *Did ever wanderer find again*
> *The path he left of old?*

Only perhaps in Lewis Carroll's poem *The Hunting of the Snark*[1] do
we get so distinct and critical an image of romantic presumption as we
find in Anne's stanzas quoted here. The Baker, it will be remembered,
is depicted by Carroll, 'On the top of a neighbouring crag,

> *Erect and sublime, for one moment of time.*
> *In the next, that wild figure they saw*
> *(As if stung by a spasm) plunge into a chasm,*
> *While they waited and listened in awe.*'[2]

The image and criticism of the Spirit of Earth is more dispersed in
treatment than the above, but this in itself helps to suggest the multiple
activities and defects of its nature. Something of Carlyle's gospel of
work – the idea of industriousness as being a self-sufficient good –
seems to be implied here:

> *Striving to make thy way by force,*
> *Toil-spent and bramble-torn,*
> *Thou'lt fell the tree that checks thy course*
> *And burst through brier and thorn:*
> *And, pausing by the river's side,*
> *Poor reasoner! thou wilt deem,*
> *By casting pebbles in its tide,*
> *To cross the swelling stream.*

Anne criticizes this view of life also for want of an interior sense.
It is all external action, all bustle and 'output':

> *If to the breezes wandering near*
> *I listened eagerly,*
> *And deemed an angel's tongue to hear*
> *That whispered hope to me,*
> *That heavenly music would be drowned*
> *In thy harsh, droning voice;*
> *Nor inward thought, nor sight, nor sound*
> *Might my sad soul rejoice.*

[1] The symbolic and subconscious levels in this poem are now generally
recognized.

[2] It is interesting to compare Anne's and Carroll's statements with Nietz-
sche's words, '6,000 feet beyond man and time!' affixed as an epigraph to
one of his books.

Anne's poem 'Self-Communion' is her longest composition. She
was nearly six months writing it,[1] from November 1847 to 17 April
1848. As a psychological document, it is Anne's most interesting
poem; for what it consists of is nothing less than a retrospective view
of her life in the light of her growth of moral ideas. The signature
of personal experience is stamped strongly on this composition,
causing the poet to cancel, as it were, the petition of one vain hope
after another. The poem is in the form of a debate between the
natural instincts of the being and 'Reason, with conscience by her
side'.

It begins with a meditation upon 'the wasting power of time',
which has brought the poet – in the figure of a pilgrim – so far
through 'the weary desert' of life 'that awes the brave and tires the
strong'. The spokesman of instinct is led to describe the workings of
time upon the feelings:

> *I see that time, and toil, and truth*
> *An inward hardness can impart, –*
> *Can freeze the generous blood of youth,*
> *And steel full fast the tender heart.*

The answer of 'Reason, with conscience by her side' is both
logical and pragmatic:

> *Canst thou that softness so deplore –*
> *That suffering, shrinking tenderness?*
> *Thou that hast felt what cankering care*
> *A loving heart is doomed to bear,*
> *Say, how canst thou regret*

Against this, the feelings urge that:

> *Love may be full of pain, but still*
> *'Tis sad to see it so depart, –*

In reply, we are given an account of some of the discords of unequal
love:

> *And sometimes it was grief to know*
> *My fondness was but half returned.*
> *But this was nothing to the woe*
> *With which another truth was learned: –*

[1] Her labour at it was, of course, intermittent.

That I must check, or nurse apart,
Full many an impulse of the heart
And many a darling thought:
What my soul worshipped, sought, and prized,
Were slighted, questioned, or despised; –
This pained me more than aught.
And as my love the warmer glowed
The deeper would that anguish sink,
That this dark stream between us flowed,
Though both stood bending o'er its brink;
Until, at last, I learned to bear
A colder heart within my breast;
To share such thoughts as I could share,
And calmly keep the rest.
I saw that they were sundered now,
The trees that at the root were one:
They yet might mingle root and bough,
But still the stems must stand alone.[1]

But in spite of observing these discrepancies, the poem contains a long paean on the affections. 'Oh, love is sweet of every kind!' writes Anne, passing on to consider the fortunate condition of those between whom it may flow, 'Unchecked, unchilled, by doubt or fear.' Love of this order, Anne remarks, she has only known momentarily in dreams.

Turning from the past to the future, the instinctive side of Anne sees only a diminishing perspective of hope, leaving 'above the dark hill's brow'

A rayless arch of sombre grey.

This last image, with its suggestion of funeral masonry, serves to mark the turn of the poem. Hitherto, the tone had been one of alternate lament and reason. Now – in the exhortation which follows, an exhortation to duty, at all costs – the note is urgent, grim, and bracing.

Toil is my glory – Grief my gain,

writes Anne, who views them as the only way, at the late barren stage of her life, to God.

A comparison between Anne Brontë and Christina Rossetti might

---

[1] It is interesting to compare the last four lines with Emily's poem 'Death'. (See especially the lines 'Strike again/Time's withered branch dividing/From the fresh roots of Eternity!') Emily's lines, in some sense, may be read as a metaphysical projection of these four lines by Anne.

furnish much of interest. As religious poets, both of them were largely concerned with renunciation. But the moral passion was probably stronger in Anne. There is not the same morbidity in her, the same weird relishing of the thought of death, which we encounter in the later poet. Anne's *ascesis* is of a less luxuriant order.

In Anne's poem 'The Narrow Way' (1848), we have the exercise of a moral resolution more firmly carried out than anywhere in Christina Rosetti. If we compare it with the latter's well-known anthology-piece 'Up-hill', its own sure clear determination becomes the more apparent. Referring to the emanation of the virtues, Anne writes

> *On all her breezes borne,*
> *Earth yields no scents like those;*
> *But he that dares not grasp the thorn*
> *Should never crave the rose.*

Christina Rosetti's poem has a vein of wit in it – a sinister life-mocking type of wit, which is like the skeleton's grin:

> *Shall I meet other wayfarers at night?*
> *Those who have gone before.*
> *Then must I knock, or call when just in sight?*
> *They will not keep you standing at that door.*

This is superior poetry to Anne's, but morally it is not so tonic. There is less of the presence of a will informing it.

The Religious Poems

Most of Anne's religious poetry is in the nature of a prayer for assistance. 'Lord, I believe; help, Thou, my unbelief' is the substance of much of this verse. Then, again, we find her using the idea of God as a stimulus to her tired moral will. In this sense, the chief function of Anne's religion seems largely to have been the provision of a super-natural sanction for the dictates of her conscience.

The glory of God – that other side to religious meditation – was less manifest to her. Between confession of her sins or her weakness, and petitions for greater resources of faith, her spiritual energies were used up. There was, perhaps, too much restlessness in her, for feelings of beatitude to find a home in Anne. Her religious life was such an up-hill struggle, so full of anxieties concerning her shortcomings, that the wholly transcendental or imminent presence of God was seldom felt by her in its entirety.

But there is one poem by Anne, 'In Memory of a Happy Day in February' (1842), which is modestly abundant in its sense of revelation. Beginning as a simple record of joy, felt in the face of natural scenery, the poem goes on to speak of the intimation which the scene and the moment carry for her:

> *It was a glimpse of truths divine*
> *Unto my spirit given,*
> *Illumined by a ray of light*
> *That shone direct from Heaven!*
>
> *I felt there was a God on high*
> *By whom all things were made;*
> *I saw His wisdom and His power*
> *In all His works displayed.*
>
> *But most throughout the moral world*
> *I saw His glory shine;*
> *I saw His wisdom infinite,*
> *His mercy all divine.*

It is in the wording of the last stanza here that we see the difference between Anne and the Romantic poets of the nineteenth century, whose apprehension of deity was pantheistic rather than ethical. 'But most throughout the moral world' singles out Anne as belonging to quite a different tradition of thought – to one, in fact, which has more affinity with the eighteenth-century didactic poets such as Johnson.

In such a mood of gratitude and joy, Anne was able to feel secure in her possession of God. The fear of her own spiritual inadequacy – of her occasional inability to believe – seemed completely lifted from her. Instead of the face of justice, which one aspect of Deity showed, she saw only the countenance of love. And in this transport of illumination, the horror of death was utterly removed, and resurrection appeared a certainty:

> *And while I wondered and adored*
> *His Majesty divine,*
> *I did not tremble at His power:*
> *I felt that God was mine.*

I knew that my Redeemer lived;
  I did not fear to die;
I felt that I should rise again
  To immortality.

Anne tried always to hold to the image of God as a being of love rather than as an avenging judge. In her less self-tormented moments, she succeeded in doing this; and at such times she was eager to convince all whom she could, that final salvation was intended for everyone. In her novel, *The Tenant of Wildfell Hall*, Anne – through the lips of the heroine – repudiates the doctrine of eternal punishment; and in her poem 'A Word to the "Elect" ', she is attacking a cardinal Calvinistic notion. That certain souls, from the beginning of the world, were destined by God to achieve salvation, while others were intended for damnation, seemed to her a horrible idea.[1] But even more horrible to Anne, was the thought that those who believed themselves saved should find their security enhanced by the reflection that many were excluded from it.

From piety of such a kind, Anne hastened to separate herself:

> *And, when you, looking on your fellow-men,*
> *Behold them doomed to endless misery,*
> *How can you talk of joy and rapture then? –*
> *May God withhold such cruel joy from me!*[2]

Her next reflection is that

> *. . . none shall sink to everlasting woe,*
> *That have not well deserved the wrath of Heaven.*

But this, it seems, was still too harsh an admission for Anne to conclude upon. Breaking off and beginning again, with a fresh rhythm, she asserts a personal hope over and above orthodox belief; her hope being

[1] It is necessary to distinguish between the Calvinistic doctrine of 'predestination', and the Anglican belief in eternal damnation not as part of God's predestined plan, but as a punishment for conscious sins committed by a man during his life-time. The chief of the sins, of course, was reckoned to be rejection of God. Belief in eternal punishment was current in the Church of England until the last quarter of the nineteenth century, and still has its firm adherents today.

[2] The idea, of course, was not exclusive to Calvinism. It is to be found in the Catholic Dante.

That when the cup of wrath is drained
The metal purified,
They'll cling to what they once disdained,
And live by Him that died.

Charlotte – so often Anne's well-wishing Bad Fairy – has been responsible for the belief that her sister was a religious melancholic. That Anne thought seriously about religion, as it applied to her, is evident enough. Then, too, both Anne and Charlotte lived at a time when religious questions had the force of personal issues. Charlotte herself had experienced a period of deep religious despondency, as we know from letters which she wrote to Ellen Nussey; but her taste of this form of indisposition does not appear to have made her more understanding of her sister's problem. In Charlotte's Introduction to the selection she made of Anne's poems (by no means an unimpeachable choice), she concentrates on this aspect to the exclusion of other elements. Charlotte is often represented as acting the salesman to her sisters' posthumous works, and the various liberties she took with their text tend to be excused on this account. But, as always, when Charlotte is dealing with Anne, we observe the note of exoneration, of vicarious apology, and faint praise. No literary salesman could do much worse than Charlotte to damn the goods he was seeming to offer. As Charlotte's words are of some interest (since later criticism has honoured her opinion), perhaps the reader will forgive my requoting – after Miss Harrison and her gloss upon it[1] – Charlotte's Introduction to the poems entire.

'In looking over my sister Anne's papers', wrote Charlotte, 'I find mournful evidence that religious feeling had been to her but too much like what it was to Cowper – I mean, of course, in a far milder form. Without rendering her a prey to those horrors that defy concealment, it subdued her mood and bearing to a perpetual pensiveness; the pillar of a cloud glided constantly before her eyes; she ever waited at the foot of a secret Sinai, listening in her heart to the voice of a trumpet sounding long and waxing louder. Some, perhaps, would rejoice over these tokens of sincere though sorrowing piety in a deceased relative. I own to me they seem sad, as if her whole innocent life had been passed under the martyrdom of an unconfessed physical pain. Their effect, indeed, would be too distressing, were it not combated by the certain knowledge that in her last moments this tyranny of a too tender conscience was overcome;

[1] See pages 50–52.

this pomp of terrors broke up, and passing away, left her dying hour unclouded. Her belief in God did not then bring to her dread, as of a stern Judge, but hope, as in a Creator and Saviour; and no faltering hope was it, but a sure and steadfast conviction, on which, in the rude passage from time to eternity, she threw the weight of her human weakness, and by which she was enabled to bear what was to be borne – patiently, serenely, victoriously.'

After the damage has already been done, we note that Charlotte lets up on Anne a little. 'Her belief in God', she writes of her sister's 'last moments', 'did not then bring to her dread, as of a stern Judge, but hope, as in a Creator and Saviour.' After coming near to suggesting that Anne's religious disposition was a kind of mania, and that this *malaise* of hers blighted her verse, Charlotte is content to allow her sister the marginal honours of a staunch Christian death-scene. No presentation could render worse service.

To say this is not to imply that Anne's poetry records no spiritual dilemma. It most clearly does; but where Charlotte is wrong is in locating this dilemma incorrectly. By linking Anne's name with that of Cowper, Charlotte implies that her sister's religious 'problem' was that of the poet who died insane; in other words, that Anne's obsession was not really in the nature of a problem, but constituted an aberration. If this aberration was the same as Cowper's (though 'in a far milder form' as Charlotte charitably adds), then Anne's preoccupation was with the idea of predestination, with the question of whether she was saved or damned.

This I consider an erroneous reading of Anne's religious difficulties. Her poem 'A Word to the "Elect" ' should be quite sufficient to rebut this charge. As I interpret her poems, Anne's cause for despondency was the recognition of her own fallible nature; and, more than this, her comparative *lack of faith*. Far, then, from being the result of what we incline to term fanaticism, Anne's religious dilemma arose from her own tincture of disbelief.

A casual reading of her poem 'To Cowper' might, truly, support the conclusion that Anne's religious troubles were the same as that poet's. But no second reading would endorse this opinion.

> *The language of my inmost heart*
> *I traced in every line;*
> My sins, my *sorrows, hopes, and fears,*
> *Were there – and only mine.*

she writes in the second stanza. But both the third and fourth stanzas forbid us to establish a close identification:

> *All for myself the sigh would swell,*
> *The tear of anguish start;*
> *I little knew what wilder woe*
> *Had filled the Poet's heart.*
>
> *I did not know the nights of gloom,*
> *The days of misery;*
> *The long, long years of dark despair,*
> *That crushed and tortured thee.*

Furthermore, the next two stanzas reject the notion that Cowper – in the self-delusion of feeling himself damned – might, after all, have been right:

> *But they are gone; from earth at length*
> *Thy gentle soul is passed,*
> *And in the bosom of its God*
> *Has found its home at last.*
>
> *It must be so, if God is love,*
> *And answers fervent prayer;*
> *Then surely thou shalt dwell on high,*
> *And I may meet thee there.*

And here it is important to observe that Anne believes Cowper's spirit 'Has found its home at last', not because the poet was really one of God's 'elect' (while all the while mistakenly thinking himself damned), but because the very doctrine of 'election' is wrong, since 'God is love', and love implies salvation. Admittedly, Anne's premise here is conditional, being prefaced by an 'if'; but positive assertion and dogmatic utterance was never Anne's manner.

The next stanzas establish that Cowper is not unworthy of salvation by means of a pragmatic argument:

> *Is He the source of every good,*
> *The spring of purity?*
> *Then in thine hours of deepest woe,*
> *Thy God was still with thee.*
>
> *How else, when every hope was fled,*
> *Couldst thou so fondly cling*
> *To holy things and holy men?*
> *And how so sweetly sing*

Of things that God alone could teach?
And whence that purity,
That hatred of all sinful ways —
That gentle charity?

Are these the symptoms of a heart
Of heavenly grace bereft:
For ever banished from its God,
To Satan's fury left.

'By their fruits. . . .' Anne is reasoning here, with that practical sense of the good which the Anglican tradition has always cherished. By a like method of inference, Anne deduces God's intentions to men from His qualities as described by Scripture. If 'God is love', if 'He (is) the source of every good', if He 'answers fervent prayer' — then He will not destine any of His creatures to damnation. If God is the being we are told He is, His actions must partake of His attributes. Anne's argument is simple, but quite consistent.

In the last stanza, Anne returns to Cowper's hypothesis; yet more, we feel, for dramatic effect, than out of respect for its possibility:

Yet, should thy darkest fears be true,
If Heaven be so severe,
That such a soul as thine is lost, —
Oh! how shall I appear?

It rounds off the poem, and serves to save Anne's long-range Christian optimism from any suspicion of complacency. From such assumption, her humility always saved her.

In using the term 'optimism', I refer to Anne's objective beliefs — not to any institutional doctrine (though, as we remember in *The Tenant of Wildfell Hall*, the heroine had found 'nearly thirty passages' going to suggest that the flames of Hell were cleansing rather than everlasting — a significant fact, since the Church of England has always claimed that the source and authority of its teaching are, first and foremost, Biblical), but to certain ideas made clear in her own mind. Subjectively, Anne's temperament was far from being optimistic. There was too little of the sanguine element in her constitution for that. A frail but determined Christian stoicism was the nearest she could get to optimism in action.

In spirit, she was often despondent: either on account of her weakness — her inability to maintain the standards she had set herself;

or because of her relative lack of faith. Both of these causes of depression are recorded in her poems.

'Despondency' (1841) confesses,

> *I have gone backwards in the work,*
> *The labour has not sped;*
> *Drowsy and dark my spirit lies,*
> *Heavy and dull as lead.*

In this poem, she speaks of the hold-up of belief, as if by an internal obstacle that keeps the spirit from communication with God. The dark night of negativity, as we may call it, is something that many mystics and saints have experienced. But Anne's trouble was not quite orthodox, since, she unlike them, seems to have placed small importance upon the Church as an intermediary body. It is clear from her novel *Agnes Grey* that the corporate worship of a congregation appeared always as good and pleasing to her; but in questions of personal intercourse with God, the Church did not quite answer her need.[1]

For along with her feelings of despondency, there came, at intervals, moments of doubt as to whether God existed at all. If He did exist, then Anne was persuaded that His nature partook of love and mercy, rather than of arbitrary wrath. Her intuition about God's attributes, Anne felt to be correct; but could she be certain of His being, without which her inference was so much 'vain delusion'?

> *What shall I do, if all my love,*
> *My hopes, my toil, are cast away,*
> *And if there be no God above,*
> *To hear and bless me when I pray?*

('The Doubter's Prayer' (1843))

Earlier in this poem, she prays for faith; and reflects, as in her piece on Cowper, that this desire itself betokens God's presence, however obscure or hidden, within her:

> *Without some glimmering in my heart,*
> *I could not raise this fervent prayer;*
> *But, Oh! a stronger light impart,*
> *And in Thy mercy fix it there.*

[1] One must, agreed, be careful not to read too much of an autobiographical meaning into a passage from a novel. Nevertheless, we recall how Mr Hatfield (a symbol of formal ecclesiasticism) in Anne's story *Agnes Grey*, can only tell a poor distressed old woman, as a remedy for the worries on her soul, to attend church regularly. Mr Weston (the more inward-minded curate) expounds and reasons with her *à deux*.

If Anne's doubt partook of an intellectual element, her method of solving it was not by argument, but by direct appeal and prayer:

Oh, help me, God! For Thou alone
Cans't my distracted soul relieve;
Forsake it not: it is Thine own,
Though weak, yet longing to believe.

Oh, drive those cruel doubts away;
And make me know that Thou art God!
A faith, that shines by night and day,
Will lighten every earthly load.

From the standpoint of her bigoted liberalism,[1] Charlotte found Anne's very real religious misgivings akin to those of Cowper. As I hope to have indicated, they were of a subtle and different order, and even if they were allied to a low constitutional vitality, this was not their source, nor were they in any way pathological like Cowper's madness.

In another poem 'If This be All' (1845), Anne surveys the course of her past life, heavy with toil, and lacking in love and friendship – a life in which she feels she receives

No freshening dew from Thee.

Reflecting on the barrenness of existence, she senses the death-wish gaining upon her:

If life must be so full of care,
Then call me soon to Thee;

Then it seems as if alarmed at what she had written, she shifts the meaning in the last two lines of the stanza begging that the wind be tempered to the shorn lamb:

Or give me strength enough to bear
My load of misery.

Even so, the shape of her thoughts, set down in writing, may have appalled her; for, in the original MS, the last four lines are lightly cancelled.

Hard upon the heels of this poem (some twelve days later), comes

[1] I am very far from implying that all liberalism is bigoted. My meaning is that Charlotte's was.

one with a more cheerful theme. Included in the *Congregational Hymnary*, and in other collections, this piece, entitled 'Confidence', expresses Anne's trust in the mercy of God:

> *Far as this earth may be*
> *From yonder starry skies,*
> *Remoter still am I from Thee*
> *Yet Thou wilt not despise*

> .   .   .

> *In my Redeemer's name*
> *I give myself to Thee;*
> *And all unworthy as I am,*
> *My God will cherish me.*

Anne's last poem was a religious composition. It was written on 28 January 1849; and four months later, to the day, she was dead, 'These lines written, the desk was closed, the pen laid aside – for ever' observes Charlotte, in her selection of her sister's verse, with that touch of the melodramatic that was second-nature to her. But if the first stanza of 'Last Lines' is rhetorical in tone, there is no hint of the melodramatic. It speaks with a fearful directness, with a chill full prescience of dissolution which is pathetic in the extreme. But there is much more in this stanza than the clear intuitive apprehension of death. Anne knew that the final stage of her illness would prove a greater testing to her will and her faith than all the previous misfortunes of her life. She knew that before her lay

> *That inward strife against the sins*
> *That ever wait on suffering,*
> *To strike wherever first begins*
> *Each ill that would corruption bring.*

Pain, frustration, disappointment: these she knew would be waiting to way-lay her; and any prospect that included all these would be sufficient for the average mortal. But much as she dreaded these terrors a greater fear stood facing her. Anne trembled to think that in her ordeal she might lose her faith completely, or that her faith in God might undergo a change. She had always set herself to believe that God was mercy, love, and salvation. Did she, under the threat of the future, doubt whether she could retain that image? Was she afraid, that, after all, God might reveal himself a God of wrath? And did she fear that then, she might be led to reject Him, or rebel?

One cannot quite know what was in Anne's mind when she wrote the first stanza of 'Last Lines'. We can only catch, in the reverberation of these dark words, some hint or suspicion of her meaning. Charlotte, in her selection of Anne's poems, omitted this first stanza; though she might have printed it as evidence of her sister's so-called religious melancholia. I conclude that she decided it was 'too terrible', and in the interests of public health and the general Brontë reputation, suppressed it.

> *A dreadful darkness closes in*
> *On my bewildered mind;*
> *O let me suffer and not sin,*
> *Be tortured yet resigned.*

The ease and pleasures of life had long deserted Anne when she came to write this poem. In place of the fruits of joy she had come to hope for the fruits of duty, but even these were denied her. She was not to be allowed a harvest of 'good works':

> *I hoped amid the brave and strong*
> *My portioned task might lie*
> *To toil amid the labouring throng*
> *With purpose keen and high.*

But see how she continues this inner debate, with regret and acceptance answering each other:

> *But Thou hast fixed another part,*
> *And Thou hast fixed it well;*
> *I said so with my breaking heart*
> *When first the anguish fell.*
>
> *O Thou hast taken my delight*
> *And hope of life away,*
> *And bid me watch the painful night*
> *And wait the weary day.*
>
> *The hope and the delight were Thine:*
> *I bless Thee for their loan;*
> *I gave Thee while I deemed them mine*
> *Too little thanks I own.*

By the end of the poem acceptance is complete. If her return to health is possible, she vows herself to greater humility; but if it is her fate 'thus early to depart', she asks for the fortitude to make of that departure itself a service to God.

This service was to be required of her.

XIV

The Verbal Texture

THE FORMAL MERITS of Anne's poetry have been neglected in the past. They tend to be over-looked today; and the reason for this, in both cases, I think, is that they are judged by wrong or irrelevant standards.

If we go to Anne's poems in search of some common Brontë feature – the drama of Emily or the rhetoric of Charlotte – we shall, often, be disappointed. And if we discover these elements, the traces of them will be so slight as to lead us to discount Anne as a poet. Again, if we expect from Anne the peculiar gifts and characteristics of her own Romantic century – the loaded epithet, the rare and brilliant image, or the come-and-go of haunting music – we shall anticipate in vain. But because Anne seems colourless in the light of these expectations, we must not conclude that she has been tried and found wanting.

For all its accumulated beauties, the nineteenth-century mode of expression is not the only one that poets have honoured. The eighteenth century favoured other merits, practising them with nicety; and if the precise perfections of the eighteenth century seem slight in comparison with the riches of Romantic poetry, they are still by no means to be ignored.

Harmony, clarity, economy, precision: these are the eighteenth-century virtues, both in poetry and in prose. Wit and paradox, in both these media, as employed by the eighteenth-century writer, often assumed the nature of excrescence; and the snap and crackle of imposed epigrams can prove just as burdensome to the reader as Romantic over-ornamentation. Both of these hold the poem up; they arrest the flow of communication; and – to the historically unprejudiced purist – both are reprehensible.

Now it is the distinction of Anne's poetry that, while we largely discover in it the former group of eighteenth-century virtues – namely, harmony, clarity, economy, and precision – we are not distracted by the impositions of paradox and wit. To many, this will seem to mean an absence of savour, but piquancy can prove a burden when purity is already present. At least, with Anne we never feel, as we do with so many eighteenth-century poets, 'if only she would stop being clever, and get on with the argument, the moral, or the story'. Without keeping her eye upon the entertainment-value of her verse, Anne effortlessly succeeded in achieving the public virtues in her writing: clearness, neatness, directness, and elegance. And this she did without any self-conscious straining. Because she was interested, first and foremost, in her own problems, and their solution (and these were not chiefly poetic problems), she spoke naturally and to the point. She did not regard the art of poetry as a craft of affectation (which, all too often, was the eighteenth-century custom), nor yet as a mode of self-dramatization (which was the Romantic nineteenth-century habit).

In saying this, I would not seem to claim too much for Anne vis-à-vis those more gifted poets who sinned largely and frequently in these directions – Pope and Byron, for example. It is just that her style is remarkably pure. And after the paraded pretensions to cleverness (on the part of the typical Augustan poet), and to feeling (on the part of the nineteenth-century Romantic), there is a certain pleasant relief to be had in reading her poetry.

Her style, as a whole, has been described as colourless, neutral, or weak; but I would prefer to speak of it as limpid. It seems that between her words and her intention no discrepancy has crept in. Her meaning appears to shine quietly through her verse with a very minimum of loss. There is nothing to impede it, on its passage to the reader: no ornamentation, no melodramatics. Naturally enough, this virtue of her style has its own reverse side. A style with so rapid a reading-speed as Anne's must travel, so to speak, comparatively light. It cannot carry some of poetry's more interesting luggage. Even the compactness of metaphor would weight down the line too much, presenting a density of implication, which is foreign to Anne's unambiguous directness. There is nothing complex, then, in the texture of Anne's style. To some, it may wear a look of thinness; and none of the grander veins of poetry have, indeed, clothed themselves so sparsely as Anne's. But as a mode of minor poetry, Anne's lightweight medium is agreeable enough.

As an artist, Anne's chief gift was her sense of rhythm. This was apparently instinctive to her; for in her writing-span of thirteen years, her first poems reveal it as neatly as her last.

Sometimes her delicate awareness of it is shown by the exquisite right choice of the sort of rhythm her subject demands, as in her poem 'Lines composed in a Wood on a Windy Day' (1842), where the excitement of her theme seems to have entered into the alliteration of the title:

> *My soul is awakened, my spirit is soaring*
> *And carried aloft on the wings of the breeze;*
> *For above and around me the wild wind is roaring,*
> *Arousing to rapture the earth and the seas.*
>
> *The long withered grass in the sunshine is glancing,*
> *The bare trees are tossing their branches on high;*
> *The dead leaves, beneath them, are merrily dancing,*
> *The white clouds are scudding across the blue sky.*
>
> *I wish I could see how the ocean is lashing*
> *The foam of its billows to whirlwinds of spray;*
> *I wish I could see how its proud waves are dashing,*
> *And hear the wild roar of their thunder to-day!*

The feminine rhyme of the first and third lines to every stanza is very effective here; and the present-participle form maintained throughout helps to create the sense of constant motion.

In Anne's poetry, we find repetition employed in a variety of ways. The use of adjectives in the same place in the line, in all four lines of the second stanza, is one example of this, as is the employment of identical construction in the first and third lines of the fourth stanza.

But more often, Anne's feeling for rhythm is revealed by a change of movement in the one poem. Sometimes it is the rhythm of a single line which she lightly varies; sometimes she varies or alters a whole stanza, introducing a new rhyme-scheme. Above all poetry in the English language, the verse of the Border Ballads presents us with the greatest variety of rhythmical effects within a simple verbal structure. Anne, like Emily, learned much from ballad poetry, as it came to her in Scott's *Minstrelsy of the Scottish Border*. Some of her best rhythmical effects are obtained in her practice of the ballad form. Her early poem 'The Parting' is an admirable example of this practice. Changing the length of her stanzas, and her rhyme-scheme, as occasion directs, Anne charms us with that combination, difference and sameness, which is one of poetry's principal hypnotics.

> *For three years she has waited there.*
>   *Still hoping for her lord's return;*
> *But vainly she may hope and fear,*
>   *And vainly watch and weep and mourn.*
> *She may wait him till her hairs are grey,*
> *And she may wear her life away,*
> *But to his lady and his home*
> *Her noble lord will never come.*

Note, in the fifth line, the alteration in rhythm, which serves to carry forward the movement of the poem, while at the same time it repeats and stresses the meaning of the line before.

The other poems which exhibit a like masterly change of rhyme and rhythm are 'The North Wind' and 'I Dreamt last Night', from both of which I have quoted.

Besides possessing a feeling for rhythm, Anne had a native niceness of approach to the use of language in general. This is often made plain in her precise choice of a word, against the force of more popular usage. In the passage quoted from 'The Parting', we have the line, 'She may wait him till her hairs are grey', where it would have been more 'normal' to find the noun in the singular form. But Anne's choice of the plural was deliberate and functional, for, by it, she conveys an effect of years of waiting while the hairs go grey, one by one.

Another instance of this fine correctness is discoverable in 'Verses by Lady Geralda', the earliest poem of Anne's we have.

> *Why did the unexpected tear*
> *From my sad eyelid start?*

she writes, when the majority of poets would probably have been satisfied with the word 'eye'. But Anne's choice is the more exact; giving us an image of the tear, as it pauses, pendant for a moment; instead of being shot forward like the waters of a fountain, which the words of many poets suggest.

This aspiration after exactness of meaning occasionally leads Anne into the employment of italics. Generally, we feel this to be a mistake. Striving for complete exactitude, Anne tries to make some ordinary

word bear a more than ordinary stress of meaning. So, in 'The Arbour'
(1845), she writes:

> *'Tis but the* frost *that clears the air,*
> *And gives the sky that lovely blue.*
> *They're smiling in a* winter's *sun,*
> *Those ever-greens of sombre hue.*

This poem, which deals with the illusion of a summer feeling in
wintertime, might profit from the italics if they were taken merely as
hints to the reciter, like the *fortissimo* and *pianissimo* in music; but
they do not add to the merit of the lines. In fact, they apprise us of
Anne's own misgivings.

Anne's passion for transparency of meaning had happier results,
however, than to tempt her into a wrong sort of emphasis. It drove
her also to revise much of her work; and when we compare an
original version of some line of hers with its revision, we never fail to
note the improvement. Occasionally, the revision achieves a greater
euphony only, but most often the gain is in preciser meaning as well.

Thus, in the poem 'Self-Communion', where Anne is speaking of
time, the first version was as follows:

> *His footsteps in the ceaseless sound*
> *Of yonder clock I seem to hear,*
> *That through this stillness so profound*
> *So keenly strikes the vacant ear.*

In the revised version, Anne has changed the last line to

> *Distinctly strikes the vacant ear.*

Not only is this more melodious by reason of the recurring 'ts' but it is
also more suggestive as to meaning. The repetition of the consonant
't' is like the tick-tock sound of the clock, marking off the passing
seconds. And the opposition of 'Distinctly' and 'vacant' evokes the
idea of a drum-stick striking a drum. For this, we derive an added
feeling of the resonance and reality of time.

In the same poem we find further proofs of Anne's striving to
improve on her original perceptions more unequivocally. The cliché
'angry passions' yields place to the more specific 'jarring discords'. The
looser line 'For things I worshipped, sought, and prized' is changed for
the more economical 'What my soul worshipped, sought, and prized'
('soul' is both stronger and less reducible than 'I'). The less compact

line 'Nay, welcome labour, grief, and pain' is changed for the aphoristic 'Toil is my glory – Grief my gain'. Musically, too, with other things equal, Anne's revision always shows an improvement.

> *O toil! and if thy strength be small,*
> *Toil yet the more, and spend it all*

becomes

> *O strive! and if thy strength be small,*
> *Strive yet the more, and spend it all*

– an investment in alliteration, where the gain is obvious. Similarly, by repeating the broad vowel ("wide" and "wild"), she improves

> *However wide this rolling sea,*
> *However bleak my passage be*

to

> *However wide this rolling sea,*
> *However wild my passage be.*

At the same time, Anne knew that there are occasions when the general is more telling than the specific.

> *Earth hath too much of sin and pain:*
> *This bitter cup – that binding chain*

is altered to

> *Earth hath too much of sin and pain:*
> *The bitter cup – the binding chain.*

As it now reads, the line presents a balanced summary of afflictions; more evenly disposed, as it were, throughout existence.

These points might be dismissed as small; but it is by attention to such details that the poet achieves his own kind of purity. To cultivate one's garden in poetry, however narrow it may be, can bring no guarantee of greatness, but it does make attainable the promise of good verse. When it is remembered that all these revisions (and there are plenty more) have been taken from one poem, and that it is Anne's last poems which bear the evidence of fullest revision, the concentration of her mind on such problems can be properly appreciated. If the work of Anne's later years has not the spontaneity of her early period, it achieves its validity in a highly conscious manner – by the force of a literary and moral self-criticism.

I have spoken already of some of the uses of repetition to be found in Anne's poems. One I have not as yet mentioned is that of the repetitive construction employed for narrative purpose. This is a very old device; a very elementary one, perhaps; but Anne handles it in 'An Orphan's Lament' (1841) with what may be termed an artful simplicity:

> *She's gone; and twice the summer's sun*
> *Has gilt Regina's towers,*
> *And melted wild Angora's snows,*
> *And warmed Epina's bowers.*
>
> *The flowerets twice on hill and dale*
> *Have bloomed and died away;*
> *And twice the rustling forest leaves*
> *Have fallen to decay.*
>
> *And thrice stern winter's icy hand*
> *Has checked the river's flow,*
> *And three times o'er the mountains thrown*
> *His spotless robe of snow.*
>
> *Two summers, springs, and autumns sad,*
> *Three winters, cold and grey:*
> *And is it then so long ago*
> *That wild November day?*

This is the means that many ancient story-tellers used to introduce, and locate, their story; and Anne imitates their garrulity well.

Aspiring to a form of poetry that should be simple in structure as the Border Ballads, Anne was concerned to 'fit it out' as conscientiously as possible. The straightforward clarity of her poetry (which some critics have considered barren), was largely the result of such care, and this quality has led to some of her poems being used as hymns.[1] As such, they cannot compare with those of a great practitioner of this art, and if we contrast them with the hymns of Isaac Watts and Charles Wesley, we see the smallness of their scope. Their lack of dogma and exposition and their avoidance of the general statement limits their applicability. But the more personal note, which they contain, gives them a slender fervid grace.

As a lyric poet, Anne's range was narrow; and her gifts, here,

---

[1] 'A Prayer' (1844) is included in the *Baptist Hymnal*; 'Confidence' (1845) in the *Congregational Hymnary* and Dr Hunter's *Glasgow Hymnal*; and parts of the address to the Spirit of Faith in 'The Three Guides' (1847) have been similarly adapted.

though genuine, were hardly intense. Indeed, one critic[1] has written that the only real poetry to be found in Anne is comprised in the two lines from her poem 'Memory' (1844):

> *For ever hang thy dreamy spell*
> *Round golden star and heather-bell,*

It is true that this couplet possesses a prettiness which we seldom find in Anne's sparse verse, but to make this prettiness our criterion is just to judge Anne by those Romantic standards which we have seen to be irrelevant.

Reticence, restraint, and the virtue of omission can work as effectively in a poem as those talents that 'load every rift with ore'.

This dramatic and artistic delicacy – a knowledge that teaches the time to break off – is evinced by Anne in her early narrative poem 'Alexander and Zenobia'. The young lovers have vowed to meet at a given trysting-place after two years' separation. The heroine awaits her friend's arrival, fearful that he will not come. Anne describes the young girl's vigil, and then takes the reader to meet her lover who, faithful to his word, makes for the chosen spot:

> *He has journeyed on unweariedly*
> *From dawn of day till now,*
> *The warm blood kindles in his cheek,*
> *The sweat is on his brow.*
>
> *But he has gained the green hill top*
> *Where lies that lonely spring,*
> *And lo! he pauses when he hears*
> *Its gentle murmuring.*
>
> *He dares not enter through the trees*
> *That veil it from his eye.*
> *He listens for some other sound*
> *In deep anxiety.*
>
> *But vainly – all is calm and still;*
> *Are his bright day-dreams o'er?*
> *Has he thus hoped and longed in vain?*
> *And must they meet no more?*

[1] Phyllis Bentley.

One moment more of sad suspense
And those dark trees are past;
The lonely well bursts on his sight
And they are met at last!

'And they are met at last!' is conclusive. Anne retires on a well-timed curtain. Though the bias of her poetry is intensely personal, Anne understood, in an un-looked-for manner, the impersonality of her craft.

XV

Comparison and Status

ANNE'S VOICE, IN poetry, is a still small voice. Compared with it, many other voices 'of louder lay', however much lacking in purity or integrity, have often seemed more important.

During her life-time, Anne's verse was neglected, and after her death it received no recognition. Unlike the poetess Felicia Hemans, Anne had no influential critic, such as Jeffreys, to laud her work in the *Edinburgh Review*. (He had written that 'she [Felicia Hemans] is, beyond all comparison, the most touching and accomplished writer of occasional verses that our literature has yet to boast of'.)

For the nineteenth century in general, Anne's claims as a poet were as nothing compared to those, say, of Mrs Barbauld, Joanna Baillie, Jean Ingelow, Hannah Moore, and Caroline Norton. And over these popular dispensers of sentimentality and the commonplace, Mrs Hemans queened it, without a doubt. Like her own poem 'Graves of a Household', her name became a household-word. Yet if we set a stanza of Mrs Hemans' beside a stanza by Anne, the latter's superiority is clearly apparent. Here is Mrs Hemans, in her poem 'The Hall of Cynddylan':

> *The Hall of Cynddylan is gloomy to-night;*
> *I weep, for the grave has extinguished its light;*
> *The beam of the lamp from its summit is o'er,*
> *The blaze of its hearth shall give welcome no more.*

and here is Anne, in the opening stanza of her poem 'The Parting' (Part II):

> *The lady of Abyerno's hall*
> *Is waiting for her lord;*
> *The blackbird's song, the cuckoo's call,*
> *No joy to her afford.*

She smiles not at the summer's sun,
Nor at the winter's blast;
She mourns that she is still alone
Though three long years have passed.

As Arthur Symons remarked of the former, it is 'a kind of prattle'; and, what is more, a prattle that is based on impurer models than Anne employed in her poems. 'Living much of her life in Wales, and caring greatly for its ancient literature, she loses', observes Arthur Symons,[1] 'whatever is finest and most elemental in her Celtic originals.'

The loss is incurred through Mrs Hemans' imitation of the strain of Thomas Moore. Anne went to Scott and the Border Balladists for inspiration and assistance in her poem 'The Parting', and Scott is purer and nearer to the source of the ancient ballad literature than was Moore to the older Irish minstrels. It is this – as well as Anne's honesty of mind – which makes of her poem a more 'real' experience. Contrasted with it, Mrs. Hemans' poem is a tawdry affair. Anne's poems, as Charlotte observed to Mrs Gaskell, 'have the merit of truth and simplicity'; and it is the presence of these qualities which distinguish even such a work as 'The Parting' which quite undisguisedly takes its cue from previous examples of ballad poetry.

But if Anne emerges an easy winner when matched with this concourse of Victorian ladies, she cannot claim to hold a position equal to that of Elizabeth Browning. By reason of her greater variety of tones, her greater human curiosity, and perhaps her fuller experience, the wife of Browning takes precedence over the spinster Anne. Nor was it only a narrow range of human experience which limited Anne. Christina Rossetti, a spinster likewise, is superior to her as a poet. There is neither the same originality of expression, nor power of invention, in Anne's verse. Her faculty for poetic dreaming seems to have been nipped in the bud.

Even George Eliot can, momently in verse, attain to a note beyond Anne's reach:

The world is great: the birds all fly from me,
The stars are golden fruit upon a tree
All out of reach: my little sister went,
And I am lonely.[2]

[1] *The Romantic Movement in English Poetry* (1909).
[2] I do not quote this stanza from 'Pablo's Song' as an example of first-rate poetry, but rather to show that even mediocre verse could sometimes achieve an atmosphere or magic beyond Anne at her most 'poetical'.

But if we compare the bulk of George Eliot's verse, sprawling and miscellaneous, with Anne's slighter poems, we see that the victory stays safely with Anne. Her scope is narrow, but verse is for her a natural medium and allows the consummation of her small talents. George Eliot, on the contrary, gains nothing from verse as a medium. Her poems have an occasional rewarding richness, but such general strength as they possess owes more to the prose-writer than the poet.

An irresistible comparison would be with Charlotte's poetry. In 'Pilate's Wife's Dream', the author of *Jane Eyre* has certainly composed a poem whose narrative holds us more firmly than any which Anne essayed to tell in verse. But again, as with George Eliot, we feel that this superiority has unpoetic sources. Charlotte's triumph is the triumph of the novelist. And if Anne cannot be reckoned on to make the most of a tale in verse,[1] with her we are safe at least from the barn-storming into which Charlotte could allow herself to fall :

> *I, who sat by his wife's death-bed,*
> *I, who his daughter loved,*
> *Could almost curse the guilty dead,*
> *For woes the guiltless proved.*

> *And heaven did curse: they found him laid,*
> *When crime for wrath was ripe,*
> *Cold, with the suicidal blade*
> *Clutched in his desperate gripe.*

> ('Mementos')

Comparison with Emily's verse is less pointless than might be expected. The second of the Brontë sisters is, of course, a major-poet, but only by reason of six poems[2] which are among the greatest of nineteenth-century lyrics. After these half-dozen exceptional pieces, there comes a secondary body of work, comprising poems which are sometimes better than the best of Anne's verse, and sometimes worse. A third section of Emily's poetry includes pieces whose flaws of taste and silly Byronic affectations could never be found in Anne :

[1] Save in her early poem 'Alexander and Zenobia'. Neither 'The Parting' nor 'I Dreamt last Night' are well contrived *as stories*.

[2] 'There let thy bleeding branch atone', 'Cold in the earth . . .', 'Death that struck when I was most confiding', 'No coward soul is mine', a sequence of seven stanzas from the poem 'Julian M and A. G. Rochelle' and 'Often rebuked yet always back returning'. For a defence of this choice, see *Emily Brontë: her Life and Work*, by Muriel Spark and Derek Stanford (1953).

I flung myself upon the stone,
I howled and tore my tangled hair,
And then, when the fierce gush had flown,
Lay in unspeakable despair.

This is Emily at her worst: Anne exhibits no such 'tantrums', not even in her Byronic pastiche in blank-verse, 'The Captain's Dream'. If purity of diction, and control of expression, count for anything in poetry (and I am not claiming that they count decisively), then Anne is not an inconsiderable poet.

But there are fuller, more humane, attractions present in Anne's poetry than merits of diction. Choice and graceful as is her formal sense, it is not this virtue, in isolation, that guarantees an interest and pleasure for many who have come, or may come, to read her. Her subject also has a call upon us.

If we respond sympathetically to aspirations after the 'good life', if the existence of sin appears real, and the idea of deity desirable but distant, if hope seems difficult and human love unsmooth, we shall not read Anne Brontë's poems unrewarded.

ANNE BRONTË AS NOVELIST

XVI

THE BRONTËS, LIKE Shakespeare himself, pose a question: how did the people we believe them to have been come to write their remarkable works? Daughters of a sparsely tenanted moorland, dwellers in a bleak and lonely parsonage, their image has a way of asserting itself interrogatively in the reader's mind. How, we ask ourselves, on putting down their writings, should these provincial girls have accounted between them for a batch of books whose richness and merit have been surpassed by no single family of authors?

With Emily, the question is usually answered by means of that evasive term 'imagination'; with Charlotte, we may catch a reference to what the psychologists describe as sublimated feeling or wish-fulfilment, and hear a rumour concerning a passion for her Belgian professor. When we come to Anne, however, no ready-made reply offers.

Briefly, the problem may be attempted by means of a short digression. For the sake of convenience, we may distinguish three different workings of the artistic mind, which our three authors may be said respectively to illustrate. The first is responsible for the creation of a world without reference to things outside it. Its universe is original – a virgin territory of imagination. Emily's mind, perhaps, worked in this way; for although we may all recognize the outward features of Haworth and its people in the scenes, moors, and characters of *Wuthering Heights*, the true protagonists of its drama, engaged in their essential and elemental conflict, can hardly be said to reproduce a cast or pattern familiar to the author.

The second of these workings is answerable for a world which repeats – but in heightened or idealized form – a reality known to the author already. Composition would seem to take place at a tension; and recalling the romanticized orphan Jane Eyre, who improbably captures her master's heart, we may venture to place Charlotte's procedure within this creative category.

The third type of creative activity produces a world that tallies at many points with the world inhabited by the author. For such a writer, we may say, experience is both imagination and invention; instead of imagination being – as it was for Emily – the single true experience. Provisionally, then, we shall think of Anne as illustrating this last type of activity; a mind for whom art appears as recollected experience.

But experience, of itself – even great experience – cannot produce or guarantee creation. 'To experience,' wrote Walter Bagehot, 'one thing is essential, an experiencing nature'; and this very sense of registering things; this gift of feeling in any occurrence, combined with a power to reflect on what she felt, were the properties special to Anne as an author.

Thus it comes about that the lonely years which Anne was to spend in service as a governess, years away from home and away from her sisters; years, it seemed, of exile for mind and heart, were not, after all to be just so much time wasted; but were rather to provide the substance for her works.

Agnes Grey, her first novel – according to what Charlotte told Mrs Gaskell – 'pretty literally described' Anne's own experience as a governess.

The plot of the novel *Agnes Grey* is simple and straightforward. It recounts the casual domestic adventures of a young intelligent girl, like Anne, the daughter of a poor parson. In order to alleviate the family burden she takes a post as governess with a vulgar family who have made their money in trade, and are both pretentious and ignorant. After a while she leaves them to serve in a more aristocratic household. Here in the course of visiting the poor of the district, she meets and falls in love with the new curate. At first she feels her love endangered by the activities of the coquette; but all turns out happily in the end, and the couple are married with affectionate decorum.

The novel records not a few of the painful incidents suffered by Anne, and the deep petty cruelties to be endured by a governess at the hands of her employer.

Anne had been in love with her father's curate, William Weightman. The lover in the book is also a cleric. How far Anne may have drawn on him, how far she deliberately avoided drawing on him, whether or not she filled out her figure in the external likeness of another local curate are all matters of interest but were not decisive factors in giving her character authenticity.

That Anne, as artist, stood in little need of any direct experience in order to present in sympathetic light the passionate love-affairs of others, her second book, *The Tenant of Wildfell Hall,* can prove. Conceived at the time of her stay at Thorp Green, where Branwell was deep in an amorous intrigue with his employer's wife, the novel would appear to exploit and employ the situation in two distinct ways. Firstly, the image of her brother, in his capacity of rake and wastrel, is taken and transferred into her story where we see him as the dissolute Mr Huntingdon. This, indeed, is all that most critics have seen, thrown off the second scent, so to speak by the words which Charlotte came to pronounce in her *Biographical Notice of Ellis and Acton Bell.* 'The choice of subject', she wrote of this novel, 'was an entire mistake. Nothing less congruous with the writer's nature could be conceived. The motives which dictated this choice were pure, but, I think slightly morbid. She had, in the course of her life, been called on to contemplate near at hand, and for a long time, the terrible effects of talents misused and faculties abused; hers was naturally a sensitive, reserved, and dejected nature; what she saw sank very deeply into her mind; it did her harm. She brooded over it until she believed it to be a duty to reproduce every detail (of course, with fictitious characters, incidents, and situations) as a warning to others. She hated her work, but would pursue it.'

In interpreting *The Tenant of Wildfell Hall* as a didactic novel *manqué*, Charlotte, it seems, missed the positive side, the fructifying aspect of Branwell's passion, as far as the novelist in Anne is concerned. For just as the sister regarded her brother with pity, disapprobation, and shame; so, too, she was moved and excited by witnessing his passion; even in the midst of her distress her imagination was stirred by the atmosphere of longing and the currents of desire. The nature of the creative mind is such that those events which are torture to the person may prove the artist's greatest gain. This appears to have held true for Anne, who though tormented by having to observe her brother's degraded and illicit passion, was able to use her understanding of it to portray its nobler variations in the passion of her hero Gilbert Markham for her heroine Helen, the widow of Huntingdon.

That the subject-matter of her novel both repelled and fascinated Anne is something that Charlotte could not admit. It was something that not even Anne—with her greater degree of truthfulness – could admit to herself or her public. The workings of the subconscious mind, answerable for so much in art, was a factor the Victorians were seldom aware of. But the presence of this factor, hidden from Anne, has not escaped the notice of a later, more emancipated mind; and George Moore – a connoisseur and specialist in these matters – has observed the element of 'heat' with which the story of the lovers unfolds. Describing it rather in negative terms, he speaks of this 'rarest of literary qualities' as something we must not confuse with 'violence, rhetoric or vehemence'. To attempt to formulate more neatly what Moore could only vaguely suggest would no doubt prove a hazardous task. Edmond Gosse, with whom he shared this *Conversation in Ebury Street* (from the text of which these remarks are taken) seems to have found Moore's comments rather puzzling. Perhaps they are easier to understand if we go back to Moore's *resumé* of the first part of the story.

'As you haven't read the book for a long time, Gosse, you will allow me to recall to your remembrance the theme', he writes. 'The tenant of Wildfell Hall is a young and handsome woman who has rented the hall and lives in almost complete seclusion, making no acquaintances; she is rarely seen except when she goes forth to paint. The lonely figure painting woods and fields becomes a subject of gossip, and it is not long before the imaginations of the people discover in her the heroine of a sinful story – a discovery which helps, I take it, to plunge the young farmer headlong into that torment of passion which men rarely, if ever, have the power, I will not say of feeling, but of transferring into written words.'

Those literary occasions on which we find the 'heart's heat' translated 'without loss' are, according to Moore, few and far between. St Paul possesses it, he tells us, and it is to be found in St Teresa and in the letters of Héloise to Abelard. More surprisingly, we learn that it is to be discovered in the incident in which Marianne goes up to London in search of Willoughby in *Sense and Sensibility*, but that 'it doesn't exist in Shakespeare, in Dante, in Homer'. Moore tells us that he doesn't put it forward 'as a very high literary quality' but merely as the rarest one. Faced with such subtle and extraordinary distinctions, Gosse can only reply, 'An emotion enkindled by spiritual or physical love. I think you exaggerate its rarity.'

But whatever value we are prepared to allow to this quality of 'heat' in fiction, we feel that Moore was right in detecting its presence. The illicit relationship of Branwell and Mrs Robinson did not leave Anne untouched. With one side of her being she reacted morally against the affair by her creation and censure of Huntingdon; with another, she embodied in Gilbert Markham the atmosphere of passion with which the clandestine lovers were surrounded.[1]

If Anne, as was first advanced, obtained her data in experience rather than in imagination, we must allow that observation can itself constitute vivid experience. It was not, in other words, only those things which happened to herself that provided material, but those things, too, which happened to others. To see things done was to feel and understand them – an emotional knowledge from whence sprang her art.

For Moore, in this case, the novel's excellence lay in 'the first hundred and fifty pages of *The Tenant of Wildfell Hall*, whose "weaving of the narrative reveals a born story-teller, just as the knotted and tangled threads in *Wuthering Heights* reveal the desperate efforts of a lyrical poet to construct a prose narrative". The author,' Moore continued, 'broke down in the middle of her story, but her breakdown was not for lack of genius but of experience. An accident would have saved her; almost any man of letters would have laid his hand upon her arm and said: You must not let your heroine give her diary to the young farmer, saying, "Here is my story, go home and read it." Your heroine must tell the young farmer her story. . . . The diary broke the story in halves. . . .'

With this stricture Gosse agrees (a decision to which the present writer cannot lend his own humble support. Admitted that the narration of the story, through the medium of the diary, does amount to an hiatus – a set-back, even – its great interest and desperate events offer rich compensation for this. In every way, the characters and events which we encounter at one remove, here, are possessed of greater interest than those met with in the first part of the book. Helen, the author of the diary, who appeals so much more to our sympathy than does the image of her girlhood past, appears to us as a tragic figure. Gilbert's erstwhile unrequited love has not the same

---

[1] This is, confessedly, a conjecture. There is no final evidence, one way or the other, that Branwell and Mrs Robinson were lovers. That Branwell was clearly infatuated, and that this infatuation may, at the least, have been partly provoked by a certain flirtatiousness on the part of Mrs Robinson (whose husband was old and feeble), is not an unlikely guess. That Mrs Robinson's good name (which she had somewhat lost as a result of rumour and gossip) was restored to her, some years afterwards, by public investigation cannot, I think, be taken as conclusive, concerning her innocence or non-participation in the affairs. Matters of so intimate a nature can seldom be definitely pronounced on.

sort of pathos about it. Then, too, the lesser characters in the early chapters of the novel are quite uninspiring village figures. They are well but not deeply portrayed; and Fergus, Gilbert's younger brother is a facetious bore. Compared with these, the group of cronies that surround Huntingdon – Hargrave, the urbane sententious seducer; Lord Lowborough, trying to live down his evil past, and his wife Anabella who plays him false; the violent, gruff, but loyal Hattersley whose love for his meek and uncomplaining wife finally leads to his change of heart – are engaged in a moral drama of more vital significance than the affairs of Gilbert Markham's friends).

XVII

O NE OF THOSE errors of literary judgement, which criticism
appears to have honoured for something like a hundred years,
is to have regarded Anne as an artistic adjunct to the elder
Brontës; a sort of humble footnote to her sisters' pages. It is true
that George Moore did not consider her later novel a complete
success; but whether or no one agrees with him as to the merits of
The Tenant of Wildfell Hall, it is he who has struck the most resound-
ing blow for the restitution of the youngest Brontë in her capacity as
novelist. Anne, he claimed, 'had all the qualities of Jane Austen and
other qualities', and again, 'If Anne Brontë had lived ten years longer
she would have taken a place beside Jane Austen, perhaps even a
higher place.' The judgement is unusual but not extravagant, and of a
kind that is fertile in the comparisons to which it prompts us.

'If Anne had written nothing but *The Tenant of Wildfell Hall*,'
Moore maintains in the same talk with Gosse, 'I should not have been
able to predict the high place she would have taken in English letters.
All I should have been able to say is: An inspiration that comes and
goes like a dream. But, her first story, *Agnes Grey*, is the most perfect
prose narrative in English letters.' 'The most perfect prose narrative
in English literature, and over-looked for fifty-odd years!' retorts
Gosse; a statement which Moore, in his turn, nicely capped by
remarking that 'the blindness of criticism should not surprise one as
well acquainted with the history of literature' as he presumed was his
dear friend Gosse. '*Agnes Grey*,' continued Moore, 'is a narrative
simple and beautiful as a muslin dress. . . . The arrival of Agnes at the
house of her employer (she is the new governess) opens the story, and
the first sentences convince us that we are with a quick, witty mind,
capable of appreciating all that she hears and sees; and when Agnes
begins to tell us of her charges and their vulgar parents, we know that
we are reading a masterpiece. Nothing short of genius could have set
them before us so plainly and yet with restraint – even the incident of

227

the little boy who tears a bird's nest out of some bushes and fixes hooks into the beaks of the young birds so that he may drag them about the stable-yard. In writing it Anne's eyes were always upon the story itself and not upon her readers; a thought does not seem to have come into her mind that a reader would like a little more drama, a little more comedy, that a picnic or a ball would provide entertainment.'

The cruelty of Agnes Grey's first pupils brings out the gentle mildness of her nature (which is not without its own persevering streak of moral fortitude or toughness). Her second appointment, in a fresh house, to the charge of two growing girls serves to elicit her shrewdness and balance, her very ungirlish powers of judgement, and (more adult still) her suspension of opinion when there is not enough evidence to go on. These mental and temperamental gifts were qualities equally manifest in Agnes Grey and her author; and sometimes the expression of them is left to the governess-heroine while, at others, it is placed in the mouth of another character. One of Miss Grey's new pupils is about to leave the paddock of the school-room for the wider expanses of the social world, while the other – as George Moore puts it – is 'a sort of tomboy who likes kittens and puppies, and the society of the stable-yard and harness-room better than that of the drawing-room, her hour not having yet come'.

After a short holiday at home, Agnes returns, very tired from her journey, to have the elder girl's excitable reactions to her first ball unleashed upon her. The passage describing this recital was especially dear to George Moore for the quiet but brilliant note on which it closes. The young lady, the elder Miss Murray, is so absorbed in relating all the small details of her 'coming-out': her dress, her partners, the flowers she was given, the compliments which she received, that her governess's fatigue goes unnoticed by her. 'Agnes Grey,' Moore observes, 'gives all the attention she can give to her pupil, but is too tired to respond, and Miss Murray, feeling, no doubt, that Agnes thinks she is exaggerating her successes, insists still further : "As for *me*, Miss Grey, – I'm so *sorry* you didn't see me ! I was *charming* – wasn't I, Matilda?" And the younger sister, who had not been to the ball, answers: "Middling."

'The word lights up the narrative like a ray of light cast by Ruysdael into the middle of a landscape.'

'Middling', in fact, seems to have been one of Anne's most effective counters. It is part of her technique of reduction, one of the quiet ways in which she punctures pretence. ('Note her scorn for the falsely romantic,' remarked Phyllis Bentley in a broadcast upon her. 'Agnes describes herself as having "ordinary brown hair". Few are the heroines of fiction to whom their creators allow the reality of "ordinary brown hair"! The dissipated Sir Thomas Ashby, too, is a real roué, not a romantic one; his face is blotchy, his eyelids disagreeably red.' 'One is tempted to wonder,' continues Miss Bentley, 'what Anne would have made of Mr Rochester – I think she would have taken him down several pegs.') 'What relentless honesty informs that word,' she exclaims of its use in the following conversation between the governess and a pupil who is enquiring about the fiancé of Agnes's loved sister:

> ' "Is he rich?"
> ' "No, only comfortable."
> ' "Is he handsome?"
> ' "No, only decent."
> ' "Young?"
> ' "No, only middling." '

It is this demure irony that prevents the gentle even motion of the prose in *Agnes Grey* from producing a monotony of effect. Under the cover of unhurried statement, there lurks in the dialogue of the novel a tempered impatience with affectation. Unepigrammatic as are the answers of Agnes Grey in conversation, they are primed with the nicest balanced rebuke. Her mild reflective words are always on the side of sanity, good-naturedness, and thoughtful judgement:

> ' "Well, Miss Grey, what did you think of the new curate?" asked Miss Murray on our return from church the Sunday after the recommencement of our duties.
> ' "I can scarcely tell," was my reply. "I have not even heard him preach."
> ' "Well, but you saw him, didn't you?"
> ' "Yes; but I cannot pretend to judge a man's character by a single cursory glance at his face."
> ' "But isn't he ugly?"
> ' "He did not strike me as being particularly so; I don't dislike that cast of countenance. But the only thing I particularly noticed about him was his style of reading, which appeared to me good. . . ." '

Nothing too much! In more ways than one, Anne was a very classical spirit.

For all his ardent partisanship, it is probable that Moore's high-spirited defence was received by many minds with a small pinch of salt, his eloquence possibly smacking too much of paradox and special pleading to persuade the average sober-tempered critic. The result of this is that even today Anne has not been seriously considered as an artist. She has not so much as been weighed and found wanting, as rather unthinkingly put to one side.

A factor, doubtless, in this misconstruction is the habit of looking to find in her novels qualities present in Emily's and Charlotte's : their headlong poetry and fiery rhetoric, their highly-coloured palette and air of storm-and-stress. Of this fallacy of false approach, the critic Saintsbury is representative, for in his book *The English Novel* (1913), he writes that the 'third Brontë sister is but a pale reflection of her elders', and merely leaves the matter at that without further comment on her work. Anne, whose art participates so little in the family characteristic – the Brontë inclination towards the dramatic – is misjudged when placed side by side with her sisters. Her properties, her merits, are of another order : she is not their weak reflection, their sedulous echo, but a writer of an almost completely different sort.

Any man, Robert Louis Stevenson observed, who was truly able to remember his childhood could write an incomparable book. What Anne remembers to perfection are the incidents and state of late adolescence and early womanhood under certain forms of stress. In the story of the governess in *Agnes Grey*, we meet with all those moments of hope and fear, those happenings, productive of keen joy or pain, which a young susceptibility and lack of experience inevitably guarantee to their possessor. But the two things mainly remarkable about this record of early impressions is the accurate, sober, unmisted fashion with which each detail is presented ; and the stoic and un-self-pitying manner in which these griefs and hardships are described. With Thackeray or with Dickens, for example, the narration of such sad situations would be the occasion for some purple passage, some lachrymose lament, or some indignant sermon. With Anne, the elegy is largely implicit. She holds on always to the thread of her tale ; her style never registers hysterics ; and even through tears her eye is on the object.

This self-control which we know was hers in life, and this self-knowledge which her writings reveal, prevented her from ever attempting any kind of excellence foreign to her nature. Without her sisters' driving imagination – she was careful never to be decoyed into trying to step up the current of her story. Knowing very well she was no *tragédienne*, no glamorous *femme fatale* of fiction, she serenely ignored all temptations to melodrama. It is this certain consciousness of her own pitch, this natural rise and fall of her voice on paper, that gives to *Agnes Grey* so consistent a texture, so smooth, so unhurried, so classic a strain.

Yet, when all is said and done, the main attraction of Anne Brontë's novels does not solely depend upon her style. Eager as the born bookman may be concerning the technique of his own art, few works have exerted a popular appeal without the possession of wider human traits than virtues of style. In the work of Anne this broader attraction resides in her sense of character, of character chiefly understood in the light of moral development. This latter adjective, applied to fiction, is one we are somewhat wary of these days; and recalling the manner in which the moral content was abused and exploited by Victorian authors, our caution is not simply to be considered as symptomatic of a more degenerate age. Yet with Anne we have no need to be wary. Moralist, as she undoubtedly was, she avoided the pitfall of making her creations into the stock figures of an ethical scheme. She did not, in other words, cut her figures to ready-made shapes of vice or virtue; but exhibited them, rather, as manifesting a certain tendency towards good or bad; a tendency that time and experience strengthen, until it hardens into a habit, which in turn absorbs the whole personality. It is just this process which her novels set out to trace.

The method Anne chose by which to present this sphere of internal activity and change is that of introspective narration – a 'first person singular' confession or recital. This device, she employs throughout her first novel *Agnes Grey*, and with modification in *The Tenant of Wildfell Hall* (where the story is unfolded by two tellers, each of them in turn speaking in the 'first person'). It is the means by which her characters confess, explain and justify their lives and it is also a discipline through which they arrive at a state of fuller self-awareness – at a knowledge of existence and their own nature, and of how these may best come to terms. Such an exposition of moral growth does not lead in the novels of Anne – as it does in so much introspective modern fiction – to a somewhat sterile analysis of self in which the personality appears to deliquesce. In spite of occasional religious doubts, Anne knew – in the long run – what she believed; and that she believed was a bedrock conception, upon which her idea of man was founded. We do not discover, then, in her pages any of those brilliantly iridescent studies of character-structure in decay (such as Proust magnificently gives us); but find, rather, character in the act of growth; in the act, we may say, of becoming itself; of becoming responsible, moral, and adult; of being weaned from illusion and dream, and adapting itself to reality.

This simple saga of moral development is best seen in *The Tenant of Wildfell Hall,* in which the heroine starts her life as an easily impressionable romantic miss, a lovely unconscious little pagan. Experience deceives and injures her, and at one stage of the story she seems to have escaped from the follies of the heart only, as it were, 'to wither into truth'. But if experience is injury, it is also, for the thoughtful spirit, instruction; and by its lesson she eventually achieves a new and informed light-heartedness of being, a kind of happiness which comes, like the runner's second-wind, after pleasure and despair.

With this development of moral stature in the character of Anne's heroine, we find an accompanying commentary upon the stages of her erotic development. After she has been profoundly disillusioned in her love for her dissolute husband, she separates from him, and for a time we see her hard and invulnerable as stone. During this period all men repel her; and even her future lover, Markham, meets only with an outward unmitigated scorn. Little by little, she learns to soften, finding in her second love an image of the good. For a shy unsought-after governess, this itinerary of spirit is a veritable triumph; and for the age in which she lived this build-up and analysis of feeling is most rare. Infatuation, blind and unheeding; a passionate frigidity of the heart; and, lastly, a reborn, well-founded passion: all three emotional stages are uncovered for us here.

Nor was Anne slow to seek the application of her psychological insight – a species of knowledge which, when transferred to the drawing-room levels of Victorian fiction – assumed a quite devastating air. What English novelist of that time, prior to the advent of Thomas Hardy, would have dared – well mindful of the unwritten law concerning conjugal obedience – to have shown the heroine bolting the door against her rightful but vicious husband, determined that a man so false and debauched should enjoy intimacy with her no longer. In a similar way, for sheer and simple frankness – a purposive outspokenness in no manner brazen – we shall find no Victorian, again before Hardy, capable of treating so unsavoury a scene as that in *The Tenant of Wildfell Hall* where the drunken husbands break in upon their wives after a much-protracted session with the bottle. Their brutalities, stupor, and acts of violation are described in a fashion which Zola might have admired. How much more convincing to us today is Anne's description of this stupid carouse than Charlotte's midnight coming and going in the pages of *Jane Eyre* where Rochester's mad wife nearly burns down the house. ('Why ever,' we feel, when this female bogey escapes a second time, 'doesn't her caretaker keep her locked up better! And how unlikely that Rochester, no incapable a person himself, should have entrusted his wife to the care of a servant who is almost an alcoholic!') Reading the following masque of sottishness, one thinks of the scene in *Nana* where the prostitute, seated on the back of Count Muffat, rides him around the apartment on all fours:

'At last they came; but not till after ten, when tea, which had been delayed for more than half an hour, was nearly over. Much as I had longed for their coming, my heart failed me at the riotous uproar of their approach; and Milicent turned pale and almost started from her seat as Mr Hattersley burst into the room with a clamorous volley of oaths in his mouth, which Hargrave endeavoured to check by entreating him to remember the ladies.'

The scene begins with a description of harmless though inane imbecilities perpetrated by the drunken Mr Grimsby who propounds a new theory of inebriation and mistakes the sugar-basin for his teacup. But as the evening advances, and the minds of the drunken men grow more fermented, an element of temper and violence enters in:

'Lord Lowborough had entered a moment or two before, unobserved by anyone but me, and had been standing before the door, grimly surveying the company. He now stepped up to Annabella, who sat with her back towards him, with Hattersley still beside her though not now attending to her, being occupied in vociferously abusing and bullying his host.

' "Well, Annabella," said her husband, as he leant over the back of her chair, "which of these three 'bold, manly spirits' would you have me to resemble?"

' "By heaven and earth, you shall resemble us all!" cried Hattersley, starting up and rudely seizing him by the arm. "Hallo, Huntingdon!" he shouted – "I've got him! Come, man and help me! And d——n me if I don't make him drunk before I let him go! He shall make up for all past delinquencies as sure as I'm a living soul!"

'There followed a disgraceful contest; Lord Lowborough, in desperate earnest, and pale with anger, silently struggling to release himself from the powerful madman that was striving to drag him from the room. I attempted to urge Arthur to interfere in behalf of his outraged guest, but he could do nothing but laugh.

' "Huntingdon, you fool, come and help me, can't you!" cried Hattersley, himself somewhat weakened by his excesses.

' "I'm wishing you God-speed, Hattersley," cried Arthur, "and aiding you with my prayers: I can't do anything else if my life depended on it! I'm quite used up. Oh, ho!" and leaning back in his seat, he clapped his hands on his sides and groaned aloud.

' "Annabella, give me a candle!" said Lowborough, whose antagonist had now got him round the waist and was endeavouring to root him from the door-post to which he madly clung with all the energy of desperation.

' "I shall take no part in your rude sports!" replied the lady, coldly drawing back, "I wonder you can expect it."

'But I snatched up a candle and brought it to him. He took it and held the flame to Hattersley's hands till, roaring like a wild beast, the latter unclasped them and let him go. He vanished, I suppose to his own apartment, for nothing more was seen of him until the morning.'

Foiled of his prey, the drunken Hattersley now commences to torment his wife. She is crying with mortification and distress at his behaviour, and he man-handles her in his endeavour to make her openly confess the sad fact. The hostess intervenes to prevent the wife from receiving physically harsher treatment:

' "I'll tell you, Mr Hattersley," said I. "She was crying from pure shame and humiliation for you; because she could not bear to see you conduct yourself so disgracefully."

' "Confound you, Madam!" muttered he, with a stare of stupid amazement at my 'impudence'. "It was not that, was it, Milicent?"

'She was silent.

' "Come, speak up, child!"

' "I can't tell you now," sobbed she.

' "But you can say 'yes' or 'no' as well as 'I can't tell' – Come!"

' "Yes," she whispered, hanging her head, and blushing at the awful acknowledgment.

' "Curse you for an impertinent hussy, then !" cried he, throwing her from him with such violence that she fell on her side; but she was up again before either I or her brother could come to her assistance, and made the best of her way out of the room, and, I suppose, upstairs, without loss of time." '

Hattersley then turns on Huntingdon, the heroine's vicious self-indulgent husband, who has been laughing at his bearish antics.

' "Oh, Hattersley !" cried he, wiping his swimming eyes – "You'll be the death of me."

' "Yes, I will, but not as you suppose : I'll have the heart out of your body, man, if you irritate me with any more of that imbecile laughter ! – What ! are you at it yet ? – There, see if that'll settle you," cried Hattersley, snatching up a footstool and hurling it at the head of his host; but he missed his aim, and the latter still sat collapsed and quaking with feeble laughter, with the tears running down his face ; a deplorable spectacle indeed.'

Finally, the heroine can endure the scene no longer : 'I thought I had witnessed enough of my husband's degradation; and, leaving Annabella and the rest to follow when they pleased, I withdrew, but not to bed.'

The passage ends with the host being helped to his bedroom by his drunken cronies :

'At last he came, slowly and stumblingly, ascending the stairs, supported by Grimsby and Hattersley, who neither of them walked quite steadily themselves, but were both laughing and joking at him, and making noise enough for all the servants to hear. He himself was no longer laughing now, but sick and stupid.'

There is no young-lady-like squeamishness and no puritanical indignation (there are even occasional touches of humour).

As for sermonizing – her age's stock response – we find it present here in no degree at all. Instead, we witness the situation through the eyes of one who saw things neither with cynical distortion nor in sentimental terms. Anne, we may say, possessed the power of looking facts fully in the face; of keeping her gaze steadfastly upon them, however the sight might offend her. She refused to bury her head in the sand: refused even so much as to look the other way; and though she had few illusions about life, she would not permit her disenchantment to find an easy outlet in romantic grief.

Seen in this light, her claim to be regarded as our first realist woman author is not one that we can glibly ignore. Published in 1848, *The Tenant of Wildfell Hall* appeared some ten years before George Eliot's novels. Indeed, the only challenger to her position is Mrs Gaskell whose *Mary Barton* appeared in the same year as Anne's second book. But *Mary Barton* – Mrs Gaskell's first work – was rather a story of social reform than a deep and subtle study of human intimacies. Lay bare, as she might, the awful conditions of employment and poverty in Manchester, an exposure of the motives of domestic drama was a business in which she could not compete with Anne. In support of this view, we find May Sinclair writing, in her book *The Three Brontës* (1914), 'There was, in the smallest . . . of the Brontës, an immense, a terrifying audacity. Charlotte was bold, and Emily was bolder; but this audacity of Anne's was greater than Charlotte's boldness or than Emily's, because it was willed, it was deliberate, open-eyed. Anne took her courage in both her hands when she sat down to write *The Tenant of Wildfell Hall.*' This lifting-off the lid from the human saucepan earned Anne all that petty opprobrium which a dishonest age reserves for those who cannot respect its shibboleths.

To be attacked in such a way today might almost guarantee the sale of a book; but in Anne's time, when public opinion was ruled more severly than it is now by the government of cant, such a verdict was a sort of intellectual ostracism.

None the less, when it came to entering on her defence, Anne was well able to act as her own counsel.

'My object in writing the following pages,' she states in the Preface to the so-called second edition of *The Tenant of Wildfell Hall*, 'was not simply to amuse the Reader; neither was it to gratify my own taste, nor yet to ingratiate myself with the Press and the Public: I wished to tell the truth, for truth always conveys its own moral to those who are able to receive it. But as the priceless treasure too frequently hides at the bottom of a well, it needs some courage to dive for it, especially as he that does so will be likely to incur more scorn and obloquy for the mud and water into which he has ventured to plunge, than thanks for the jewel he procures; as, in like manner, she who undertakes the cleansing of a careless bachelor's apartment will be liable to more abuse for the dust she raises than commendation for the clearance she effects. Let it not be imagined, however, that I consider myself competent to reform the errors and abuses of society, but only that I would fain contribute my humble quota towards so good an aim; and if I can gain the public ear at all, I would rather whisper a few wholesome truths therein than much soft nonsense.

'As the story of *Agnes Grey* was accused of extravagant over-colouring in those very parts that were carefully copied from the life, with a most scrupulous avoidance of all exaggeration, so, in the present work, I find myself censured for depicting *con amore*, with "a morbid love of the coarse, if not of the brutal", those scenes which, I will venture to say, have not been more painful for the most fastidious of my critics to read than they were for me to describe. I may have gone too far; in which case I shall be careful not to trouble myself or my readers in the same way again; but when we have to do with vice and vicious characters, I maintain it is better to depict them as they really are than as they would wish to appear. To represent a bad thing in its least offensive light, is doubtless, the most agreeable course for a writer of fiction to pursue; but is it the most honest, or the safest? Is it better to reveal the snares and pitfalls of life to the young and thoughtless traveller, or to cover them with branches and flowers? Oh, reader, if there were less of this delicate concealment of facts – this whispering "Peace, peace" when there is no peace, there would be less of sin and misery to the young of both sexes who are left to wring their bitter knowledge from experience.

'I would not be understood to suppose that the proceedings of the unhappy scapegoat, with his few profligate companions I have here introduced, are a specimen of the common practices of society – the case is an extreme one, as I trusted none would fail to perceive; but I know that such characters do exist, and if I have warned one rash youth from following in their steps, or prevented one thoughtless girl from falling into the very natural error of my heroine, the book has not been written in vain. But, at the same time, if any honest reader shall have derived more pain than pleasure from its perusal, and have closed the last volume with a disagreeable impression on his mind, I humbly crave his pardon, for such was far from my intention; and I will endeavour to do better another time, for I love to give innocent pleasure. Yet, be it understood, I shall not limit my ambition to this – or even to producing "a perfect work of art": time and talents so spent, I should consider wasted and mis-applied. Such humble talents as God has given me I will endeavour to put to their greatest use; if I am able to amuse, I will try to benefit too; and when I feel it my duty to speak an unpalatable truth, with the help of God, I *will* speak it, though it be to the prejudice of my name and to the detriment of my reader's immediate pleasure as well as my own.'

Dignified and demurely outspoken, Anne by-passes the claims of aesthetic realism ('I shall not limit my ambition . . . to producing "a perfect work of art" ') which Flaubert, de Goncourts, and Maupassant were later to narrow their work by maintaining.

But not only does this Preface of hers – so full of strength without rhetoric – assert her moral position as a writer; in addition, it makes a plea for the literary equality of the sexes. This emancipated view of artistic creation was something again quite startling in its day; for although it had long been taken for granted that the feminine mind might engage in novel writing, it was thought that its products should be restrained to a kind of sampler-stitching in words, a form of occupa-tion as truly harmless and limited in scope as that 'refined' accomplish-ment. Not so Anne, who quietly argued that, 'If a book is a good one, it is so whatever the sex of the author may be. All novels are, or should be, written for both men and women to read, and I am at a loss to conceive how a man should permit himself to write anything that would be really disgraceful to a woman, or why a woman should be censured for writing anything that would be proper and becoming for a man.'

Realist as we have called Anne, the truth is that her attitude has little in common with the art of such novelists as Maupassant and George Moore. To express this distinction very briefly, we can say that the latter were concerned with the authentic presentation of a scene according to the canons of good writing; whereas Anne, who was deeply concerned with presenting the scene as she knew it, de-sired, in addition, to bring to light the moral significance latent in it. If, then, we describe these later authors as subscribing to a sort of aesthetic realism, we shall properly describe Anne as a moral realist.

Of the serious way she regarded her own writing, especially the writing of her second novel, we know from what Charlotte has to impart. 'She wrote it,' we are told by her, with reference to *The*

Tenant of Wildfell Hall, 'under a strange, conscientious, half-ascetic notion of accomplishing a painful penance and a severe duty'; and indeed of Anne – as of few Victorian authors – we feel she never wrote for the sake of writing. Her words are always a token of goodwill – of the knowledge of something she has to tell us; a something observed or experienced by her, through which she desires to instruct us for our good.

As might have been expected of a mind as bold as Anne's, her audacity of presentation was matched by an intellectual daring which repudiated certain semi-sacrosanct opinions of her age. One of these, as we have seen, was the notion of conjugal obedience : the belief that a wife had at no time the right – the human, not the legal privilege, that is – of denying herself to her husband. This myth Anne certainly exploded in her novel *The Tenant of Wildfell Hall,* showing how continued intimacy with a worthless husband one has come to despise is a most contagious form of degradation. 'If thy right hand offend thee, cut it off'; and Anne had the courage to insist upon this precept.

It must not be surmised, however, that because Anne held ideas on marriage which her own age did not share, that these ideas are therefore ours. As a matter of fact, her thoughts upon marriage are perhaps more practical than those which either her own or our time have espoused. More romantic than Jane Austen, and more 'commonsensical' than her sisters, she is probably, in this respect, more 'knowing' than they are, and even worthy of attention in these matters today. 'When I tell you not to marry without love,' one of her characters advises another, 'I do not advise you to marry for love alone – there are many – many other things to be considered.'

Another question, on which she differed from the adamant convention of her day, was the Anglican conception of Hell as a place, not of temporary, but of eternal punishment. To Anne, this seemed but a poor crowning proof of the sure existence of the Christian God of love; and in *The Tenant of Wildfell Hall* the heroine asserts she has found in her Bible 'nearly thirty passages' going to show that the threatened fires of Hell are purgative rather than everlasting. And again, Huntingdon's unregenerate death seems bearable to Helen only on the supposition that, 'through whatever purging fires the erring spirit may be doomed to pass – whatever fate awaits it, still, it is not lost, and God, who hateth nothing that he hath made, will bless it in the end !'

This interpretation is a good example of the way in which she combined an instinctive and personal philosophy of love with the dictates of her Christian conscience. With Christian theology in her time, as represented by the Anglican Church; such a synthesis had not yet been effected; for it was not until 1877 (nearly thirty years after Anne's novel) that Dean Farrar, in his book *Eternal Hope* startled the ranks of the orthodox by suggesting that salvation was appointed for all.[1]

[1] As late as 1853, F. D. Maurice had been deprived of his professorship at King's College, London, for proclaiming his disbelief in Everlasting Damnation.

XVIII

HOWEVER SOLICITOUS for Anne's welfare we may allow Charlotte to have been, we cannot avoid the unfortunate suspicion that, so far as Anne the artist was concerned, the elder sister proved something of an evil fairy.

George Moore was the first to hint at Charlotte's inadequate handling of Anne's reputation. 'Critics,' he remarks, 'follow a scent like hounds, and I am not certain that it wasn't Charlotte who first started them on their depreciation of Anne. I cannot give chapter and verse here, but in one of her introductions she certainly apologizes for *The Tenant of Wildfell Hall*, pleading extenuating circumstances: Anne's youth, her sickness, her inexperience of life. Three phthisis-stricken sisters living on a Yorkshire moor, and all three writing novels, were first-rate copy, and Charlotte's little depreciations of the dead were a great help, for three sisters of equal genius might strain the credulity of the readers of the evening newspapers. Such insight as would enable the journalist to pick out the right one would be asking too much of journalism.' This, of course, may be dismissed as one of Moore's fancies, and the positive service which Charlotte lent her sisters be instanced as sufficient defence.

We know that their first publication in book form – a volume of poems which the three sisters shared – was due to Charlotte's initiative; and that she generally seems to have acted as publicity-agent to them all. At the same time, though, we cannot but recall the words of faint praise or condonation in which she inevitably speaks of Anne. Her character, she tells us – comparing her with Emily – in her *Biographical Notice of Ellis and Acton Bell*, 'was milder and more subdued; she wanted the power, the fire, the originality of her sister, but was well endowed with quiet virtues of her own. Long-suffering, self-denying, reflective, and intelligent, a constitutional reserve and taciturnity placed and kept her in the shade, and covered her mind, and especially her feelings, with a sort of nun-like veil, which was rarely lifted.' This, one may see, from the briefest study of Mrs Gaskell's *Life of Charlotte Brontë*, was the kind of statement she was always to make: a note of praise for Anne as a human being; a slighting apology for her as artist.

And when 'the milder and more subdued' Anne, the Anne who wanted 'the power, the fire, the originality of her sister', made a fair bid to extend her scope from the pastoral cameo of *Agnes Grey* to the larger fuller canvas of her second novel, Charlotte's response was still belittling. *The Tenant of Wildfell Hall*, she wrote in her *Biographical Notice*, had 'an unfavourable reception. At this I cannot wonder. The choice of subject was an entire mistake.' When reasoned with on the incongruity of her subject, Anne – Charlotte tells us – 'regarded such reasonings as a temptation to self-indulgence. She must be honest: she must not varnish, soften, or conceal. This well-meant resolution brought on her some abuse, which she bore, as it was her custom to bear whatever was unpleasant, with mild steady patience.'

This was written after Anne's death, but while she was still alive Charlotte had started to circulate her exaggerated report (which critics were to take at its face value) of her sister's limitations. 'That it had faults of execution,' she wrote in a letter to W. S. Williams (31 July 1848)[1] of *The Tenant of Wildfell Hall*, 'faults of art, was obvious, but faults of intention or feeling could be suspected by none who knew the writer. For my part, I consider the subject unfortunately chosen – it was one the author was not qualified to handle at once vigorously and truthfully. The simple and natural – quiet description and simple pathos – are, I think Acton Bell's forte. I liked *Agnes Grey* better than the present work.'

This was the substance of Charlotte's judgement. Anne was all very well when it came to something simple and pathetic (though we note that Charlotte never offers any positive praise of *Agnes Grey*), but when she tried her hand at anything larger, anything more vigorous and truly worth while, then she was out of her proper depth, and only able to perpetrate blunders.

In another letter to Williams, dated 18 August 1848, Charlotte abruptly, if not indignantly, repudiates the idea of a resemblance between the heroine's first husband in *The Tenant of Wildfell Hall* and the hero of *Jane Eyre*:

[1] For the preceding and succeeding part of this epistle, see Part I, pages 124–5.

'You say Mr Huntingdon reminds you of Mr Rochester. Does he? Yet there is no likeness between the two; the foundation of each character is entirely different. Huntingdon is a specimen of the naturally selfish, sensual, superficial man, whose one merit of a joyous temperament only avails him while he is young and healthy, whose best days are his earliest, who never profits by experience, who is sure to grow worse the older he grows. Mr Rochester has a thoughtful nature and a very feeling heart; he is neither selfish nor self-indulgent; he is ill-educated, misguided; errs, when he does err, through rashness and inexperience: he lives for a time as too many other men live, he does not like that degraded life, and is never happy in it. He is taught the severe lessons of experience and has sense to learn wisdom from them. Years improve him; the effervescence of youth foamed away, what is really good in him still remains. His nature is like wine of a good vintage, time cannot sour but only mellow him. Such at least was the character I meant to portray.

'Heathcliff, again, of *Wuthering Heights* is quite another creation. He exemplifies the effects which a life of continued injustice and hard usage may produce on a naturally perverse, vindictive, and inexorable disposition. Carefully trained and kindly treated, the black gipsy-cub might possibly have been reared into a human being, but tyranny and ignorance made of him a mere demon. The worst of it is, some of his spirit seems breathed through the whole narrative in which he figures: it haunts every moor and glen, and beckons in every fir-tree of the Heights.'

This is a fair enough working discrimination; but it totally fails to consider, either the representative status of Huntingdon, or Anne's achievement in creating him. Yet the fact remains that for every five rough idealists like Rochester, and for every single (and incredible) Heathcliff, there exist a score of Huntingdons.

The Brontës have been censured – and censured rightly – for their inability to create convincing male characters 'to take the lead'. The old man-servant Joseph in *Wuthering Heights* is certainly a more real character than the glamorized Byronic gipsy Heathcliff, whom I find almost too bad to be true. From this specific criticism, Anne is largely to be exempted. There is nothing to strain our credulity about the figure of Huntingdon. He represents the man more than *moyen sensuel*, the male whose carnality has been allowed to develop to excess. Not that he is shown as a high-society Don Juan, trailing a string of broken hearts behind him. There is nothing at all single-minded, let alone romantic, in his character. The drive of his instinct is broken up by random dissipation and casual promiscuity. His affair with Lady Lowborough is not a grand passion. There is not sufficient force of unity in him ever to will for one thing only.

Of Anne's success in creating Huntingdon, and the means she employs to achieve her effect, Charlotte is totally unaware. Unlike her elder sisters, who liked to trace the lines of titanic evil — the power to work a large-scale wrong — within the male characters they depicted, Anne had a way of exposing vice in terms of its often attendant pettiness. What could be better than the picture she gives us of Huntingdon returned to the country, after his six months' debauchery in London, a petulant neurasthenic wreck:

'On the following morning, I received a few lines from him myself, confirming Hargrave's intimations respecting his approaching return. And he did come next week, but in a condition of body and mind even worse than before. I did not, however, intend to pass over his derelictions this time without a remark; — I found it would not do. But the first day he was weary with his journey, and I was glad to get him back: I would not upbraid him then; I would wait till tomorrow. Next morning he was weary still: I would wait a little longer. But at dinner, when, after breakfasting at twelve o'clock on a bottle of soda-water and a cup of strong coffee, and lunching at two on another bottle of soda-water mingled with brandy, he was finding fault with everything on the table, and declaring we must change our cook — I thought the time was come.

' "It is the same cook as we had before you went, Arthur," said I. "You were generally pretty well satisfied with her then."

' "You must have been letting her get into slovenly habits, while I was away. It is enough to poison one, eating such a disgusting mess!" And he pettishly pushed away his plate, and leant back despairingly in his chair.

' "I think it is you that are changed, not she," said I, but with the utmost gentleness, for I did not wish to irritate him.

' "It may be so," he replied carelessly, as he seized a tumbler of wine and water, adding, when he had tossed it off, "for I have an infernal fire in my veins, that all the waters of the ocean cannot quench!"

' "What kindled it?" I was about to ask, but at that moment the butler entered and began to take away the things.

' "Be quick, Benson; do have done with that infernal clatter!" cried his master. "And don't bring the cheese, unless you want to make me sick outright!" '

As a realist, Anne had the knack of being faithful in little things.

It is difficult to reconcile one's idea of a person with that image of them contained in their art. For some reason, Charlotte made no effort to do so, or made the effort and failed lamentably. Perhaps her failure was due to the fact that, being an author in her own right, she could not readily appreciate another who held quite different ends in view. Be that as it may, there is not the slightest doubt that her words – repeated parrot-fashion by the critics, or echoed with a kind of timid variation – have kept the stone at the mouth of Anne's tomb for something over a hundred years. It is time the stone was rolled away.

Selected Bibliography

Works by Anne Brontë (pseud. Acton Bell)

Poems by Currer, Ellis, and Acton Bell, Aylott and Jones, 1846.

Agnes Grey – A Novel, first published as Vol. III of Emily Brontë's *Wuthering Heights*, Smith, Elder, 1847.

The Tenant of Wildfell Hall, 3 vols., Newby, 1848. (Novel.)

Complete Poems, edited by C. K. Shorter and C. W. Hatfield, Hodder and Stoughton, 1921.

Works by the Brontës

The Shakespeare Head Brontë. Novels, 11 vols.; Lives and Letters, 4 vols.; Poems of Emily and Anne Brontë, 1 vol; Poems of Charlotte Brontë, 1 vol.; Miscellaneous and Unpublished Writings of Charlotte and Patrick Branwell Brontë, 2 vols. Edited by Wise and Symington. Blackwell, 1934–8.

The Brontë Letters, edited by Muriel Spark, Peter Nevill, 1954.

Works on the Brontës

Gaskell, Mrs E. C. *The Life of Charlotte Brontë*, Smith, Elder, 1857.

Sinclair, May. *The Three Brontës*, Hutchinson, 1914.

Moore, George. *Conversations in Ebury Street*, Heinemann, 1936. (There are original and valuable pages in this work on Anne and her novels.)

Ratchford, Fannie Elizabeth. *The Brontës' Web of Childhood*, Columbia University Press, New York, 1941.

Bentley, Phyllis. *The Brontës*, Home and van Thal, 1947.

Harrison, G. Elsie. *The Clue to the Brontës*, Methuen, 1948.

Hanson, Lawrence and E. M. *The Four Brontës*, Oxford University Press, 1949.

Bentley, Phyllis: *The Three Brontës* (*Writers and their Work* series. British Council, published by Longmans), 1950. (There is an excellent short bibliography of Brontë works and Brontë studies in this short monograph, as well as a host of illuminating insights by a leading Brontë scholar.)

247

Index